This-Worldly *Nibbāna*

This-Worldly *Nibbāna*

A Buddhist-Feminist Social Ethic for
Peacemaking in the Global Community

Hsiao-Lan Hu

Published by State University of New York Press, Albany

For information, contact State University of New York Press, Albany, NY
www.sunypress.edu

Production by Diane Ganeles
Marketing by Anne M. Valentine

Library of Congress Cataloging-in-Publication Data

Hu, Hsiao-Lan.
    This-worldly nibbāna : a Buddhist-feminist social ethic for peacemaking in the global community / Hsiao-Lan Hu.
        p. cm.
    Includes bibliographical references and index.
    ISBN 978-1-4384-3933-4 (hardcover : alk. paper)
    ISBN 978-1-4384-3932-7 (pbk.: alk. paper)
    1. Peace—Religious aspects—Buddhism.   2. Buddhism—Social aspects.
3. Women and peace.   4. Feminism.   I. Title.

BQ4570.P4H8 2011
294.3'37273082—dc22   2011004869

10 9 8 7 6 5 4 3 2 1

To all "helpful friends" who have shown me, with their actions,
the endless and multidirectional reverberations
of positive *kamma*

Contents

Acknowledgments

In Chinese, a mentor or a friend who provides help at crucial points of one's life is called *guiren* (or *kuei-jen* in Wade-Giles), often rendered "helpful friend." I am extremely fortunate to have encountered an unusual number of *guiren*-s in my life. To say the least, I have yet to meet another person who would say she or he had four advisors in graduate school and all four had read multiple revisions of every chapter in her or his dissertation. Dr. John C. Raines was officially the chair of my doctoral advisory committee, and I can never thank him enough for all the guidance he has provided me over the years. I have been moved by, and benefited from, his commitment to social justice and his care for underprivileged students. I am equally indebted to Dr. Rita M. Gross, who took a chance on me and agreed to sit on my committee before she even met me. Her works have influenced numerous feminist Buddhists around the world, and she has certainly inspired me in many regards. It was an honor to be her student. Dr. Rebecca T. Alpert is in every way my role model. I wish one day I could approximate her wisdom and strength in tackling all the difficulties in life, and I wish I will have the same kind of humor and patience as she does. Dr. Laura S. Levitt's energy and passion have always amazed me. She has read more revisions of all of my chapters than anyone else, with unparalleled enthusiasm. More than once she pointed out the potentials of my work that I myself did not see. These four mentors critiqued my work from four very different angles, which made my dissertation, the former version of this book, much broader and richer.

I am extremely thankful for the friends I encountered in recent years who have helped me in my professional and personal life. Venerable Karma Lekshe Tsomo is loving-kindness embodied. Her presence is always assuring and her words are always wise and affirming. She is also a superhuman in terms of the various services she has provided to humanity in general and Asian Buddhist women in particular. Dr. Carol Winkelmann "adopted" me as a sister because I have no family in the U.S., and so for the first time I actually feel that I have a "home" here. I still cannot believe how quickly our friendship developed. The friends I met through Sakyadhita have enriched my world tremendously and prompted me to integrate more fully my theory with my practice: Dr. Christie Chang, Dr. Yuchen Li, Dr. Susanne Mrozik, Dr. Elise A. DeVido, Charlotte B. Collins, Roseanne Freese, etc. Dr. David R. Loy is a knowledgeable and fun friend whose works have influenced my own thinking. Dr. Douglas L. Berger has always been generous in sharing with me his insights and experiences. Jamie Dylenski was kind enough to read through my manuscript and offer her feedbacks. Dr. Gloria H. Albrecht, Dr. Audrey Brosnan, and Pamela A. Wilkins have provided me with a sense of stability. Dr. James B. Tubbs is the best department chair one could have. Friends at the Lansing Buddhist Association and Muddy Water Zen have provided me with places for practice and made me feel at home. I am especially grateful for Dr. Lina Wu, Dr. Chungwen Chen, Anna Fisher, Hae Doh Sunim, and Dr. George Sanders.

I thank Nancy Ellegate and Diane Ganeles, editors at the State University of New York Press, for their kind assistance. Elise Brauckmann's cover designs were thoughtful and beautiful, and I am grateful that she worked patiently with me and responded to my multiple requests for change. I also want to thank copyeditor Sharon Green of Panache Editorial, Inc., and typesetter Sue Morreale of Partners Composition for their meticulous and expedient work.

My father had a paralyzing stroke in August of 2005 and passed away in May of 2006. When I was young, neither he nor my mother really thought that a girl's place could be in the academia, and yet it was them who equipped me with the aptitude and discipline that I would need for advanced studies. I am grateful that their belief in education outweighed all other presumptions and concerns. It could not be not easy for them to deal with the fact that I did not fit into either of their preconceived notions of a daughter, and it certainly was unsettling to know that their daughter was leaving them, both physically and ideologically, and yet they let her go anyway. After my father's passing, I realized that I am in no small way indebted to my only brother. Since the onset of my father's illness, he has made life easier for me. His way of making peace with the manifold obstacles in his life while maintaining remarkable warmth and sensitivity in his personality, moreover, has been a continuous inspiration.

It was Dr. Theresa Der-Lan Yeh who initiated me into religious studies, gender studies, cross-cultural communication, and peace studies. Inadvertently, she was also the one who made me acutely aware of the ways in which social classes could affect the construction of people's gender identities as well as their senses of deservedness and their overall approaches to people and to life. More importantly, she familiarized me with life in America. I was one of the few students in the Department of Foreign Languages and Literatures at National Taiwan University who could not afford consuming American cultural commodities. As a result, I was awkwardly unfamiliar with the daily life in the United States when I first set foot on this land. Dr. Yeh's own experience as a doctoral student in the U.S. and her encyclopedic knowledge helped me on numerous occasions. Even more fundamentally, it was thanks to the various forms of financial and social aids she had provided or procured for me, including her sister Terry's expertise, that I could afford coming to the United States for an advanced degree in the first place. I could not have done what I have done without her.

1

Introduction

> Do not go by oral tradition, by lineage of teaching, by hearsay,
> by a collection of scriptures, by logical reasoning, by inferential
> reasoning, by reflection on reasons, by the acceptance of a view
> after pondering it, by the seeming competence of a speaker, or
> because you think, "The ascetic is our teacher." But when you
> know for yourselves, "These things are unwholesome, these things
> are blamable; these things are censured by the wise; these things,
> if undertaken and practised, lead to harm and suffering," then you
> should abandon them. . . . when you know for yourselves, "These
> things are wholesome, these things are blameless; these things are
> praised by the wise; these things, if undertaken and practised,
> lead to welfare and happiness," then you should engage in them.[1]

Having renounced the conventional ways of thinking and behaving,
a human teacher gives the above advice about taking actions and
accepting views. He is concerned with the prevalence and causes of
dukkha (Sanskrit: *duhkha*), the unsatisfactoriness of ordinary life, the dis-
ease and anguish of conventional existence, the suffering particularly
pronounced at the troubled time in which he lived.[2] He affirms that
nibbāna (Sanskrit: *nirvāna*), the cessation of *dukkha*, is achievable, and
he teaches the practices and views that can lead all sentient beings
to it. At the same time, however, he discourages blind faith in any
tradition, teaching, or teacher, himself and his own teachings included.
He does not encourage wayward dismissal of all practices and doctrines, either.[3] Rather, he teaches his followers to reflect critically on
the consequences of the actions they take and the ramifications of the
views they accept.

This human teacher is the Buddha, "the awakened one." He is also known as Siddhāttha Gotama (Sanskrit: Siddhārtha Gautama) and Sākyamuni (Sanskrit: Śākyamuni), the silent sage of the Sākya (Sanskrit: Śākya) tribe at the foothill of the Himālayas. He is popularly dated in the sixth to fifth centuries BCE according to Buddhist traditions, albeit exact dates are still disputed.[4] His oral teachings have attracted so many followers that he is retrospectively considered the teacher and founder of a religious tradition. His followers are now commonly called Buddhists in the English language, and their practices and views are now collectively termed Buddhism. Followers of the Buddha's teachings, however, refer to the Buddhist views and practices as the *Dhamma* (Sanskrit: *Dharma*). Rooted in the verb *dhr*, meaning to support or to sustain, the word *dhamma* has the connotation of the natural order or cosmic law that underpins the operation of the world in both the physical and moral senses. It is a multivalent word in both Hindu traditions and Buddhist traditions. In Hindu traditions, it can mean religious-social duties, the customary observances of a caste or sect, law usage and practice, righteousness, justice, norm, morality, virtue, religious or moral merit, piety, religion, sacrifice, and so forth. In Buddhism, it is used to denote the totality of the Buddha's teachings and the Buddhist path, or any one of Buddhist principles, or any individual element or phenomenon that collectively constitutes the empirical world and existence, including physical objects, activities, circumstances or conditions of life, as well as mental objects, psychological processes, and character traits. In the Mahāyāna Buddhist tradition, *Dhamma* also designates the reality of Buddhahood.[5] In this book I distinguish between *Dhamma* and *dhamma*, with the former referring to the Buddha's teachings, and the latter referring to the individual element that constitutes the empirical world.

In the long history of Buddhism, the most prominent exegetes of the *Dhamma* have largely been monastic males who were most likely from the upper strata of their societies. Buddhist scholar Roger R. Jackson notes that, in pre-modern times, the major theorists and disseminators of the Buddhist *Dhamma*, whom he terms "theologians," were "an élite within an élite, for they were among the very few people within their societies who were able to separate themselves from lay life to follow the monastic calling, and they were, unlike the majority of the populace (and probably the majority of monastics)[,] literate."[6] In addition to being separated from the majority of people and having the education and leisure to tackle the voluminous Buddhist literature, they were befriended by the political and economic élite in their societies because they were seen as "sources of spiritual power and temporal legitimation."[7] This privileged group usually had been culturally conditioned to identify with the existing social orders and not to question them. As a result, Buddhist masters in history have been known more through their teachings about, and pursuit of, individual inner peace in various adverse situations, than through their effort in challenging and restructuring the social institutions at their times. Most of them also uncritically inherited an androcentric bias that has been persistent in most societies and in most ages. The privileged androcentric perspective of the major transmitters of the *Dhamma*, which focused on individual spiritual transformation and paid little attention to structural problems and gender inequity, has been kept alive in their commentaries and translations.[8] Being the *Dhamma* teachers and lineage patriarchs, those privileged men were (and still are) much revered in most Asian cultures where Buddhism has been influential, and as such their teachings sometimes became utterly unchallengeable. Thus, even though the transmitters of the Buddhist *Dhamma* of later times were not necessarily of the upper classes, and even though some of them were not even male, they inherited their masters' blind spots together with their insights. As a result, they took the existing social orders and gender roles for granted, focused on inner peace *only*, overemphasized isolated meditation and individualistic intellectual study, and devalued social relationships.[9] Even among traditional Asian Mahāyānists, who often self-proclaimed to be committed to "liberating all sentient beings," the *socio*-ethical implications of the Buddha's teachings were often downplayed, and the cultivation of the mind was often propped up as the sole point of the Buddhist *Dhamma*. Socio-ethical engagement was thus rendered secondary by some, if not utterly unimportant.

Western colonialism in Asia, unfortunately, pushed Buddhism further down the path of social indifference and individual purification. Edmund F. Perry relates this recent history in his foreword to Walpola Rāhula's *The Heritage of the Bhikkhu*:

> The image of the Buddhist monk as a public leader engaging in social and political activities had been obscured, deliberately so, by Western colonialists and their accompanying Christian missionaries. By imposing a particular type of Christian monasticism upon the Buddhist clergy, restricting the clergy's activity to individual purification and temple ministries, the colonial administrators dispossessed the

> *bhikkhus* of their influence on the public life of their people
> and actually succeeded in instituting a tradition of Buddhist
> recluses, to the near exclusion of other types of clergy.
>   . . . The conspiracy to "convert" the Buddhist monk
> from public leader to disengaged recluse prevailed so widely
> and pervasively that today even in independent countries
> the monks have to struggle against so-called Buddhist
> politicians who, still possessed by the "heritage" left by
> the imperialists, want, more than the colonial Christians,
> to silence and seclude the monks as though the monk
> constitutes a public menace.[10]

Under Western colonial rule, Buddhism was branded as a religion
that lacked a social ethic and thus irrelevant to modern society.
That misrepresentation was furthermore taught to the colonized,
especially the élite who received "modern" education and learned
to see their own traditions through the colonial lens.[11] To this day,
"Western scholars of Buddhism tend to perpetuate the image of the
Buddhist monk as something like the medieval mystic recluse of the
Christian faith,"[12] and "Popular literature in the West often presents
the 'essence' of Buddhism as primarily about inner experience rather
than its institutional and social realities."[13]

However, the historical and social reality is that the Buddhist goal
of the cessation of *dukkha* has never been disregarded, even though at
times it was turned inward and individualized. Prior to the colonial
presence, Buddhism in Asia had had a "considerable history of social
involvement."[14] In Theravāda countries, such as Ceylon (Sri Lanka),
bhikkhu-s (Sanskrit: *bhikṣu*-s; male Buddhist renunciates) had served
as the ethical and spiritual educators of the masses, preservers of
cultural heritages, main providers of medical care and social services,
and advisors to the rulers.[15] Even in East Asian countries where the
Confucian tradition is said to have dominated the social, ethical, and
political spheres, *bhikkhu*-s, *bhikkhunī*-s (Sanskrit: *bhikṣunī*-s; female Buddhist renunciates), and lay followers often engaged in social work and
disaster relief as an effort to fulfill the Mahāyānist bodhisattva vow of
"liberating all sentient beings." Engaged Buddhist theorist Ken Jones
observes, "in both Theravada and Mahayana scripture, the practical
relief of suffering is commonly given first priority."[16]

In the Buddhist *Dhamma*, ethical discipline is an indispensable
part of the path that leads to *nibbāna*, and inner peace and social
well-being are positively correlated. Part of understanding non-Self
(Pāli: *anatta*; Sanskrit: *anātman*) and interdependent co-arising (Pāli:

paṭiccasamuppāda; Sanskrit: *pratītyasamutpāda*; also translated as dependent origination, interconditionality, or simply co-arising) is to see the mutual generations and mutual reinforcements between the "inner" states of an individual and her or his "outer" behaviors, between an individual's behavior and the social realities, and between the seemingly "external" socio-cultural phenomena and the seemingly "internal" mental processes of individuals. As such, individual transformation includes ethical dealing with one's surroundings, and social well-being is a *bona fide* Buddhist concern. Robert Magliola observes that the globally influential engaged Buddhists "were *perhaps* inspired *in part* by western models, but they have *revived* (long-untapped) political/ social reserves in their own Buddhism."[17] (Emphasis added.) That is, rather than being a purely modern invention inspired by Protestant Christian values,[18] social ethics has been ingrained in the Buddhist *Dhamma* since its inception.

In this book I draw from the foundational teachings recognized by all Buddhist schools in order to revive its social ethics that has often been downplayed and neglected. In this regard, this book provides a theoretical and textual foundation of socially engaged Buddhism and its ethics. Christopher Ives aptly critiques that engaged Buddhist discourses so far largely deploy a rather nebulously defined concept of "interdependence" and thereby "step onto a slippery rhetorical slope and, by extension, run the risk of succumbing to slippery argumentation."[19] A theoretical work that grounds the ethics of socially engaged Buddhism in foundational Buddhist texts is therefore much needed. At the same time, heeding the Buddha's own injunction as quoted at the beginning of this chapter, I will maintain a spirit of inquiry taught by the Buddha[20] and think critically about traditional materials, keeping in mind that the true criteria for Buddhist views and actions are alleviating *dukkha* and contributing to welfare of all sentient beings.[21] In this effort, I am joining those who engage in critical and constructive Buddhist thinking, exploring the ways in which the Buddhist teachings can be understood and revalorized to help deal with various forms of social *dukkha* in today's much globalized and still patriarchal world. The critical-constructive Buddhist thinking, otherwise termed "Buddhist theology," involves "critiquing past elements of tradition inappropriate to a new time, recovering or re-emphasizing other elements, critiquing Western models inadequate for a fuller understanding of Buddhism, and exploring the potential of Buddhist experience to shine new light upon a host of contemporary cultural and religious concerns."[22] This approach to the Buddhist *Dhamma*, as I will show in the section "Dhammic Exegesis" below, is completely grounded in the Buddha's own teachings and examples as recorded in the earliest Buddhist literature, even though some may consider it a form of "Buddhist Modernism" that emerged newly "out of an engagement with the dominant cultural and intellectual forces of modernity."[23]

In the same effort of taking up the Buddha's injunctions to alleviate *dukkha* and work for the well-being of all, male and female, this book also seeks to address the social expectations and impositions of gender roles, which have resulted in much suffering for women and sometimes for men also. The concept of *kamma* (Sanskrit: *karma*), in particular, has been frequently misused to justify male dominance. A female rebirth has been commonly viewed as the unavoidable result of negative *kamma* from past lives, and the purported negative *kamma* from past lives is used to justify the mistreatments that a woman endures in this life.[24] In light of these abuses and in the spirit of alleviating suffering, a feminist critique is necessary in the revitalization of the socio-ethical dimensions of the Buddhist teachings. Gender is a very basic aspect of individual identity to which a person may tenaciously cling,[25] and yet the central Buddhist teaching of non-Self has never been consistently applied to gender, which is rather questionable for a tradition dedicated to analyzing the constructedness of self-identity and discouraging all forms of self-clinging.[26]

I will build on the work of liberal and liberationist feminist scholars of Buddhism, particularly Rita M. Gross, and extend their effort by referencing recent feminist analyses of gender construction and socio-economic ramifications of sexism and rigid gender roles. In particular, theories inspired by poststructuralism and Foucault, such as constructivism posed by Judith Butler, provide a richer language for explicating the socio-ethical implications of basic Buddhist teachings such as non-Self, five aggregates, *kamma*, and the significance of the *Sangha*. These feminist theories can form a more nuanced and yet more radical critique of gender hierarchy (and any other form of social inequity that claims to be based on inherent nature). More importantly, they can better capture the dynamic complexities that are conveyed by the teaching of interdependent co-arising: relations among beings are as dynamic and ever-changing as beings themselves are. Thus regarded, ethics in Buddhism is not about abiding by a set of rigid, inalterable rules, but *an ongoing process of striving to be ethical in the midst of ever-changing relations among ever-changing beings. Sangha*, one of the Three Jewels in which all Buddhists take refuge, then, is not a closed community bound by geographical proximity, much less by blood relation, but is *an unending effort of building communities and working interconnections.* It follows that *nibbāna,* the cessation of *dukkha,* is not a static existence where nothing happens, but *a dynamic endeavor of alleviating dukkha and making peace that requires the participation of everyone entangled in the interconnected web of life.* Recent poststructuralist feminist theories serve as an interpretive tool that demystifies and yet brings forth the insights of Buddhism. They can be very helpful in my revitalization of this-worldly Buddhist social ethics informed by interdependent co-arising. They can also make basic Buddhist teachings accessible and acceptable to people who are concerned with their own and/or global social well-being but do not identify themselves as Buddhists.

Aiming at ceasing the *dukkha* that is present in social realities, the Buddha's teachings cannot be separated from social interactions, but they cannot be reduced to social interactions, either. *Nibbāna* is unattainable through "external" structural and behavioral changes alone, in the same way that it is unattainable through "internal" emotive and conceptual changes alone. To say the least, *nibbāna* literally means "blowing out" or "extinguishing," and in the canonical understanding what is blown out or extinguished is the three "fires" of delusion (*moha;* synonymous with ignorance [Pāli: *avijjā;* Sanskrit: *avidyā*] in Buddhist usage), greed/lust (*lobha;* synonymous with *rāga*), and hatred/ill will (Pāli: *dosa;* Sanskrit: *dveṣa*). These three "fires" are also called three "poisons" and three "root vices" (Pāli: *akusala-mūla;* Sanskrit: *akuśala-mūla*). Together, they comprise *taṇhā* (Sanskrit: *tṛṣṇā*), the deeply seated fixations that cause *dukkha.* Immoral conducts occur "through a misapprehension of the facts [i.e., delusion] . . . together with an emotional investment," which swings to the extremes of greed/lust and hatred/ill will.[27] The cessation of *dukkha,* therefore, concerns "the destruction of lust, the destruction of hatred, [and] the destruction of delusion."[28] That is to say, *nibbāna* requires not only behavioral transformation, but also emotive and conceptual transformations. The Buddhist Noble Eightfold Path (Pāli: *ariya-atthangika-magga;* Sanskrit: *ārya-astanga-mārga*), through its Three Learnings (Sanskrit: *triśiksā*) of ethical discipline (Pāli: *sīla;* Sanskrit: *śīla*),[29] mental training (Pāli/Sanskrit: *samādhi*),[30] and wisdom development (Pāli: *paññā;* Sanskrit: *prajñā*),[31] is a holistic program that guides behavioral, emotive, and conceptual transformations altogether. Ethical social interaction is certainly not all there is in the Buddhist path to the cessation of *dukkha,* just as individual inner peace is not. The Buddhist *Dhamma* teaches that the "internal" and the "external" are interconnected, and therefore we need to work on both at the same time.

Foundational Texts and Basic Teachings:
Nikāya-s in the Pāli Canon

Buddhist literature is traditionally divided into three groups, called the Three Baskets (Pāli: *Tipiṭaka*; Sanskrit: *Tripiṭaka*): the *Vinaya Piṭaka* (the Basket of Disciplines for Renunciates), the *Sutta Piṭaka* (Sanskrit: *Sūtra Piṭaka*; the Basket of the Discourses of the Buddha), and the *Abhidhamma Piṭaka* (Sanskrit: *Abhidharma Piṭaka*; the Basket of Higher Teachings, referring to scholastic and philosophical renditions of the Discourses of the Buddha). The three major branches of Buddhism, Theravāda, Mahāyāna, and Vajrayāna, however, do not recognize the exact same set of texts. The Mahāyāna and Vajrayāna collections, in fact, contain many more texts than the Three Baskets, even though the term "Three Baskets" is often used as a generic term for the whole collection of Buddhist teachings. Theravādins generally consider the Pāli Canon to be the authentic teachings of the Buddha and remain suspicious of many of the texts preserved in the Mahāyāna and Vajrayāna collections. Mahāyānists and Vajrayānists, on the other hand, generally do not question the legitimacy of the Pāli Canon, even though they may consider their respective tradition to be the ultimate form of Buddhism and may consider the Pāli Canon a product of the Buddha's "skillful means" that caters to people of lesser capacities.[32] That is, Buddhists across traditions recognize early Buddhist literature as the basic and foundational texts of Buddhism, and more often than not they "see themselves as directly in the line of that early Buddhism."[33] More importantly, various forms of "Modern Buddhism," such as the multiple strains of "Engaged Buddhism" taking place simultaneously in different regions, "Critical Buddhism" in Japan, and "Buddhism for the Human Realm" in Taiwan, all see themselves as a return to the Buddhist *Dhamma* practiced at the time of the Buddha and all appeal to the early Buddhist literature.[34] Therefore, in order to make the Buddhist social ethics revitalized in this book recognized as *Dhammic* (that is, in accordance with the Buddhist *Dhamma*) by Buddhists across traditions, I will mainly reference the Pāli Canon for the key concepts of Buddhism.

Among the Three Baskets, the *Vinaya Piṭaka* is most readily associated with ethics since it contains behavioral codes. In fact, most of the discussions about Buddhist ethics available either focus on the *Vinaya* alone or rely heavily on it.[35] However, it is not very practical to extract Buddhist social ethics from the *Vinaya* for the simple reason that the majority of Buddhists in the world are not renunciates and do not abide by the hundreds[36] of precepts contained in the *Vinaya*

Piṭaka. Moreover, many of the rules in the *Vinaya*, such as the practice of rain retreat, were simply customary practices among wandering ascetics in Northeastern India at the time of the historical Buddha or later.[37] A kind of Buddhist social ethics that may be recognizable by Buddhists in the modern world, who are predominantly lay and mostly do not live in Northeastern India, has to be extracted from the *Dhamma* contained in the *Sutta Piṭaka* acknowledged by all those who walk the Buddhist path.

To extract Buddhist social ethics from the *Dhamma* rather than the *Vinaya* is in fact a valid approach in Buddhists' own terms. The *Dhamma* and the *Vinaya* are traditionally mentioned together as "*Dhamma-Vinaya*."[38] Ian J. Coghlan expounds the mutually dependent and mutually enhancing relation between *Dhamma* and *Vinaya* as such:

> If ethics [as reflected in the Vinaya] is not extensively taught, it is difficult to establish the basis for generating the correct view of dhamma, in accordance with the progressive development of the three higher trainings. If dhamma is not extensively taught, it is difficult to understand the need for ethics and the very nature of dhamma itself. Without a stable understanding of these two, negative internal and external conditions will tend to quickly undermine the spiritual life. Aspirants, therefore, need to train for a long period within a proper training structure overseen by others adequately. trained in ethics and dhamma. Such realized guides are capable of directly demonstrating the path in accordance with their realization.[39]

Thai scholar-*bhikkhu* Phra Prayudh Payutto (Rājavaramuni) also explains the connection and distinction between the Buddha's teaching and the precepts he laid down over time: "Buddhism in its entirety consists of the *dhamma* and the *vinaya*. . . . The *dhamma* deals with ideals and principles, whereas the *vinaya* deals with rules and circumstances in which these ideals and principles are practiced and realized."[40] The *Vinaya* is the *Dhamma* spelled out in detail for a particular group of people in a particular socio-cultural context at a particular time, but the overarching principles of the *Vinaya* were contained in the *Dhamma* recorded in the *Sutta Piṭaka*. Étienne Lamotte therefore asserts, "While the Vinaya is only a convention (*saṃvrti*) adopted as a line of conduct, the Dharma as propounded in the Sūtra represents the absolute truth (*paramārthasatya*)."[41] Therefore, even though the *Vinaya* is ostensibly more relevant in the discussion and construction of Buddhist ethics, it is the *Dhamma* recorded in the *Sutta*s that provides the rationales for the ethical codes in Buddhism.

The *Sutta Piṭaka* in the Pāli Canon consists of four major collections of *sutta*s called the *Nikāya*-s. They are called *Āgama*-s in the Sanskrit Buddhist texts and are preserved in the Chinese *Tripitaka*. Despite the variations in arrangement, Étienne Lamotte observes, "The doctrinal basis common to the āgamas and nikāyas is remarkably uniform."[42] The Pāli *Sutta Piṭaka* contains a fifth collection of short texts, such as *Theragāthā* and *Therīgāthā*. It has been recognized by scholars of the Pāli Canon that each of the four major *Nikāya*-s carries its own distinctive immediate objectives. The *Dīgha Nikāya* (The Long Discourses of the Buddha[43]) "is permeated by a concern with the propagation of Buddhism."[44] Suttas in this collection either portray the Buddha in debate against brāhmins or glorify the Buddha profusely. The *Majjhima Nikāya* (The Middle-Length Discourses of the Buddha[45]) "has its spotlight directed towards the Buddhist community itself,"[46] and so its suttas deal largely with the fundamentals of the Buddha's teachings, including the building of communities according to Buddhist ideals. The *Samyutta Nikāya* (The Connected Discourses of the Buddha[47]) would have served as a reference for those "who were capable of grasping the deepest dimensions of Buddhist wisdom and who were charged with clarifying for others the subtle perspectives opened up by the Buddha's Teaching."[48] As such, it contains suttas pertaining to philosophical theories and structures in which the *bhikkhu*-s and *bhikkhunī*-s are trained. The *Anguttara Nikāya* (The Numerical Discourses of the Buddha[49]) focuses more on what is practical in terms of "personal edification,"[50] and hence the suttas in this collection teach basic ethical observances as well elucidate the methods of rigorous mental training. The fifth collection, consisting of fifteen or fourteen or nineteen or twelve books, is named *Khuddaka Nikāya* in the canon of some schools, *Ksudraka Piṭaka* in the canon of some other schools that use Sanskrit texts, and excluded from the canon of still others, such as the Sarvāstivāda.[51]

More often than not, instructions contained in the *Anguttara Nikāya* were directed toward renunciant and lay male brāhmins who were most concerned with self-purification. The abundance of instructions on self-purification in this collection, then, is better understood as the result of the Buddha's attempt to appeal to those male brāhmins, rather than the overall focus of the Buddha's teachings. Targeting mainly at male brāhmins wary of temptation and contamination, not surprisingly this collection also contains the majority of the rather misogynist statements that can be found in the *Nikāya* literature.[52]

Likewise, it would be erroneous if one concludes, based on the *Dīgha Nikāya* that aimed at propagating Buddhism, that the Buddha was only concerned with glorifying himself. It is probably best to look to the *Samyutta Nikāya* for doctrinal nuances, and the *Majjhima Nikāya* for the Buddha's instructions on community building. The exposition of central Buddhist teachings such as co-arising and five aggregates in this book, therefore, will be drawn primarily from the *Samyutta Nikāya* and the *Majjhima Nikāya*. The *Dīgha Nikāya* and the *Anguttara Nikāya* will be referenced when the main issue is the Buddha's skillfulness in communicating with privileged non-Buddhists as well as with male Buddhists with strong brāhmanic backgrounds.

Citing the *Nikāya* texts in the Pāli Canon as the foundational teachings of the Buddha is not the same as endorsing the claim made by some Theravādins that Theravāda Buddhism is the "authentic" or "pure" Buddhism that has preserved the Buddha's original teachings without change.[53] First of all, in terms of basic Buddhist teachings, one of the "Three Marks of Reality" (Pāli: *tilakkhaṇa*; Sanskrit: *trilakṣaṇa*; also translated as the "Three Characteristics of Existence"[54]) in Buddhism is that everything in the phenomenal world is impermanent; every phenomenon co-arises with its material and socio-cultural surroundings and therefore changes together with them. From a Buddhist perspective, that is, it is rather delusional for one to claim that something has never changed for two thousand five hundred years. Many Western scholars on Buddhism have also seen Theravāda as preserving original Buddhist teachings with little change,[55] to the extent that the Theravādin emphasis of individual effort and its practice of not acknowledging women's equal potential have been retrospectively, and quite inaccurately, attributed to early Buddhism. The prevalence of equating Theravāda Buddhism with early Buddhism is evidenced by the fact that a search of "early Buddhism" in a library catalogue is likely to bring forth entries on Theravāda Buddhism.

Additionally, in terms of historical evidence, Theravāda Buddhism in Southeast Asian countries has been compromised by political powers and reshaped by the existing local cultures as much as Mahāyāna Buddhism in East Asian countries has.[56] To say the least, the vestiges of Brāhmanism, especially its over-emphasis on individual purity and its hierarchical social structure, are still readily discernible today in Theravāda countries such as Sri Lanka, Thailand, Laos, and Cambodia. Brahmā, the "creator" according to brāhmins' construction, is commonly worshiped in Theravāda countries under the misleading title of "The Four-Faced Buddha." Even Tavivat Puntarigvivat, who claims that Theravāda Buddhism has preserved the Buddha's teachings "without any significant change," acknowledges that in Theravāda countries such as his home-country Thailand, "monks not sympathetic to state policies are structurally excluded from senior administrative positions within the *Sangha*, just as monks supportive of the regime in power receive material and career advancement in the *Sangha* hierarchy."[57]

One of the most salient proofs of Theravāda having been reshaped by the cultural and political norms in its locality is the position and title of *Sangharāja* (literally, "the king of *Sangha*") within the Thai Theravādin *Sangha* hierarchy, officially appointed by the king.[58] This office is a direct contradiction to the Buddha's own teachings and practices as recorded in the Pāli Canon. It was recorded that the Buddha said, "It does not occur to the Tathāgata, 'I will take charge of the Bhikkhu Sangha,' or 'The Bhikkhu Sangha is under my direction,' so why should the Tathāgata make some pronouncement concerning the Bhikkhu Sangha?"[59] The Buddha considered himself a teacher and not a ruler of the *Sangha*; therefore it would not be in conformity with his role as a teacher to appoint a successor. Furthermore, his final injunction to the *bhikkhu*-s and *bhikkhunī*-s was, specifically, "Dwell with yourselves as your own island, with yourselves as your own refuge, with no other refuge; dwell with the Dhamma as your island, with the Dhamma as your refuge, with no other refuge."[60] Similarly, in the *Mahāparinibbāna Sutta* the Buddha was recorded to have instructed, "What I have taught and explained to you as *Dhamma-Vinaya* will, at my passing, be your teacher."[61] It is recorded in the *Majjhima Nikāya* that, by not appointing a successor, the Buddha intended (or so as the compilers of the *Nikāya* texts understood it) for his disciples to lead a relatively egalitarian communal life according to the *Dhamma-Vinaya*, rather than to have a hierarchical structure with a king-like figure.[62]

Related to the above is another glaring counterproof to the claim that Theravāda has transmitted the original Buddhist teachings without change: the current male *sangha* hierarchy's opposition to the restoration of the *bhikkhunī sangha*,[63] which was established by the Buddha himself as recorded in the Pāli Canon. For this reason, Rita M. Gross points out that "contemporary Theravādin Buddhism is not identical with early Buddhism, especially in practices regarding women."[64] It might seem that male dominance was sanctioned by the Pāli Canon, which the Buddhist traditions in general and the Theravāda tradition in particular believe to have reached its current content and format at the First Council held immediately after the Buddha's death. Presumably, the Canon thus constructed carries the Buddha's words as his own direct disciples remembered them, and therefore the misogynist attitude contained in the Canon was from the Buddha himself. However, one has to keep in mind that the Pāli Canon had been orally transmitted for at least four hundred years before it was committed to writing. In fact, very few Buddhist texts in their present form can be definitely dated to earlier than the fourth or fifth centuries CE. Some of the early texts may have been committed to writing in the first century BCE, approximately four hundred years after the Buddha's passing. The *Vinaya* texts were codified in their present form even later, in about the fourth to fifth centuries CE.[65] Peter N. Gregory thus questions the validity of equating the Pāli Canon with the Buddha's own words:

> Although the Pāli canon may, as a whole, be closer to the Buddha's "word" than any other extant textual corpus, it is still mediated by the collective memory of the community that compiled, codified, redacted, and transmitted it orally for hundreds of years before ever committing it to writing, and even when finally put into writing, it did not remain static but continued to be modified by the tradition over the ensuing centuries. As we have it today it is thus far removed from the Buddha, and we have no way of gauging how close or how distant any given statement is to the words of the Buddha.[66]

Nyanaponika Thera and Bhikkhu Bodhi also point out in the introduction to their translation of the *Anguttara Nikāya*, "it is essential to realize that they [the Pāli texts] are the products of an oral tradition."[67] For the sake of oral transmission, "These were streamlined, condensed and standardized, cast into a format suitable for memorization; hence the prevalence of stock phrases, formulaic definitions and frequent repetition."[68] The suttas in the *Nikāya*-s themselves contain evidences of extensive editing for the purpose of memorization. David R. Loy further observes that the history of oral transmission provided "many opportunities for some passages to be intentionally or unintentionally 'corrected' by monks less enlightened than the Buddha."[69] In other words, the Pāli *Nikāya*-s, the earliest Buddhist literature traditionally held to be the most authentic, are not the exact recording of the Buddha's exchanges with his followers, but are products of a later period.[70] The *Vinaya* texts, in fact, supply the information that the *Dhamma* was not only uttered by the Buddha, but also by his direct followers, wise recluses (*rsi*), gods (*deva*), and apparitional beings (*upapāduka*).[71] What might have actually taken place at the First Council, Bhikkhu Bodhi suggests, "was the drafting of a comprehensive scheme for classifying the suttas . . . and the appointment of an editorial committee (perhaps several) to review the material available and cast it into a format conducive to easy memorization and oral transmission."[72]

Moreover, according to the tradition, the First Council was attended by five hundred *bhikkhu*-s, and *bhikkhu*-s only. The prominent *bhikkhu*-s at the time of the Buddha were largely of upper-class backgrounds,[73] and it was highly likely that they had been heavily influenced by the androcentric culture in the larger society.[74] It was a culture, *bhikkhunī* scholar Karma Lekshe Tsomo points out, in which women "were classified as dependents either under the protection of their father, their husband, or, upon a husband's death, their husband's brother."[75] In that culture, women existed largely as men's property, which was subject to plunder and abuse if the "ownership" was not clear or was not firmly established. In the *Mahāparinibbāna Sutta*, for instance, the Vajjians' "not forcibly abduct[ing] others' wives and daughters and compel[ling] them to live with them" was extolled as a "virtue,"[76] which evinces that in India at that time it was not uncommon for men to use violence to snatch women from other men and force them to provide menial and/or sexual services.

Needless to say, privileged men were more likely than women to have the freedom of leaving home and becoming renunciates if they so desired. Men in that society generally enjoyed much greater mobility, as well as safety, than women. In addition, upper-class families, having control over lower-class people and practically living off of their labors, could afford losing one man or two in the family to spiritual pursuits. By contrast, it was much more difficult for women to break the confines of their homes to follow the Buddha around since permission from the male kinsmen in charge was required in order to join the Buddhist *Sangha* as a renunciate.[77] "[I]n a patriarchal society, men simply left their wives, without a mutual agreement . . . By contrast, wives who wished to become nuns usually had to wait until their husbands died or granted them permission to leave."[78] Even if a woman did successfully leave home, she was at a much greater risk of being assaulted in a society where women had to be owned by men and guarded by their "owners." Incidents of male violence against female renunciates were recorded, and some regulations were designed to prevent it as a result.[79]

In a culture so deeply entrenched in these forms of sexism, it should not come as a surprise that the compilers of the Canon, who were very likely to be men from upper-class families, retained an androcentric or even misogynist attitude. To make things worse for women, celibacy was the norm amongst the anti-Brāhmanic renunciates

(Pāli: *samaṇas*; Sanskrit: *śramaṇas*) at the time. The Buddhist *Sangha*, being one of the only two religious orders that accommodated female renunciates (the other one was Jainism), was likely to incur suspicion and criticisms both from other celibate renunciates and from the larger androcentric society.[80] Wijayaratna points out that the first group of women who joined the monastic sangha were relatives of the Buddha from the Sākyan tribe, which incurred suspicion from outsiders regarding the seriousness of their renunciation.[81] It was highly probable that the Buddha tailored his teachings to suit the mentality of his predominantly male audience on the one hand, and to respond to the criticisms coming from the non-Buddhist society on the other. It was also highly probable that, in order to guard the reputation of the Buddhist *Sangha* under the societal expectation of establishing the ownership of women, the male compilers further sought to control and subordinate the female renunciates among them. Perhaps the male compilers did so also to help themselves deal with the requirement of celibacy at the close proximity of women:

> The compilers of the various Buddhist monastic codes that we have appear to have been very anxious men. They were anxious about—even obsessed with—maintaining their public reputation and that of their order, and avoiding any hint of social scandal or lay criticism. They were anxious about their body and what went into it; and they were anxious about women. They appear, moreover, to have been particularly anxious about nuns, about containing, restraining and controlling them. At every opportunity they seem to have promulgated rules towards these ends.[82]

According to the Theravāda tradition, the five hundred *bhikkhu*-s at the First Council reprimanded Ānanda for the "offense" of introducing women into the Buddhist *Sangha*,[83] which reflected the anxiety that Gregory Schopen, scholar of early Buddhist monasticism, poignantly points out in the quote above. The male compilers' effort of keeping women contained and controlled is also reflected in the later interpolation, roughly in the first century BCE, of the *aṭṭhagarudhammā* (Sanskrit: *aṣṭaugurudharmāḥ*), the eight revered conditions that intended to subordinate *bhikkhunī*-s under *bhikkhu*-s and may have indirectly contributed to the demise of the *bhikkhunī sangha* in the Theravāda tradition.[84] Scholars concluded that misogyny grew more pronounced after the first few hundred years of Buddhism, and "[t]he positive attitude toward women evident among the early Buddhists seems to have declined sharply around the time written Buddhism literature began to appear."[85]

The Pāli Canon recorded largely upper-class androcentric understandings and redactions of the Buddha's teachings. It does not preserve the exact words of the Buddha without change and does not reflect the Buddha's own position in every regard. Furthermore, it is worthwhile to bear in mind that, in the Buddhist worldview, texts are also phenomena (Pāli: *dhamma*-s; Sanskrit: *dharma*-s) that have been interdependently co-arisen, which means that texts also bear the "Three Marks of Reality," i.e., unsatisfactoriness, impermanence, and lack of self-essence. In other words, from the Buddhist perspective, no text is sacred if the word "sacred" means in and of itself holy, permanently true, and worthy of unconditional veneration. To say that texts are not "sacred" in Buddhism is not to suggest that textual study bears no importance for Buddhists. Buddhism, as other religions, is to some extent defined by its texts and Buddhists do commonly use traditional texts to gauge their understandings and guide their practices. In Buddhist terms, now that the Buddha entered *parinibbāna* and is no longer in the world, a follower aspiring to realize Buddhahood can only learn the *Dhamma* from Buddhist texts or from knowledgeable practicing Buddhists, whose knowledge is likely to have been based on their study of Buddhist texts. Moreover, in the contemporary world of rising literacy rate and increasingly individualistic approach to religious traditions, more and more Buddhists are turning to texts by themselves for insights and guidance.[86] Discourses that are based on the study of classical texts still carry more weight than those that are not, and discourses that invoke the Buddha and appeal to the core teachings can speak to Buddhists across traditions. Even though the Buddha's own position remains unknowable due to the history of oral transmission, in the absence of archaeological evidences from the early period, "the texts are all we have."[87]

Besides, it is worth noting that the Pāli texts do contain some egalitarian and protofeminist statements alongside the androcentric or even misogynist regulations. The very appearance of egalitarian statements in a highly patriarchal society, and the survival of them, suggest either that the Buddha himself had not been as misogynist as the later compilers of the Pāli Canon were, or that at least some compilers understood the Buddha's teachings very differently. Alan Sponberg maintains that early Buddhist literature recorded a multiplicity of voices rather than one ambivalent, uncertain voice.[88] At any rate, the fact that those egalitarian statements appeared and survived speaks volumes.[89] It refutes an entirely misogynist reading of Buddhist teachings and can support a gender-inclusive ethic that is well grounded in early Buddhist texts. Moreover, all of the core teachings of the Buddha support an all-inclusive revalorization of Buddhist ethics, as shown in the following section.

Dhammic Exegesis: Interdependent Co-Arising and the Cessation of *Dukkha*

The singular goal of the Buddha's Teaching is *nibbāna*, the cessation of *dukkha*. Therefore, a view or practice that is not conducive to the cessation or alleviation of *dukkha* is not worth endeavoring, let alone holding onto.[90] That is, according to the Buddhist *Dhamma*, the cessation of *dukkha*, rather than religious identity or cultural boundary, is the criterion for adopting a view or practice.

The Buddha on numerous occasions discouraged his followers from dogmatically clinging to philosophical views or religious doctrines. In the *Anguttara Nikāya*, for instance, the Buddha said that religions came into dispute with one another "because of lust for views, because of adherence, bondage, greed, obsession and cleaving to views."[91] In the *Majjhima Nikāya*, the Buddha said it was in terms of not propounding "full understanding of clinging to views" and not propounding "full understanding of clinging to rules and observances" that a teaching would be "unemancipating" and "unconducive to peace."[92] Even when talking about his own teachings, the Buddha cautioned against clinging and then reiterated that the purpose of imparting or learning or practicing the *Dhamma* was emancipation and cessation of *dukkha*:

> Bhikkhus, both formerly and now what I teach is *dukkha* and the cessation of *dukkha*. If others abuse, revile, scold, and harass the Tathāgata for that, the Tathāgata on that account feels no annoyance, bitterness, or dejection of the heart. And if others honour, respect, revere, and venerate the Tathāgata for that, the Tathāgata on that account feels no delight, joy, or elation of the heart.[93]

And the Buddha went on to suggest that his listeners adopt the same attitude. He taught the *Dhamma* in order to cease *dukkha*, not to provide an anchor for identity clinging or any form of self-absorbed dejection or elation. And his followers were instructed to do the same.

The Buddha likened his *Dhamma* to a raft, which was built solely for the purpose of crossing a great expanse of dangerous water and reaching the far shore that was safe and free from fear. He asked his listeners to reason about the proper use of the raft:

> By doing what would that man be doing what should be done with that raft? Here, bhikkhus, when that man got across and had arrived at the far shore, he might think thus: ". . . Suppose I were to haul it onto the dry land or set it adrift in the water, and then go wherever I want." Now, bhikkhus, it is by so doing that that man would be doing what should be done with that raft. So I have shown you how the Dhamma is similar to a raft, being for the purpose of crossing over, not for the purpose of grasping.
>
> Bhikkhus, when you know the Dhamma to be similar to a raft, you should abandon even the teachings, how much more so things contrary to the teachings.[94]

The Buddha gave teachings for people to practice and utilize so that *dukkha* would cease in their lives. The teachings in and of themselves were not meant to be sacred or inalterable, not to mention the written texts that carried those teachings. They could be abandoned, as the simile showed, once they served the purpose of transporting people across the *dukkha*-filled body of water. In fact, they *should* be abandoned if they did not help alleviate *dukkha* or, worse, ended up producing more of it.

Having the cessation of *dukkha* as the criterion also means that a teaching helpful in removing *dukkha* from life should be learned and put into practice, even if it was not given by the Buddha or a Buddhist master. As reflected in the opening quote, the Buddha taught his followers not to cling to or dismiss a teaching on account of the identity, lineage, school, or denomination of the teacher. Whether a teaching is to be accepted and practiced depends on whether it is conducive to the cessation of *dukkha*. Whether or not the teaching is given by someone in one's own philosophical, religious, ethnic, social, or cultural group is ultimately irrelevant.

What kind of teaching would be considered conducive to the cessation of *dukkha*? The Buddha was reported to have said that it is through not understanding interdependent co-arising that "this generation has become like a tangled ball of string, covered as with a blight, tangled like coarse grass, unable to pass beyond states of woe, the ill destiny, ruin and the round of birth-and-death."[95] For as long as people do not understand the ways in which persons and psycho-socio-cultural forces co-arise and inter-condition one another, they keep behaving themselves in such ways that produce and reproduce *dukkha* for others as well as for themselves. Eventually the vicious cycle of *dukkha* production is formed and people are caught up in it and unable to "pass beyond states of woe." If not understanding interdependent co-arising leads to *dukkha*, as it is presented in the quote, then the cessation of *dukkha* cannot be effected without understanding interdependent co-arising.

It has been established among both early Buddhists who compiled the *Nikāya*-s and contemporary Buddhist scholars that interdependent co-arising is the central teaching of the Buddha that can string all of his teachings together. In the *Majjhima Nikāya*, the collection of suttas that was directed toward the Buddhist community itself, Sāriputta (Sanskrit: Śāriputra), who traditionally has been recognized as the wisest and most scholarly among the Buddha's direct disciples, reported: "this has been said by the Blessed One: 'One who sees dependent origination sees the Dhamma; one who sees the Dhamma sees dependent origination.' "[96] Similarly, in the *Samyutta Nikāya*, the collection that carried nuances of the Buddha's teachings, Ānanda, reportedly the Buddha's closest disciple and his personal attendant, was amazed at the fact that the entire meaning of the Buddha's teachings could be stated by a single phrase, i.e., dependent origination.[97] David J. Kalupahana, author of *Ethics in Early Buddhism* and *A History of Buddhist Philosophy*, states, "The Buddha's explanation of the nature of existence is summarized in one word, *paṭiccasamuppāda* (Sanskrit: *pratītyasamutpāda*),"[98] i.e., co-arising. Thai Buddhist activist-scholar Sulak Sivaraksa, founder of the International Network of Engaged Buddhists and twice nominee of Nobel Peace Prize in 1993 and 1994, writes, "The concept of interdependent co-arising is the crux of Buddhist understanding."[99] Engaged Buddhist scholar Joanna Macy points out that *paṭiccasamuppāda* was what the Buddha realized under the *bodhi* tree,[100] and that it serves not only as an explanation of human existence, but also the ground for Buddhist morality and the means for liberation.[101]

Interdependent co-arising is the core, the summary, and the logic of the Buddhist *Dhamma*. Some may think that the Four Noble Truths are the summary of the Buddha's teachings, and many Buddhist masters begin their series of *Dhamma* talks with the Four Noble Truths, honoring the tradition that they were the first *Dhamma* talk given by the Buddha after his *nibbāna*. However, that first *Dhamma* talk was first directed at the five wandering ascetics with whom the Buddha had once practiced austerities and meditation. According to the early texts, all of them had attained very advanced levels of ethical discipline and mental training. The very concise first *Dhamma* talk directed at those advanced practitioners might not be suitable as the first talk to average people who have little or no background in mental training and whose level of ethical discipline is probably not comparable to that of those five ascetics. The Four Noble Truths are undeniably central in the Buddhist *Dhamma*, but the reasoning behind the Four Noble Truths, behind the arising and cessation of *dukkha*, is interdependent co-arising. In fact, "wisdom" in Buddhism is frequently defined as seeing co-arising, seeing "into the arising and passing away of phenomena, which is noble and penetrative and leads to the complete destruction of suffering."[102] In the *Samyutta Nikāya*, it is said that having "correct wisdom" means one is able to see, as it really is, "this dependent origination and these dependently arisen phenomena."[103] Likewise, being mindful in Buddhism is to be mindful of the formation or arising of phenomena in the world, including one's body, one's mind, and one's very own existence.[104]

Since any one phenomenon depends on multiple causes and conditions to come into existence and in turn is merely one among many causes or conditions for other phenomena, the "logic" revealed by the teaching of interdependent co-arising is not a logic of linear causality, but a logic of network causality. "Buddhist causality," Nicholas F. Gier and Paul Kjellberg state, "is seen as a cosmic web of causal conditions rather than linear and mechanical notions of pushpull causation."[105] Instead of seeing one and only one cause leading to one and only one effect without being affected by the effect, interdependent co-arising points to multiple causes, multiple effects, and mutual influences among phenomena in the world. To see interdependent co-arising is to see the causes, origins, and conditions[106] of phenomena, to understand the network of origination, and to comprehend under what conditions have things and events in human life come to be what they are. Therefore, from a Buddhist point of view, a teaching or analysis that presumes only one cause for all existing problems or proposes only one measure as the solution to all problems is to be viewed with more suspicion than those that acknowledge the intricate interrelations among multiple causes and recommend multiple measures simultaneously for dealing with *dukkha*-filled and *dukkha*-inducing situations.

In Buddhism, this central teaching of the Buddha is not considered a doctrine invented by the Buddha, but a realization of how things work in the phenomenal world. The *Nikāya*-s present the Buddha first and foremost as a teacher, a human being who came to understand interconditionality and sought to teach it out of compassion, not some speculator who invented doctrines or some supra-human being who imposed rules:

> Whether Tathāgata arise in the world or not, it still remains a fact, a firm and necessary condition of existence, that all formations are impermanent . . . that all formations are subject to suffering . . . that all things are non-Self.
>
> A Tathāgata fully awakens to this fact and penetrates it. Having fully awakened to it and penetrated it, he announces it, teaches it, makes it known, presents it, discloses it, analyses it and explains it: that all formations are impermanent, that all formations are subject to suffering, that all things are non-Self.[107]

The Buddhist tradition holds that people can understand the formations and cessations of phenomena on their own without receiving revelations of any kind from any specific deity or person, and the Buddha was one such person who understood, practiced, and realized a way of life that will be conducive to the cessation of *dukkha*. He taught what he had discovered and realized. He taught in order to enhance the listeners' comprehension of the conditions and conditionality of existence and to motivate them to engage in conscious, self-initiated trainings and practices that would be beneficial for all beings in the interconnected web of life.

For teachings to be understood and to serve the function of motivating the learners, they have to reflect the immediate objectives of a particular moment, to appeal to what the targeted audience would take for granted, and to suit the interests, dispositions, and capacities of the learners. David R. Loy understands that religious teachings often involve what poststructuralist feminist theorist Judith Butler would call performativity; that is, one can only get one's messages across to the audience by means of performing the established socio-cultural tropes with a difference.[108] Greg Bailey and Ian Mabbett, authors of *The Sociology of Early Buddhism*, observe that "the Buddha was fully aware of the brāhmanical cultural bedrock on which so many of his potential converts operated and knew that to extend his influence he would be required to present his teachings and normative forms of conduct within the traditionally patterned forms of behavior."[109] The Buddha was very skillful in making use of the beliefs and concepts permeating the Indian culture at his time in order to bring, gradually and gently, his interlocutors to understand

and practice the *dukkha*-alleviating *Dhamma*, whether or not they planned to become Buddhist renunciates or identify themselves as lay followers of the Buddha.[110] For example, although taking a non-theistic viewpoint and discouraging metaphysical speculations, the Buddha frequently talked about the gods in the Hindu pantheon, as well as *kamma* and rebirth, all of which were common beliefs in his day. In dialoguing with a young brāhmin named Vāsettha, the Buddha appealed to the supposed untainted nature of Brahmā, the supreme deity that Vāsettha believed in, in order to persuade Vāsettha to cultivate loving-kindness, compassion, altruistic joy, and equanimity, to discipline himself, and to give up hate, ill-will, and impurity in the sense of moral transgression.[111]

In addition to re-appropriating the accepted concepts in the larger socio-cultural context, the Buddha also adapted to the particular dispositions and capacities of his interlocutors. Nyanaponika Thera and Bhikkhu Bodhi note that the Buddha "explains the principles he has seen in the way most appropriate for his auditors."[112] The same point was made by Donald S. Lopez, Jr. in his introduction to *Buddhist Hermeneutics*: "The Buddha is said to have taught different things to different people based on their interests, dispositions, capacities, and levels of intelligence."[113] Bikkhu Ānanda observes that the Buddha, when addressing rural folks, used similes that were familiar to them, such as bullock cart, seed, or irrigation ditch, so that his teachings could be more easily comprehended.[114] For instance, in order to instruct a brāhmin named Sundarika Bhāradvāja who believed in purification through ritual bathing in the holy rivers, the Buddha spoke of "inner bathing" through moral practice:

> A fool may there forever bathe
> Yet will not purify dark deeds.
> . . .
> It is here, brāhmin, that you should bathe,
> To make yourself a refuge for all beings.
> And if you speak no falsehood
> Nor work harm for living beings,
> Nor take what is offered not,
> With faith and free from avarice,
> What need for you to go to Gayā?
> For any well will be your Gayā.[115]

In the same vein, when talking to a brāhmin named Sigālaka, who was obsessed with carrying out the ritual of paying homage to the six directions according to the "Ariyan discipline," the Buddha added an ethical thrust to the concept of paying homage to the six directions. He identified the east with parents, the south with teachers, the west with wife and children, the north with friends and companions, the nadir with servants, and the zenith with practicing religionists, and then taught that to pay homage to the six directions was to respect people and treat them in a humane way.[116] In dialoguing with another brāhmin named Kūtadanta, who was concerned with making the most profitable sacrifice, the Buddha instructed that the most profitable sacrifice was to perfect oneself in morality and wisdom, thereby successfully stopping him from carrying out an excessive sacrifice that would have involved killing seven hundred bulls, seven hundred bullocks, seven hundred heifers, seven hundred he-goats, and seven hundred rams.[117]

In order to persuade his predominantly privileged male audience to practice the *dukkha*-ceasing *Dhamma* realized by him, the Buddha appealed to their beliefs and concerns in their cultural context. The similes and concepts the Buddha used are obviously rather remote for people living in today's globalized and very much Westernized world. Targeting an audience living in Northeastern India two thousand five hundred years ago, some of the Buddha's teachings can no longer induce *dukkha*-alleviating understandings and practices, even though some other teachings transcend time and culture. That is to say, it is not being true to the Buddha's own teachings for modern-day Buddhists to strictly adhere to the languages and instructions contained in the early Buddhist texts. Following the Buddha's own example, Buddhists should not cling to "Buddhist" texts if they are no longer practical or practicable in the current contexts. Likewise, they need not hesitate to employ non-Buddhist rafts if they are conducive to ethical behaviors and the alleviation of *dukkha* in the contexts in which they find themselves.

As a result of Western domination in the past few hundred years, most privileged people around the globe nowadays have received Western education. Western philosophies and theories, therefore, are likely to be more appealing in their eyes than traditional non-Western discourses. More importantly, no matter how wise and enlightened the Buddha might be, he did not offer any analysis on the co-arising of this world we currently inhabit. That is, in revealing the interconditionality of human existence and worldly phenomena, and in explicating the ethical implications of the Buddhist teaching of interdependent co-arising, it is far more relevant and cogent to cite contemporary analyses on subjectivity, power relations, and global socio-economic interdependence, than to cite the classical presentations in the Pāli texts or any traditional Buddhist texts, particularly if the audience is the Western or Westernized élite. At the very least, citing contemporary theories and analyses may help people living in the contemporary world understand better the formation or co-arising of their own existence and the phenomena in their own world. The understanding of co-arising, as mentioned above, is a crucial compo-nent of what the Buddha would have called "wisdom" in that it can guide people to choose the most *dukkha*-alleviating courses of actions possible. In other words, incorporating contemporary Western theories in this much Westernized world may be necessary to introduce, or re-introduce, the socio-ethical dimensions of Buddhism to the educated élite who, from a Buddhist perspective, have been more responsible than others for the *dukkha*-inflicting conditions in the world (this point will be elaborated in Chapter 4), whether the élite are Western or non-Western, Buddhist or non-Buddhist. Therefore, in the process of constructing or reconstructing an ethic that is in accordance with the Buddha's teachings, relevant to the contemporary world, appealing and meaningful for people who live in the much Westernized and globalized world today, and excluding neither women nor the non-élite, I will search for insights from both the foundational Buddhist sources and contemporary Western analyses and theories, particularly socio-economic studies and poststructuralist feminist critiques.

Constructing Non-Adversarial Engaged Feminist-Buddhist Social Ethics

In order to cease or at least alleviate *dukkha* for all Buddhist and non-Buddhist beings *in this world*, followers of the Buddha need to maintain the spirit of questioning as the Buddha taught, transcend their "Buddhist" identity, and employ non-Buddhist means as the Buddha did in response to the arising of new *dukkha*-producing situ-ations. The Buddha taught that one should not speak or act for the sake of gaining worldly advantage or promoting oneself.[118] He also emphasized that the *Dhamma* was not intended for personal triumph in ego-driven debates:

> Here, bhikkhus, some misguided men learn the Dham-ma—discourses, stanzas, expositions, verses, exclamations, sayings, birth stories, marvels, and answers to ques-tions . . . only for the sake of criticizing others and for winning in debates, and they do not experience the good

for the sake of which they learned the Dhamma. Those teachings being wrongly grasped by them, conduce to their harm and suffering for a long time.[119]

Those who used the Buddhist *Dhamma* to elevate themselves and to put others down, the Buddha said, were misguided and were wrongly grasping what he taught. They were only producing more *dukkha* when they used his teachings not as means of alleviating *dukkha* but as tools for winning glory and fame for themselves, or for attacking people of different opinions or of different lineages. The practice of the Buddhist *Dhamma* itself includes restraining from egocentric opposition.

"While the Buddha is described as participating in public presentations of his experiential, dogmaless Dhamma, and thereby disagreeing with other peoples' practices or traditions," Paul R. Fleischman points out, "he never did so with an oppositional, conversional fervor. . . . He expressed his nonviolent ethics but he did not campaign for it."[120] In the examples given in the above section, the Buddha did not aggressively attack people's practices, but neither did he give his consent to all practices. His approach was generally to direct people's attention to wholesome mental, verbal, and bodily actions without blatantly demolishing others' belief systems. On occasion he would directly point out the ineffectiveness of certain practices in bringing forth *nibbāna*, but only after he had tried several other ways to get the attention of his interlocutors. Typically he sought to communicate his ethical concerns with his interlocutors in the most nonadversarial ways, which was crucial in getting his messages across to them. For instance, when Ajātasattu Vedehiputta, the king of the Magadha, planned to attack the republic of the Vajjians, he sent his chief minister Vassakāra to the Buddha, believing the Buddha would divine the outcome. Instead of vehemently condemning the militarism on the part of the Magadhan, which might have provoked him to take even more aggressive measures, the Buddha turned to his disciple and attendant Ānanda to inquire if the Vajjians had been practicing the seven ethical principles that he had taught. Eventually the Buddha led the Magadhan chief minister Vassakāra to reach the conclusion by himself: "if the Vajjians keep to even one of these principles, they may be expected to prosper and not decline—far less all seven. Certainly the Vajjians will never be conquered by King Ajātasattu by force of arms."[121] By being nonadversarial, the Buddha practiced the nonviolent *Dhamma* he taught and deterred the Magadhan king from inflicting suffering.

Sallie B. King observes that nonadversariality is one of the most important features of various forms of contemporary Engaged

Buddhism,[122] which is, not surprisingly, based on the examples set by the Buddha himself. As a matter of fact, the Buddhist *Dhamma* is often referred to as the "Middle Way" or "Middle Path" (Pāli: *majjhimā-patipadā*; Sanskrit: *madhyamā-pratipad*), which is one of the most potent phrases in Buddhism and is meaningful on many levels. It recalls the Buddha's eventual renunciation of worldly enjoyments (and attachment to the conventional way of life) on the one hand, and asceticism (and complete withdrawal from society) on the other. It also signifies the Buddha's rejection of both eternalism (that the Self exists independently, permanently, and unchangingly) and nihilism/annihilationism (that nothing exists or a person's spiritual dimension completely perishes after death), of both attachment to existence and attachment to nonexistence, of both exclusive focus on the *kamma* of oneself and exclusive focus on the *kamma* of others (to be explicated in Chapters 3 and 4), and of both aggressive confrontation and passive submission.[123] The Buddha disagreed with the conventional world in many regards, including the necessity of being oppositional or confrontational. Relating the transformation brought by practicing the Buddhist *Dhamma*, Gross remarks, "One does not have to choose between either confronting someone or getting rolled over, even though that's what the conventional world teaches us."[124] To practice the Buddha's teachings requires one to find and walk the "middle way" between confrontation and acquiescence.

Being oppositional and confrontational often aggravates a given situation in that it prompts the interlocutors to take a defensive stance and thereby obstructs the channel of communication. In addition, being adversarial will also nurture the seed of self-other opposition and thus perpetuate the pattern of conflict, which is fundamentally contradictory to the Buddhist project of nurturing *dukkha*-reducing, peace-enhancing individuals and environment. To be consistent with the Buddha's teachings means to conduct oneself in the most peaceful way possible at every moment without yielding to unwholesome, *dukkha*-producing conventions of being antagonistic and adversarial. Therefore, while attempting to maintain the spirit of critical inquiry and to employ contemporary Western studies and theories in the exegesis of Buddhist *Dhamma*, this book does not seek to instigate debates and conflicts between "Buddhist" and "non-Buddhist" systems of thoughts. That is, this book will not make unnecessary comparisons that are not conducive to *dukkha*-alleviation in the world and may increase self-other opposition.

This book studies the social and ethical implications of the core Buddhist teaching of interdependent co-arising. In order to formulate a

Buddhist social ethic that is in accordance with the most basic Buddhist teachings, I take Buddhism back to its roots, referencing mainly the earliest texts whose legitimacy in the voluminous Buddhist literature is the most widely acknowledged and the least disputable. Chapter 2 examines the "Socio-Ethical Dimensions of Early Buddhism." The ethical emphasis of the Buddha is manifested in his refusal to answer metaphysical questions, his redefinition of nobility, and his teachings with regard to the cultivation of wholesome states and wholesome conduct in this world. The Buddha's nonviolent challenge to the social hierarchies is particularly significant if the religious, political, social, and economic situations of his time are put into consideration. The repeated injunction on the importance of associating with "good friends" (Pāli: *kalyāṇa mitta*; Sanskrit: *kalyāna mitra*) testifies to his grasp of the fundamental sociality of human existence. In addition, the institution of the full *Sangha* consisting of the four assemblies to a great extent challenges the normalized and naturalized hierarchies in society, de-essentializes classes and genders, and establishes the middle path between accepting the conventional way of life in its entirety and cutting off all connections with it. The androcentrism and classism that can be observed in the history of Buddhism, inasmuch as they result in the disregard, or even justification, of the sufferings of women and lower-class people, contradict the Buddha's own teachings and therefore need to be critiqued. The Buddha recognized as being *dukkha*-producing the ways in which people had been relating to each other and treating each other, and he exemplified a way of actively responding to social problems in the world without being antagonistic.

Having grounded this social ethic in early Buddhism and its texts, starting with Chapter 3, "A Feminist Exegesis of Non-Self: Constitution of Personhood and Identity," I will cite poststructuralist feminist analyses and contemporary socio-economic studies, using them to reveal the subtleties of the Buddhist *Dhamma* as well as the blind spots of traditional Buddhist teachings and practices. Poststructuralist constructivist feminist theories can provide an exegetical framework for the Buddhist teaching of non-Self. Their convergence with the Buddhist analysis of the five aggregates helps bring forth more fully the dynamic construction of interrelational individual beings. The complex socio-psycho-physical entity that we usually call "self," including its gendered aspect, is socially constructed as well as mentally constructed. The understanding of social conditioning can call into question the validity of traditional gender roles and gender hierarchy, which still pervade many Buddhist organizations and Buddhist countries. The Buddha himself did not honor any other traditional social hierarchies,[125] and the fundamental Buddhist teaching of *anatta* clearly does not support the idea that any social group is inherently superior to another.

Neither the negation of "Self" in Buddhism nor the rejection of autonomous subject in poststructuralist feminist theories dissolves moral responsibility or moral agency. Chapter 4, "Person-in-*Kammic*-Network: Moral Agency and Social Responsibility," investigates the social meaning of *kamma*, as well as the moral agency and responsibility that a constructed subject has in the constitution and reconstitution of both herself or himself and the socio-cultural contexts in which she or he is embedded. The teaching of interdependent co-arising deconstructs the concept of independent "Self" that stays uninfluenced by its surroundings, but by no means does it dissolve moral responsibilities of individuals. Quite the contrary, what is revealed by co-arising is the fundamental sociality and interconditionality of human existence. According to co-arising, an individual is constituted in the existing socio-cultural contexts, and the socio-cultural contexts are in turn constructed and reconstructed through individuals' actions. It is in this light that the Buddha's ethicization of the long-existing term *kamma*[126] can be rightly understood. Inasmuch as a person interdependently co-arises with the contexts she or he is in, and with the people around her or him, every volitional action functions to reconfigure the socio-cultural contexts as well as one's own personality and character, and every person is directly or indirectly responsible for the well-being of others. This complex social implication of interdependent co-arising can be further accentuated by taking a look at the contemporary socio-economic and environmental studies on the global situations. What seems to be individual *kamma* more often than not has its social and even global impacts, and the cessation of *dukkha* depends on all those who are tangled in the same *kammic* web of existence realizing the social dimensions of their actions and striving to be socially aware and conscientious.

Chapter 5 considers the "Buddhist Self-Reconditioning and Community-Building." The optimal environment for the fundamental sociality to be recognized, and for the sense of responsibility to grow, is a community that is intimate enough for all members to be aware of the reverberations of their actions, and small enough for them to make decisions together. To build an intimate small community, however, is not the same as to have a closed system in which the group identity supplants all individual identities and the internal differences are homogenized. Based on the *Nikāya* texts, Buddhist community-building ideals include viewing different others as "good friends" and continuingly building connections with multiple others.

At the same time, the Buddhist *Dhamma* recognizes that factors play a significant role in the social production of *dukkha*. Consisting of the "Three Learnings" of ethic mental training, and wisdom development, the Noble Eightfold 1 a... a program that allows people to consciously and proactively recondition the individual "internal" states that build up themselves, as well as their "external" actions that build up the cultural contexts.

Chapter 6, "This-Worldly *Nibbāna* and Participatory Peacemaking," further elaborates on the participatory and dynamic nature of both *dukkha* and *nibbāna*. In line with the Buddha's this-worldly socioethical concerns recorded in the *Nikāya*-s, *nibbāna* can be understood as having a very this-worldly and dynamic character. Norwegian peace research scholar and the founder of the *Journal of Peace Research*, Johan Galtung, differentiates three kinds of violence and observes that physical violence is induced by structural violence, which is grounded, sanctioned, and justified by cultural violence. The current "culture of war," as termed by peace studies scholars, is a culture that breeds and intensifies greed, promotes egocentric attachments and oppositions, and justifies and glorifies aggression and domination. Peacemaking therefore involves far more than stopping wars and physical violence; the culture has to change. It is due to people's ongoing unreflective participation that the "culture of war" has come into existence, and so it requires all individuals' ongoing mindful participation to create and maintain the "culture of peace." Peace is therefore neither a static power structure, nor an end point that can be reached once and for all. Likewise, *nibbāna* in this world depends on all people continuingly *making* peace. Besides working on the self's behavioral, emotive, and conceptual transformations, we need to build connections throughout the web of co-arising, network with multiple others, and choose the most "wholesome" and least violent courses of actions possible in every given situation.

2

Socio-Ethical Dimensions
of Early Buddhism

Contrary to the popular misconception that Buddhism is other-worldly oriented or that Buddhism is *only* about individualistic inner peace, the early Buddhist texts bear witness to the Buddha's highly this-worldly ethical concerns and his unconventional social visions. The early texts show that the Buddhist path could not be reduced to individual inner peace only, let alone an other-worldly mystical pursuit. The practical this-worldly character of the Buddha's teachings can be seen in the Buddha's refusal of metaphysical speculations. Instead of addressing the metaphysical questions, the Buddha redirected people's attention to their own ways of behaving in the world, and he redefined nobility by associating it with wholesome mentality and wholesome conduct in this world. Ethical behavior was thus integral to the Buddha's teachings. The ethics that the Buddha taught were very social in character and not something that could be practiced in isolation. In addition to emphasizing the importance of associating with "good friends," the Buddha established the fourfold Buddhist *Sangha*, which not only altered the convention of solitary renunciates, but also challenged the prevalent gender hierarchy and class hierarchy at the time by accepting men and women from all castes. For these reasons, instead of asserting that Buddhists need to externalize or extrapolate the Buddhist inner peace (as if social ethics was nonexistent in the Buddha's teachings), I maintain that the Buddha taught peaceful engagement in the world from the very beginning and that social ethics was an indispensable part of his teachings.

The Liberative Is Ethical: This-Worldly Wholesomeness

The Buddhist path, in all branches of Buddhism, is the Noble Eightfold Path, which includes ethical discipline, mental training, and wisdom development. It may seem that ethics is only one of the three main parts of the Noble Eightfold Path. However, in the *Samyutta Nikāya*, the collection of texts in the Pāli Canon that deals with the subtlety of the Buddha's teachings, ethics is likened to earth, upon which the entirety of the Noble Eightfold Path is established and cultivated.[1] Thomas Kochumuttom therefore asserts that the practice taught by the Buddha, i.e., the Noble Eightfold Path, was ethics-based.[2] More importantly, in the *Nikāya* texts it is evident that the Buddhist goal of *nibbāna*, the cessation of *dukkha*, has a strong ethical dimension. In as much as *nibbāna* is defined as the destruction of lust, hatred, and delusion,[3] it denotes ethical transformation as much as spiritual transformation.[4] In *The Nature of Buddhist Ethics*, Damien Keown maintains, "ethical perfection is a central ingredient in the Buddhist *summum bonum*."[5]

Ethical behavior is an indispensable component of advanced "inner states" in the Buddha's teachings. Whatever meditative attainment one had, the Buddha expected it to be reflected in one's conduct:

> When a noble disciple is possessed of virtue, that pertains to his conduct. When he guards the doors of his sense faculties, that pertains to his conduct. When he is moderate in eating, that pertains to his conduct. When he is devoted to wakefulness, that pertains to his conduct. When he possesses seven good qualities, that pertains to his conduct. When he is one who obtains at will, without trouble or difficulty, the four jhānas [advanced meditative states] that constitute the higher mind and provide a pleasant abiding here and now, that pertains to his conduct.[6]

An advanced meditative state was expected to have the outward manifestation in ethical conduct, and the lack thereof was considered obstructive to the development and attainment of superior inner states. Even when instructing about loving-kindness, compassion, altruistic joy, and equanimity, all of which seemed to be "internal" mental states, the Buddha's emphasis was still unequivocally on ethical conduct: one who did evil deeds could not develop these states, and one who attained "the liberation of the mind" by the cultivation of these states would not do any evil deed.[7] In the early Buddhist discourses, the "inner" meditative states could not be separated from "outer" behaviors.

The same correlation between "inner" states and "outer" conduct was expected between wisdom and moral behavior. The Buddha said in the *Anguttara Nikāya*, "His action marks the fool, his action marks the wise person, O monks. Wisdom shines forth in behavior."[8] Wisdom and morality were so positively correlated in the Buddhist discourses that the designation "the wise" was often found in the contexts of moral issues. Wisdom was to be manifested in ethical behavior, and ethical persons were considered wise persons: "Wisdom is purified by morality, and morality is purified by wisdom: where one is, the other is, the moral man has wisdom and the wise man has morality, and the combination of morality and wisdom is called the highest thing in the world."[9] In Buddhism, both wisdom development and mental training require ethical discipline. As such, all of the "Three Learnings" of the Noble Eightfold Path are ethics-based.

Moreover, the goal that the path leads to, *nibbāna*, is inseparable from ethical behavior, too, despite the popular tendency of imagining *nibbāna* to be a purely "inner" state in which ethics does not matter at all or no longer matters, as some twentieth-century scholars of Buddhist ethics believed.[10] Many other scholars, such as Caroline Augusta Foley Rhys Davids, Hammalava Saddhatissa, Donald K. Swearer, John Ross Carter, Damien Keown, and Abraham Velez de Cea, however, do recognize ethics to be indispensable in the Buddhist *Dhamma* as a whole and *nibbāna* in particular. Keown, for example, understands *nibbāna* to be the perfection of moral and intellectual virtues, "not an ontological shift or soteriological quantum leap."[11] He and Charles Prebish point out, "it is the lived experience of the path itself that constitutes nirvana."[12] This view is supported by the Buddha's words in the Pāli Canon:

> When lust, hatred and delusion have been abandoned, he neither plans for his own harm, nor for the harm of others, nor for the harm of both . . . In this way, brāhmin, Nibbāna is directly visible, immediate, inviting one to come and see, worthy of application, to be personally experienced by the wise.[13]

A person who realizes *nibbāna* is a person who is completely rid of the three poisons of lust, hatred, and delusion and is completely ethical. In fact, in the *Nikāyas*, an *arahant* (Sanskrit: *arhat*; "worthy one," referring to one who has reached *nibbāna*) was said to be "incapable

of taking a wrong course of action on account of desire, hatred, delusion or fear."[14] Furthermore, the Buddha himself was described as one
who was pure in conduct and foremost in the highest morality (Pāli:
adhisīla; Sanskrit: *adhiśīla*).[15] That is, in Buddhist discourses, spiritual
attainments, including the ultimate goal of *nibbāna*, are expected to
go hand-in-hand with superior ethical conduct. Therefore, T. W. Rhys
Davids states,

> *Nibbāna* is purely and solely an *ethical* state, to be reached
> in this birth by ethical practices, contemplation and
> insight. . . . all expressions which deal with the realization
> of emancipation from lust, hatred and illusion apply to
> *practical* habits and not to speculative thought.[16]

The notion of *Nibbāna* being a self-existent state, Davids further suggests, was developed later in the scholastic *Abhidhamma* period.[17] Thai
Buddhist philosopher Phra Prayudh Payutto echoes Davids' understanding, "If the principles or teachings related to a quest for truth
and wisdom do not reveal ethics and a method of practice that can
be applied in daily life, then such principles cannot be considered
Buddhism—this is especially true for that which is held to be the
original body of teachings of Lord Buddha."[18]

In classical Buddhist discourses, ethical behavior was not only
expected from the Buddha's own followers, but also from non-Buddhists who claimed advanced spiritual states. With respect to what
kind of renunciates should be revered by laypeople and what kind of
renunciates should not, the Buddha set down a very simple criterion:

> Those recluses and brahmins who are not rid of lust, hate,
> and delusion . . . whose minds are not inwardly peace-
> ful, and who conduct themselves now righteously, now
> unrighteously in body, speech, and mind—such recluses
> and brahmins should not be honoured, respected, revered,
> and venerated," and those who are rid of lust, hate, and
> delusion and *consistently* conduct themselves righteously
> are worthy of reverence.[19]

In the Buddha's teachings, that is, ethics is neither only provisional
nor something that is irrelevant in the pursuit of the ultimate emancipation from *dukkha*. Ethical practices are the foundation of the Noble
Eightfold Path and are expected both in the process of pursuing
the goal and after reaching the goal. Ethical practice both leads to

nibbāna and is perfected by it. For this reason C. A. F. Rhys Davids declares that "Buddhist philosophy is ethical first and last."[20] Sallie B. King observes that this emphasis on ethics is central to modern-day Engaged Buddhisms, too: "ethical behavior ultimately leads to the transformation of liberation, which, in turn, allows a person to act skillfully, wholesomely and with wisdom, that is, in a consummately *ethical* manner."[21]

According to the *Nikāya* texts, the Buddha was in fact very much this-worldly oriented. When refuting the doctrines of nihilism, non-doing, and non-causality, the Buddha says that even if those doctrines were true, a person with bodily, verbal, and mental misbehavior is still "here and now censured by the wise as an immoral person," and a person with bodily, verbal, and mental good behavior is still "here and now praised by the wise as a virtuous person."[22] That is, in whichever way one may like to imagine the ultimate reality or speculate about the metaphysical truths, there is still this world and whatever one does, speaks, and thinks still affects others directly or indirectly in this world, just as one is still in turn affected by the wholesome or unwholesome conduct of others. By refusing to address metaphysical and/or other-worldly questions, the Buddha was redirecting people's attention to their conduct here and now, which in the Buddhist discourses was far more important and urgent.

One classical example that is often quoted to demonstrate the Buddha's practical concern and his sense of the urgency of ethical practice is the simile of the poisoned arrow. To insist on having metaphysical questions answered before starting leading an ethical life, the Buddha said, is like a person wounded by an arrow thickly smeared with poison wanting to know, before letting the surgeon pull out the arrow, every single detail about the man who shot the arrow and about the making of the bow and the arrow shaft.[23] One would have died before all the details regarding the origin of the poisoned arrow were known. It would be far more important and urgent for the wounded person to let the surgeon treat the wound and to heed the surgeon's medical instructions for the sake of recovery. In the same way, one will have died before one's metaphysical curiosity is satisfied. It is far more important and urgent that people pay attention to their actions that are here and now affecting others as well as themselves. It is far more important and urgent that people strive to conduct themselves in wholesome ways before it is too late. The following verse contained in the *Bhaddekaratta Sutta* conveyed the same point that, regardless of the past or the future, one should make the effort to be ethical right now:

> Let not a person revive the past
> Or on the future build his hopes;
> For the past has been left behind
> And the future has not been reached.
> Instead with insight let him see
> Each presently arisen state;
> Let him know that and be sure of it,
> Invincibly, unshakeably.
> Today the effort must be made;
> Tomorrow Death may come, who knows?[24]

Devoting one's energy to metaphysical speculations, in the Buddha's teachings, is "unbeneficial," because "it does not belong to the fundamentals of the holy life," and "it does not lead to disenchantment, to dispassion, to cessation, to peace, to direct knowledge, to enlightenment, to Nibbāna."[25] Metaphysical questions are therefore "unfit for attention."[26] David J. Kalupahana in *Ethics in Early Buddhism* explains that, for the Buddha, "Any conception of truth not relevant to making human life wholesome and good would simply be metaphysical and therefore unedifying."[27] What is "fit for attention," according to the Buddha's teachings in these texts of early Buddhism, is the proper way or ways to conduct oneself here and now. In addition to refusing to answer metaphysical questions, therefore, the Buddha urged people to take up wholesome conduct and associated nobility with noble actions, rather than with upper-caste origins.

In the pre-Buddhist brāhmanical discourses, nobility was claimed by the performers of sacrificial rituals who generated power via chanting and physical performance of rituals. The cosmic power generated by chanting was termed *brāhman*, and not coincidentally the ritual performers who chanted were called *brāhmaṇas* ("brāhmins" in the anglicized form). The brāhmins were said to be born out of the mouth of the primordial cosmic man Puruṣa (or, in a later rendition, out of the mouth of the creator god Brahmā). The place of their origin, mouth, supposedly defined their social function as well as justified their high social status and inherent nobility. Being born out of the mouth of Brahmā, their duty was to chant, and being born from the top portion of the primordial man or the divine body, they were inherently superior to those born out of other parts of the body.

The Buddha challenged the ritual performers' self-proclaimed nobility and redefined the word *brāhmaṇas*. In the *Majjhima Nikāya*, a young brāhmin called Assalāyana, who was said to be a sixteen-year-old "master of the Three Vedas with their vocabularies, liturgy, phonology, and etymology, and the histories as a fifth; skilled in philology and grammar,"[28] went to challenge the Buddha's teachings which, in this brāhmin's eyes, failed to heed the proper distinction of the castes. The Buddha responded first by observing that customs might vary from region to region, and then by pointing out that brāhmins were born by women just as all other castes were, and they were supposed to reap what they had sown just as people of all other castes were, too. At the same time, a fire lit by a non-brāhmin would have radiance and heat just as a fire lit by a brāhmin, and people of all other castes were as capable of developing loving-kindness and other wholesome qualities as brāhmins were.[29] Caste differences and proper intercaste relations were prescribed by the brāhmins, and the Buddha questioned whether the whole world had authorized them to prescribe things as such.[30] Based on this line of questioning and refutation, the Buddha clearly did not recognize any inherent nobility, nor did he think the proper relation between two parties should be decided unilaterally. There was no substantive difference between the four castes, and the brāhmins' prescription of proper inter-caste relations was "just a saying in the world."[31]

In terms of questioning the legitimacy of caste distinctions and repudiating the inherent superiority of privileged people, the Buddha was certainly anti-brāhmanical. However, he was not anti-brāhmanical in the sense of associating evils with privileges:

> I do not say . . . that one is better because one is from an aristocratic family, nor do I say that one is worse because one is from an aristocratic family. I do not say that one is better because one is of great beauty, nor do I say that one is worse because one is of great beauty. I do not say that one is better because one is of great wealth, nor do I say that one is worse because one is of great wealth.[32]

In the Buddha's teachings, one was "better" or nobler if one abstained "from killing living beings, from taking what is not given, from misconduct in sensual pleasures, from false speech, from malicious speech, from harsh speech, and from gossip," and one who engaged in misconduct was "worse," regardless of one's caste origin.[33]

In the same way that the Buddha referred to a renunciate's conduct to determine his or her worthiness of reverence, he used ethical conduct to redefine the term *brāhmaṇas*, disassociating it from the caste system:

> I call him not a brahmin [*brāhmaṇas*]
> Because of his origin and lineage.

If impediments still lurk in him,
He is just one who says "Sir."

. . .

Who does not flare up with anger,
Dutiful, virtuous, and humble, . . .
Who is unopposed among opponents,
Peaceful among those given to violence,
Who does not cling among those who cling:
He is the one I call a brahmin.

. . .

One is not a brahmin by birth,
Nor by birth a non-brahmin.
By action is one a brahmin,
By action is one a non-brahmin.[34]

Those aristocrats and priests who called themselves *Ariyan*s (noble-men) did not necessarily have the "Ariyan dispositions (*ariya-vāsā*),"[35] and those lower-caste people who were despised by the "Ariyans" might very well display their nobleness through moral self-conquest.[36] Thus, in the Buddha's discourses, nobility is not something one is born with, but something one has to establish and maintain through noble actions. A true brāhmin is one "who seeks enlightenment, cultivating restraint and virtue."[37] A *bhikkhu* who had expelled evil unwholesome states, for example, was called a *brāhmin* by the Buddha.[38]

Nobility is established through taking noble actions, and in the *Nikāya*s that which is acclaimed as noble is wholesome (Pāli: *kusala*; Sanskrit: *kuśala*). In the same vein, a "noble disciple" is said to be someone who feels ashamed of and dreads "bad behaviour by body, speech and mind" and "anything evil and unwholesome," and so she or he "lives with energy set upon the abandoning of everything unwholesome and the acquiring of everything wholesome."[39] The "supreme attainment" is to be perfected in what is wholesome.[40] The Buddha himself was described by Ānanda as one who had abandoned all unwholesome (Pāli: *akusala*; Sanskrit: *akuśala*) states and possessed all wholesome states.[41]

Of crucial interest here are the definitions of wholesomeness and unwholesomeness. What is first of all notable is that, in the *Nikāya* texts, the words wholesome and unwholesome are used to describe bodily, verbal, and mental actions. That is, the referents of wholesomeness and unwholesomeness include what are convention-ally considered "external" and what are conventionally considered "internal." For instance, the standard list of ten wholesome things and ten unwholesome things include three kinds of bodily actions, four kinds of verbal actions, and three kinds of mental actions:

> Killing living beings is unwholesome, abstention from kill-ing living beings is wholesome; taking what is not given is unwholesome, abstention from taking what is not given is wholesome; misconduct in sensual pleasures is unwhole-some, abstention from misconduct in sensual pleasures is wholesome; false speech is unwholesome, abstention from false speech is wholesome; malicious speech is unwhole-some, abstention from malicious speech is wholesome; harsh speech is unwholesome, abstention from harsh speech is wholesome; gossip is unwholesome, abstention from gos-sip is wholesome; covetousness [or greed] is unwholesome, abstention from covetousness is wholesome; ill will [or hatred] is unwholesome, abstention from ill will is whole-some; wrong view [i.e. delusion] is unwholesome, right view is wholesome.[42]

When the referents are mental actions, it may seem that what is whole-some is some mental state or quality that is good and praiseworthy in and of itself, and what is unwholesome is some mental state or quality that is evil and blameworthy in and of itself. For examples, generosity, loving-kindness, and wisdom are considered wholesome because they are by nature virtuous qualities, while greed, ill will, and delusion are considered unwholesome because they are vicious qualities.[43] In the *Anguttara Nikāya*, in addition to greed and ill will, eight other qualities or mental states are identified as unwholesome: sloth and torpor, excitement, doubt, anger, defiled mind, restless body, laziness, and lack of concentration. The opposites of these vices are wholesome and should be cultivated.[44]

When the referents of wholesomeness and unwholesomeness are bodily and verbal actions, the criteria are more complicated. Some-times it seems that some bodily and verbal actions, like the mental actions discussed above, are by nature blameworthy or praiseworthy. Sometimes it seems that conventional wisdom is to be followed: what is unwholesome is sometimes equated with what is "censured by the wise," and what is wholesome with what is "praised by the wise."[45] Sometimes the consideration is whether or not the action in question will lead to painful results for the self and/or for others. For instance, the Buddha instructed his son Rāhula, who had been ordained as a *bhikkhu*, to reflect before, during, and after taking every action thus:

"Does this action . . . lead to my own affliction, or to the affliction of others, or to the affliction of both?"[46] More often than not, the Buddha's advice, such as in the opening quote of this book, was to consider, simultaneously, the nature of the actions/states, the conventional wisdom, and the consequences for both the self and others.

Abraham Velez de Cea characterizes Buddhist ethics to be a combination of moral realism, virtue ethics, and utilitarianism:

> In the Pāli Nikāyas, the consideration of the wholesomeness or unwholesomeness of external bodily and verbal actions (moral realism) and internal mental actions (virtue ethics) is to be supplemented by the consideration of the consequences of actions for the happiness of oneself and others (utilitarianism).[47]

In a similar but not entirely the same way, David Loy considers Buddhist ethics a combination of deontology, virtue ethics, and utilitarianism.[48] Despite the slight difference over deontology or moral realism, both de Cea and Loy recognize virtue ethics and utilitarianism to be components of Buddhist ethics, and both recognize Buddhist ethics to be composed of aspects that can neither be collapsed into each other nor separated from each other. Peter Harvey likewise maintains that early Buddhist ethics cannot be collapsed into only one of the Kantian, Aristotelian, or Utilitarian models.[49] Quoting the Fourteenth Dalai Lama, Sallie B. King similarly observes that Buddhist ethics contains elements of teleology, deontology, and virtue ethics.[50] Christopher Ives, concurring with the scholars mentioned above, explains that Buddhist ethics exhibits characteristics of more than one branch of Western philosophical ethics:

> [W]e can argue here that Buddhists have a type of duty; they "ought to act in ways that reduce suffering" (in some cases to promote their own awakening). In this respect, Buddhist ethics takes on a deontological coloring. In addition, we can argue from such texts as Asaṅga's *Bodhisattva-bhūmi* that the over-arching Buddhist rule of thumb is to act in ways that result in the greatest cessation of suffering for the greatest number of people. Expressed negatively, one should act in ways that cause less net suffering than alternatives . . . In this respect, Buddhist ethics exhibits characteristics of utilitarianism. And Buddhist ethics, especially in the Theravada, revolves around eradicating unwholesome mental states and

cultivating wholesome states and thereby working toward the goal of nirvāṇa. In this respect, Buddhist ethics can be seen as a kind of virtue ethic.[51]

In this unique mélange of ethics of Buddhism, whether an action should be undertaken (or cultivated, if it is a mental action) or abandoned cannot be determined by only one criterion. Therefore, David J. Kalupahana states in *A History of Buddhist Philosophy*,

> For the Buddha, the rightness or wrongness of an action or a rule does not consist in its situational or contextual validity alone, but rather in what it does to the person or the group of people in the particular context or situation. Thus simply performing an act or adopting a rule because it is viewed as right does not constitute morality. It is the impact of the action or rule on the total personality or the group involved that gives it a moral character—hence the Buddha's statement, "Be moral or virtuous without being made of morals or virtues" (*sīlavā no ca sīlamayo*).[52]

That is to say, in the rubric of Buddhist ethics, an action is worth undertaking not just because it is supposed to be virtuous, or just because it is considered good by others, or just because it brings pleasant results for the self, or just because it brings pleasant results for others. Rather, an action is worth undertaking when all of these considerations are combined. Being "wholesome" involves comprehensively considering things from all angles in the web of interconditionality, including one's own motivations, the various perspectives of the people involved, and the reverberations of the action in its particular context.

Gier and Kjellberg term this type of ethics "contextual pragmatism," for in this ethical system knowing the right thing to do at any given moment entails knowing the "causal web of existence" in which one finds onesef, being keenly aware of the effects of one's actions on both oneself and others, and practically grasping "what is appropriate and what is fitting" for both oneself and one's surroundings without being tangled by egoistic attachments.[53] It is not a coincidence that each of the eight folds of the Buddhist Noble Eightfold Path starts with the Pāli prefix *sammā* (*samyak* in Sanskrit), which is often translated as "right" but in fact denotes comprehensiveness and completeness. The rightness or properness is predicated on being comprehensive and covering all grounds, not on being in accordance with any absolute truth.[54] In this "contextual pragmatism" of Buddhism, a noble person is one who is reflective of the nature of any bodily, verbal, and mental action, watchful of one's habits and intentions,[55] and mindful of both conventional wisdom and the potential consequences for the self and others, so that her or his conduct is wholesome.

With respect to the thesis of this book, what is particularly noteworthy in the Buddha's formula of wholesomeness is the consideration for others, both in terms of the moral judgments shared by "the wise" and in terms of what others may experience as a result of one's deeds, words, and thoughts. The Buddha did not at all emphasize individual effort to eclipse the sociality of human existence. An action was not to be taken simply because it might help oneself in one's individualistic pursuit of spiritual attainment. Therefore, it is inappropriate to describe Buddhist ethics as "a form of enlightened egoism."[56] The central teachings of the Buddha carried in the early and foundational *Nikāya* texts, such as interdependent co-arising, non-Self, and five aggregates, in effect, denied the very possibility of purely individualistic spiritual advancement. Moreover, the explicit instructions with regard to "good friends" and the establishment of the Buddhist *Sangha* indicate the Buddha's recognition of the sociality of human existence and testify to his unconventional social visions.

Good Friends: The Entire Holy Life

Contrary to some later misunderstandings, the Buddha himself did not unconditionally praise physical seclusion and did not teach that *nibbāna* was an outcome of solitude. In fact, seclusion was listed alongside extreme ascetic practices that the Buddha said he had experimented with but eventually rejected after his *nibbāna*.[57] He also taught that a renunciate was to be censured if she or he resorted to seclusion without first fulfilling the training in the Buddhist *Sangha*.[58] Solitary practice of purification was by no means the "authentic" Buddhist teachings. Rather, the teaching of interdependent co-arising indicated that the Buddha was aware that human existence was fundamentally social, and the Buddha often instructed his followers, renunciant and lay, to associate with "good friends," who could be either laypeople or renunciates.[59] The criteria of good friends do not include celibacy or other monastic disciplines, though it is conceivably easier for people who have renounced the conventional ways of life to match up with the criteria of good friends.

The Buddha taught that association with "good friends," otherwise called "noble friends," "spiritual friends," "virtuous companions," or "companions in the holy life," was crucial in walking the Buddhist path and reaching the ultimate goal of *nibbāna*. In a conversation with a non-Buddhist renunciate named Māgandiya, the Buddha said that association with good friends would bring one to hear the *Dhamma*, would prompt one to practice accordingly, and would allow one to know for oneself the formation and cessation of *dukkha* (i.e., co-arising).[60] In the *Samyutta Nikāya*, good friendship and ethical discipline were identified as the "forerunner and precursor" for the arising of the Noble Eightfold Path as well as the arising of the "seven factors of enlightenment" including mindfulness, discrimination of states, energy, rapture, tranquility, concentration, and equanimity.[61] Good friendship and ethical discipline were therefore praised as conditions that are the most effective in terms of bringing forth the fulfillment of the Noble Eightfold Path.[62] That is, good friendship is important not only in that it prompts one to make the effort and engage oneself in Buddhist practices, but also in that it brings those practices to fruition, i.e., *nibbāna*. Thus, when Ānanda, traditionally held to be the disciple with extraordinary memory who had served as the Buddha's personal attendant and had memorized every single one of the Buddha's discourses, reported his understanding to the Buddha by saying that good friendship constituted half of the holy life taught by the Buddha, the Buddha corrected him and instructed that good friendship was the *entire* holy life.[63]

Sulak Sivaraksa explains the importance of good friends in the Buddhist path thus:

> *Kalyanamittas,* or virtuous companions, are crucial to spiritual growth. Friends are the only people who can give us the criticism and the support that we need to transcend our own limitations and can comfort us if we fail. If we become so self-absorbed that we do not have kalyanamittas in our lives, we stagnate in complacency and self-righteousness.[64]

As aforementioned, in the Buddhist path, spiritual advancement is inseparable from ethical conduct, and whether or not a conduct is ethical and wholesome can only be decided after all dimensions and ramifications of that conduct have been considered. "Good friends" prevent purely egoistic considerations by supplementing different perspectives. They point out our "evil conducts,"[65] and they "raise embarrassing issues that we may not want to hear and remind us of the benefits of selflessness and goodness."[66] Positively, they provide support and inspiration, and sometimes serve as role models, in our cultivation of wholesomeness and wisdom. It is significant that the following passage with regard to the importance of association with good friends is found in the *Anguttara Nikāya*, the collection that was generally oriented toward personal edification and therefore was more individualistic in orientation than all other *Nikāya*s:

> The first thing . . . for making the immature mind mature for liberation is to have a noble friend, a noble companion, a noble associate. . . . When . . . a monk has a noble friend, a noble companion and associate, it can be expected that he will be virtuous . . . that he will engage in talk befitting the austere life and helpful to mental clarity . . . that his energy will be set upon the abandoning of everything unwholesome and the acquiring of everything wholesome . . . that he will be equipped with the wisdom that leads to the complete destruction of suffering.[67]

The precondition for the maturity of mind, for being virtuous, for being energetic in the cultivation of wholesomeness, and for developing mental clarity and wisdom, is association with good friends.

The functions that good friends are supposed to serve at the same time denote the criteria of good friends. They are supposed to inspire and support one to be ethical, so they need to be either accomplished in virtues or dedicated to the cultivation of wholesome bodily, verbal, and mental actions. They are supposed to inspire and help one acquire wisdom, which in the Buddhist discourses means seeing co-arising and taking the most beneficial and nonviolent course of actions, and so they need to be capable of considering things from different angles or to have a very different perspective than one's own. The passage from the *Anguttara Nikāya* quoted above was directed toward Buddhist renunciates, and the following passage, also from the *Anguttara Nikāya*, was directed toward lay followers:

> And what is good friendship? . . . in whatever village or town a family man dwells, he associates with householders or their sons, whether young or old, who are of mature virtue, accomplished in faith, virtue, generosity and wisdom; he converses with them and engages in discussions with them. He emulates them in regard to their accomplishment in faith, virtue, generosity and wisdom. This is called good friendship.[68]

Noteworthy is that the good friends recommended to Buddhist renunciates are not qualitatively different from those recommended to lay followers of the Buddha. Both groups are encouraged to associate with people who are mature in virtue as well as in wisdom, and for both groups the association with good friends is recommended because it is conducive to the development of virtue and wisdom in oneself.

It is undeniable that, while good friendship was considered most effective in prompting people to walk the Buddhist path and bringing Buddhist practices to fruition, in the *Nikāyas* seclusion was also presented as one of the bases of the Noble Eightfold Path,[69] although it was not to be taken by someone not fully trained in the monastic sangha. On occasions the Buddha explicitly told the Buddhist renunciates to "make an exertion in seclusion" so that they might develop the wisdom to see things as they really are.[70] Very often it *seemed* that seclusion was a precondition for those advanced meditative states (Pāli: *jhāna*-s; Sanskrit: *dhyāna*-s)[71] that usually preceded, but did not necessarily lead to, the experience of *nibbāna*.

The seclusion that the Buddha recommended, however, was not social isolation by cutting off all social ties or physical solitude by way of dwelling only in the forests or wilderness, as some scholars asserted.[72] In fact, the Buddha commented that he himself sometimes stayed in the mansions prepared by lay followers and commingled with male and female lay followers, political figures, and followers of other religions.[73] Physical solitude or social isolation, the Buddha taught, were not the qualities for which his disciples should honor and revere him. The qualities for which he is worthy of honor and reverence are his higher virtue, his knowledge and vision, his wisdom, and his teachings of the Four Noble Truths and the ways to develop wholesome states.[74] When seclusion was mentioned as one of the bases of the Noble Eightfold Path, it was invariably listed alongside dispassion and cessation, and the injunction "make an exertion in seclusion" was always accompanied by the injunction "develop concentration." Thus viewed, the precondition of advanced meditative states was not seclusion in the physical or social sense, but rather seclusion from sensual desires and from unwholesome states[75] such as greed and hate, anger and resentment, contempt and insolence, envy and avarice, deceit and fraud, obstinacy, rivalry, conceit and arrogance, vanity and negligence.[76] That is, the seclusion presented to be one of the bases of the Noble Eightfold Path and the precondition of advanced meditative states was not avoidance of human contact, as if human contact is in and of itself contaminating, but disassociation from the desires and emotions that would impede concentration as well as cause afflictions to self and others.[77] In fact, without seclusion from sensual desires and unwholesome states, the Buddha instructed, physical seclusion is futile.[78]

Physical solitude is not entirely without benefits, however. One of the obvious benefits of "going forth from the household life into homelessness," i.e., becoming a renunciate, is seclusion and distance from the kinds of social situations, interpersonal dynamics, and behavioral patterns that incur or reinforce egocentric oppositions and generate unwholesome thoughts, words, and deeds. Frequent contact with socio-economic élites such as brāhmins, in particular, may have the effect of leading a renunciate astray, "succumbing to craving, and reverting to luxury."[79] Even laypeople can benefit much from physical solitude or some distance from their conventional ways of life. For example, after one meditation retreat in the countryside, Sangharak-shita, founder of the Friends of the Western Buddhist Order, reports that all of the retreatants "discovered that simply being away from the city, away from the daily grind of work and home life, and being in the company of other Buddhists, with nothing to think about except the Dharma, was sufficient to raise their level of consciousness."[80] Seclusion may allow people the psychological space to develop concentration, work through their deeply-seated emotions, desires, and tendencies, and perhaps develop some insights and moral strengths for dealing with troubling situations that they could not properly deal with before. For this reason, physical seclusion was recommended by the Buddha to *some* of his followers.

Nonetheless, the Buddha did not recommend physical solitude for everyone. It may generate fear and dread, which are considered unwholesome, or it may indulge self-centered, "unpurified" thoughts, which are also unwholesome. [81] Besides, physical seclusion is not nearly as important as seclusion from unwholesome states and behaviors, and by no means was it a *sine qua non* of Buddhist practices. If the purpose of leaving the household life were simply to terminate all of one's social relations so that one could pursue mental quietude with no regard of other people, the Buddha would not have recommended the association with good friends, nor would he have established a community for his renunciant followers. After all, the norm amongst the anti-brāhmanical movements at the time was for renunciates to dwell in forests in isolation and to wander about individually. One of the attributes of *arahant*-s in general and the Buddha in particular, by contrast, was dwelling in a friendly and compassionate way among all living beings and existing for the welfare and happiness of many.[82] Neither the central Buddhist concepts nor the Buddhist institution supports an individualistic, quietist interpretation of the Buddhist *Dhamma*.

Four Assemblies of the *Sangha*: De-Essentializing Social Hierarchies

Those who interpret Buddhism as individualistic pursuit of mystical experiences generally disregard the fact that the *Sangha* is listed alongside the Buddha and the *Dhamma* as one of the Three Gems/Jewels/Treasures (Pāli: *tiratna*; Sanskrit: *triratna*), also referred to as the Three Refuges (Pāli: *tisaraṇa*; Sanskrit: *triśaraṇa*). The very grouping of the Three Jewels indicates that the Buddhist assembly or community is, or should be, of as much importance as the Teacher and the Teaching. The fact that the *Sangha* is one of the Three Gems reflects the emphasis placed on companionship and community in Buddhism.

This being recognized, the role of the *Sangha* is still subject to various misunderstandings. Some, in the spirit of considering Buddhism a world-fleeing religion, misunderstand the *Sangha* to be a collective term for the irresponsible individuals who were unwilling to take up social obligations and who loved to wander around.[83] Others, perceiving the goal of Buddhism to be an other-worldly mystical state of bliss, misrepresent the *Sangha* as a group of élite mystics under the control of the Buddha, the "king of *Dharma*," and who, by means of monastic rules, maintain their spiritual purity and claim superiority to the laity.[84] To be sure, in the long history of Buddhism it has happened that some people would join the Buddhist renunciant orders for reasons other than pursuing *nibbāna*. Some joined the Buddhist monastic orders to avoid taxes and to shun legal responsibilities. In addition, for underprivileged people who had no other access to educational resources or who were systematically subject to inhumane treatments that were not uncommon in highly stratified societies, becoming renunciates could be their only means of acquiring education and shelter. Women, in particular, had few alternatives in patriarchal societies in which their nature was defined as bearing children and serving their husband's family. Some might have found it much more preferable to become *bhikkhunīs* than functioning as baby-making machines and household servants. There have also been times when lay followers' donations would make monasteries wealthy. Combined with the great reverence paid to *bhikkhus* and *bhikkhunīs*, the flow of wealth to the monasteries would virtually make *bhikkhus* and *bhikkhunīs* the élite in their society. However, an examination of the *Nikāya* texts will reveal that, despite the later developments in some Buddhist societies, the *Sangha* was originally not established to be a group of élite mystics who were to pursue their spiritual advancement individualistically. Furthermore, the demarcation and opposition between the spiritual order and the secular society were neither posited by the Buddha nor justifiable when viewed against the Buddha's teachings.

Renunciates and Laity

Perhaps due to the widely adopted translation of the word *Sangha* as "monastic order," the Buddhist *Sangha* is often misunderstood or misrepresented as a hermitage where the "ultimate ethic of world-rejection"[85] prevails and from which laymen and laywomen are excluded.[86] From quite a different perspective, those fascinated with the egalitarian and democratic aspects of Buddhism assert the absolute equality of those who renounce and those who stay in the household life. In the former understanding, the meaning of renunciation is misconstrued as a complete rejection of social conventions and social relations. An opposition between the renunciant life and the household life is thus conceived. In the latter understanding, the significance of renunciation is downplayed, and those who do not renounce the conventional ways of life are implicitly idealized as people with stronger willpower who can overcome the impediments brought by the household life, without having to resort to renunciation.[87]

In the *Nikāya* texts, even though the Buddha manifestly showed his willingness to instruct the *Dhamma* to all those who were willing to learn,[88] he was mainly addressing those who had in fact renounced the conventional ways of life. At the same time, the importance attached to renunciation indicated neither a complete rejection of social relations, nor any intrinsic superiority of homelessness or isolation *per se*. In fact, the teaching of co-arising both provides the reason for *Dhamma* pursuers to give up the householder's life and repudiates the efficacy of cutting off all social connections with people in the larger society.

In *Buddhist Religions*, Richard H. Robinson, Willard L. Johnson, and Thanissaro Bhikkhu explain the meaning of the word *Sangha* in the Pāli usage:

> The Sangha in its ārya (ideal) sense consists of all people,
> lay or ordained, who have acquired the pure Dharma-eye,
> gaining at least a glimpse of the Deathless. In a conventional

sense, Sangha denotes the communities of monks and nuns. The two meanings overlap but are not necessarily identical. Some members of the ideal Sangha are not ordained; some monastics have yet to acquire the Dharma-eye.[89]

The full Buddhist *Sangha* as established by the Buddha consists of four assemblies: the *bhikkhu*-s (male renunciates), *bhikkhunī*-s (female renunciates), *upāsaka*-s (male lay followers), and *upāsika*-s (female lay followers). In the *ārya* sense, the *Sangha* includes all "stream-enterers" (*sotāpanna*-s), who have acquired the "pure Dharma-eye" and have known the *Dhamma* directly for themselves. By contrast, the "Dhamma-followers" (*dhammānusārī*) are those who are still investigating the *Dhamma* intellectually and experientially, and the "faith-followers" (*saddhānusārī*) are those who accept the *Dhamma* based on trust, with rather limited understanding. The stream-enterers are people who have practiced steadfastly, been virtuous, and understood "the origin and the passing away" well enough to have gained a first glimpse of *nibbāna*, meaning they will reach *nibbāna* within seven lifetimes at maximum.[90]

It seems that the all-too-common equation of modern-day Theravāda with early Buddhism has prescribed to laity a role to which laypeople in early Buddhism were not confined. For example, Damien Keown explains the role of laity in the (early) Buddhist *Sangha* as such:

> In the early tradition . . . Lay practice centres on moral conduct and providing material support for the Samgha through offerings of food and robes . . . Through the performance of good deeds of this kind it is hoped that merit (puṇya) will be gained which will secure improved material conditions in this life and the next, with the hope that at a more remote future time the opportunity will arise to renounce the world and become a monk. In Mahāyāna Buddhism, the role of the laity is more prominent . . .[91]

The passage above assumes that, before the arising of Mahāyāna Buddhism, what was practiced by renunciates was categorically different from what was practiced by the laity, who had to accumulate enough merit over many lifetimes before they could be reborn with the opportunity to become renunciates and get access to the practices pertinent to the attainment of *nibbāna*. In other words, the above quote suggests that, in the pre-Mahāyāna era, those who entered the monastic orders were necessarily superior to those who remained in the household life in the sense that the former must have had accumulated much more merit in past lives to be on the path to *nibbāna*, while the latter had no chance in becoming *arahants* in this life.

However, as Hammalawa Saddhatissa points out, "The view that the householder cannot attain to arahanthood is . . . not supported by the early scriptures. Hence, it may be a postulated view which crept into Buddhist scholarship."[92] In the *Nidānasamyutta*, the Buddha narrated that after his own *nibbāna* he had explained the *Dhamma* to the *bhikkhu*-s, the *bhikkhunī*-s, the *upāsaka*-s, and the *upāsika*-s.[93] The *Dhamma* is taught to both renunciant and lay followers, both men and women, and it is said that any person who is willing to practice as instructed "will soon know and see for himself [or herself]."[94] That is, "the possibility of realization which is accessible to the monk is also accessible to the layman."[95] As a matter of fact, as many as twenty-one lay *arahant*-s were mentioned in the *Anguttara Nikāya*. Robinson et al. observe,

> All the early lineages agreed that the laity could attain the first three degrees of Awakening and remain in the household life. Some lineages, such as the Theravāda, maintained that, although lay people could attain arhatship, lay arhats had to ordain or else die within seven days after their attainment, for the lay state could not support an arhat's purity.[96]

This view that the household life was too impure to sustain *nibbāna* and so a lay *arahant* had to enter a monastic order or die, Saddhatissa points out, is not sanctioned by the early texts, either.[97] In the *Anguttara Nikāya*, it is recorded that the Buddha, in a hall full of *bhikkhu*-s, praised a householder named Ugga for having eight "wonderful and marvellous qualities," one of which was, significantly, preaching the *Dhamma* to the *bhikkhu*-s.[98] This passage acknowledges the possibility that a layperson might exceed the renunciates in understanding and/ or conveying the *Dhamma*. Judging from the example of Ugga, the lay followers were not excluded from learning or teaching the *Dhamma* on the advanced levels. Nor were they confined to merit-making by providing material support to the renunciates. The fact might very well be that the majority of laity simply preferred merit-making to subjecting themselves to the rigorous systematic disciplines taught by the Buddha. The textual evidence does not support the depiction that lay followers at the time of the Buddha were relegated to the periphery of the Buddhist *Sangha* as a whole and excluded from the *Sangha* of stream-enterers in particular.

In addition, even those laypeople who were primarily material supporters of the early Buddhist monastic *Sangha* were by no means peripheral in the formation and operation of it. As Ian J. Coghlan argues in "A Survey of the Sources of Buddhist Ethics":

> Although the laity formally took a minor role in religious activities, it is clear they were influential during the period of the formation of the rules. The laity held strong opinions concerning what recluses could or should do, because they formed the economic support of the mendicants. By freeing them from the harvest and other economic activities, they granted the ordained *sangha* a privileged social position. However, their recognition of this status depended on the way the mendicants behaved and whether they properly represented the religious ideal held by society. In return for economic support, the laity were seen to benefit by their accumulation of merit (puñña). However, the theory of merit depended on the actual ethical status of the *sangha* in relation to whom merit was accumulated. Therefore, the laity had a vested interest in the *sangha* maintaining high religious and social standards.[99]

Granted, the majority of the laity was probably more concerned with merit-making. The concern with merit-making itself, however, prompted the laypeople to expect and even demand high ethical standards of the renunciates in the *Sangha*, for it was believed that the more ethical the recipients were, the more merit the benefactors would make. Given the fact that the renunciates in the early *Sangha* did depend on the voluntary material contributions from the laity for life subsistence, the merit-making laity actually had considerable influence over the behavioral codes of the renunciates: "When standards of behavior slipped, so did respect and donations. . . . Enforcing careful observation of the precepts ensured that high standards of conduct were kept, which would inspire the laity and, consequentially, garner sufficient material support for the Sangha."[100]

Mohan Wijayaratna, scholar of the Pāli Vinaya, more directly states, "Lay people contributed to the Community's support, indeed they assumed full responsibility for it, and *this gave them the right* to criticize monks or nuns who deviated from right conduct."[101] (Emphasis added.) As evidenced in the early texts of the Pāli Canon, the Buddha, while urging the lay followers to respect the renunciates, took the criticisms from the laity quite seriously and did not hesitate to change the monastic rules accordingly, such as establishing the rain retreat of renunciates, forbidding certain colors for monastic robes, and requiring bathing robes.[102] Bailey and Mabbett put it boldly, "the layman is both the opposite of what the monk should be and a control over the monk's behaviour[,]" even though "the monk enshrines what the layman could be."[103] That is, contrary to the belief of some Buddhists nowadays, the respect that the laity were supposed to pay to the renunciates in the *Sangha* did not include unconditional acceptance of the latter's behavior. One does not instantaneously become wholesome and noble simply by joining a monastic order, and therefore a monastic person is not off-limits for criticism.

Nonetheless, the renunciates remain at the center of the Buddhist *Sangha*. *Bhikkhu*s and *bhikkhunī*s are expected to teach the *Dhamma* to the laity and/or respond to their inquiry on a daily basis.[104] They are also expected to exemplify ethical and peaceful behavior and thereby bring positive influences to the larger society. In the *Cūḷagosinga Sutta* it was exclaimed by gods of different realms that it was "a great gain for the Vajjians" to have among them the mini-*sangha* of Anuruddha, Nandiya, and Kimbila, for they demonstrated the possibility of moral achievement and served as the model of harmonious co-existence.[105] Peter D. Hershock points out that the renunciates are at the center of Buddhist community "not because of their homelessness as such, but because of the strength of their vow—the strength of their expressed commitment to cultivating *bodhicītta* or relationships intent on enlightenment."[106] Buddhist renunciates have committed themselves to the alternative ways of living in the *Sangha*. A person reflective enough would understand the difficulty of giving up the various kinds of sensual pleasures (or the difficulty of getting rid of the *longing* for sensual pleasures in the case of the underprivileged people) in the conventional ways of life in the household, just as an alcoholic who intends to quit knows how difficult it is to fight her or his craving for, and dependency on, alcohol. That is, once laypeople recognize that they are yet to be able to part with what the renunciates have determined to give up, they would learn to admire the extraordinary determination of the latter. Moreover, after being admitted to a monastic order, a *bhikkhu* or *bhikkhunī* is circumscribed by hundreds of precepts and scriptural and mental trainings that help induce wholesome bodily, verbal, and mental states. The renunciates' commitment to all the trainings in the *Sangha* understandably would earn respect from the laity, and senior renunciates who have undergone those trainings for a long time and have successfully developed wholesome states would be revered by novices who are only at the beginning stages. It is however erroneous to confuse the effect with the cause and demand respect solely on the basis of seniority in the monastic orders, or solely on the basis of being in the monastic orders as such. A novice renunciate who has been diligent in cultivating wholesomeness may be more deserving of respect than a senior renunciate who lacks cultivation. Likewise, a committed practicing layperson, such as Ugga mentioned above, may prove to be nobler and more worthy of respect than a lax *bhikkhu*. The reason that the *Sangha* is one of the Three Gems, as Perry and Ratnayaka argue, is and should be the "spiritual attainment" of *bhikkhus* and *bhikkhunīs*,[107] which is acquired through long-term, rigorous, systematic moral and mental disciplines. The commitment to Buddhist training and development of wholesomeness should be the true criterion of worthiness of respect.

Generally speaking, though, the Buddhist monastic orders do provide an environment in which behavioral and mental transformation are far more likely to happen. Chakravarti asserts "The *sangha* was devised as a parallel society where one could construct, with immediate effect, a new structure of relations."[108] The point of renouncing the conventional way of life is not to separate oneself from the world, but to abandon the narrowly-defined self-identity so that one is no longer dictated by egoistic impulses and is able to view phenomena with a less biased mind. When the inputs that one receives are no longer about self-interests and conflicts, the outputs are less likely to be hot temper and egocentric behaviors. Factoring in the rigorous systematic trainings in the *Sangha*, renunciates are much more likely than lay followers to develop wholesome conduct, acquire an advanced understanding of the *Dhamma*, and be able to take into consideration the welfare of more and more beings in this world.

David J. Kalupahana notes that, in contrast, the larger society more often than not generates "possessive individualism"[109] and makes one attached to things (or persons[110]) one owns, caring for nothing but the interests of oneself and one's own familial, ethnic, or social group. At the Buddha's time, in particular, with the military expansion of monarchial kingdoms such as Kośala and Magadha (which were rapidly destroying the republics at the foothills of the Himālayas, including the Śākya tribe of the Buddha)[111] and the extension of agriculture by the use of iron (which were replacing the older pastoral economy, changing the landholding patterns, and creating a new group of people who were exploited and left in destitution),[112] "householder" (Pāli: *gahapati*; Sanskrit: *gṛhapati*) was in fact a status term for those males who owned property, headed agricultural productions, employed and exploited servile labors, accumulated capital, invested in trades, and were primary taxpayers in the monarchical kingdoms.[113] The stock phrases that were used to describe householders in the Pāli Canon were that they were "with a great wealth and property, with a vast number of gold ingots, a vast number of granaries, a vast number of fields, a vast amount of land, a vast number of wives, and a vast number of men and women slaves."[114] That is, a "householder" was not any layperson but a village and country élite man who had benefited from the changing social situations and thus might find it especially difficult to part with the possessive "household life" of production and reproduction. Uma Chakravarti notes that "even though the *gahapatis* dominate the pages of the Buddhist texts for their material support to the *sangha* not even one *gahapati* actually renounced the householder status and became a *bhikkhu*."[115] Contrary to the "household life" that was likely to generate and reinforce possessive individualism and social stratification, the homeless life in the Buddhist monastic order was communal, egalitarian, and without private property. According to the *Vinaya*, any gift to Buddhist monastics is supposed to be made to the monastic sangha as a whole, rather than to any individual monk or nun. In terms of socio-economic status and material attachments, the "householder" was very much "the opposite of everything for which the *bhikkhu* stands."[116] Therefore, one of the stock phrases in the early texts was: "The household life is close and dusty, the homeless life is free as air. It is not easy, living the household life, to live the fully-perfected holy life, purified and polished like a conch-shell."[117]

Thus viewed, renunciation in the Buddhist *Sangha* is by no means "world-negating"[118] in the sense of complete rejection of, and separation from, the world of the laity. For one thing, *bhikkhu*-s and *bhikkhunī*-s are required to "maintain an appropriate degree of social responsibility"[119] by way of associating with laypeople on a daily basis. Even a forest-dwelling *bhikkhu* (who does not live in the monastic community) is supposed to have this social responsibility.[120] The Buddha himself, according to the Pāli Canon, very often gave advices on worldly matters to kings and village folks alike. "Homelessness," Bailey and Mabbett note, "meant wandering (*pra-vraj*); wandering means going from place to place, not disappearing from human ken."[121] For another, laity is not separated from the renunciates in terms of practice, either. While the moral rules generally expected of the laity and renunciates are different, they differ only in degree—rules for renunciates are much more numerous and strict. For example, while the renunciates are required to keep celibacy, laypeople are only told to refrain from sexual misconduct. Yet the principle of nonattachment to sensual pleasures is the same for both groups; the difference lies in degree. Likewise, the basic principle of non-harming and watching carefully one's own actions, speeches, and thoughts is the same regardless of the number of precepts that one vows to take. What the laity need to do and can do is not categorically different from what the renunciates need to do and can do, nor are they unconnected or unbridgeable. Despite the later developments in some schools, the Buddhist monastic order was not established to replace the male brāhmins in their monopoly of religious matters and in their claim of inherent superiority to the rest of society. It was established to provide an environment that allowed men and women from all social backgrounds to reorient themselves and learn how to relate to each other in nonexploitive, nonhierarchical ways.

Class and Gender

Ancient India at the time of the Buddha was increasingly stratified. Social hierarchies were crystallized along religious, economic, and political lines, with women pushed further down the social ladder. Religiously, male brāhmins continued to monopolize religious rituals and sought to legitimize caste and gender hierarchy by claiming the innate superiority of the brāhmin caste on the one hand, and male brāhmins' exclusive efficacy in performing rituals on the other. Economically, the expansion of agriculture accelerated the breaking down of the older communal control of the land and created a new economic category of landowners and taxpayers who would use (and frequently exploit) hired laborers, accumulate capital, and engage in trade. Politically, the formation and expansion of monarchical kingdoms encroached upon the relatively democratic communal life in clan republics, heralding in the normalcy of hereditary despotic kingship and the use of military power.

The rampage of military antagonisms among kingdoms and/or clans and the increase of private property, together with the patrilineal descent system, further resulted in women's low social status and the treatment of women as property. No longer needed in production due to the use of servile laborers, women in wealthier families were now confined to home and their main function was to produce legitimate male heirs and serve their menfolk. Destitute women had to spend their entire lives in menial labor.[122] Women were considered service-providing and heir-bearing property of men, frequently acquired through violence regardless of class origins. Tighter control of women's chastity was therefore enforced in order to ensure legitimate patrilineal succession. This androcentric and sexist bias took a different form amongst various anti-brāhmanical wandering ascetics. Instead of seeing women as servants and heir-bearers, the wandering ascetics generally saw them as temptresses since asceticism was seen as a prerogative of males and celibacy was the norm amongst the male ascetics.[123]

As shown in previous sections, in addition to directly refuting the brāhmins' claim of inherent superiority, the Buddha also gave the terms *brāhmaṇas* and *ariyan* a moral thrust and demanded that the self-proclaimed nobilities should demonstrate noble behaviors. Furthermore, the Buddha instructed the well-to-do "householders" such as Sigālaka to be kind and respectful not only to those who were supposedly superior to them, but also those who were generally considered inferior. Most significant of all, the Buddha established an alternative society that was open to men and women of all castes and made it clear that, in the *Sangha* of renunciates, caste distinction was no longer relevant:

> Just as the mighty rivers on reaching the great ocean lose their former names and designations and are just reckoned as the great ocean; even so, when members of the four castes—nobles, Brahmins, commoners and menials—go forth from home into the homeless life in this Dhamma and Discipline proclaimed by the Tathāgata [another designation for the Buddha], they lose their former names and lineage and are reckoned only as renunciants following the Son of the Sakyans [i.e., the Buddha himself].[124]

In the larger society, people's social and economic standing was determined by their roles in production and reproduction. In the *Sangha*, the male and female renunciates abstained from both production and reproduction, and therefore they were not defined or stratified as they would have been in the larger society. There were no caste lineages, no noble clan names or the lack thereof, and no privileges accompanying wealth.

The very term *"sangha,"* in fact, invoked an older political ideal with which the historical Buddha was familiar. In the now-popular accounts of the Buddha's life that first appeared in the first century CE, long after monarchies had become the norm in the Indian political scene, the Buddha-to-be Siddhāttha was depicted as a prince who was to inherit the Sākya Kingdom from his father King Śuddhodana. The polity of the Śākya tribe at the time of the Buddha, in reality, was a republic (*gana-sangha*), in which means of production was held communally and political decisions were made collectively by an assembly of (male) elders called "*sangha*."[125] Other such republican self-governments include the Vajjis, the Mallas, and the Licchavis. Siddhārtha's father Śuddhodana, therefore, was not the King. He was probably one of the elders who held a seat at the assembly of the Śākyan republic. The historical Buddha was no prince accustomed to absolute power and extreme luxury in a kingdom, but an upper-caste person who was not unfamiliar with the practice of sharing economic and political resources. It should not come as a surprise that his teachings to lay followers enjoined more equity and more humaneness on the part of the men of high social status, and the institution he established for his renunciant followers conveyed the principle of sharing and collective decision-making. The Buddha may not have been a social activist in the modern sense since he did not lead any public protests or instigate rebellions, but he certainly held unconventional views with regard to the ways in which individual persons should have related to each other. Through the establishment of *Sangha*, he was pushing for a more egalitarian society through nonadversarial means.

The *Sangha* of the Buddhist renunciates in history was not completely egalitarian, though, and it is still not in most Buddhist schools. Hierarchies generally exist along the lines of seniority and gender. The "eight revered conditions" required of female renunciates, in particular, seem to have reflected the misogyny of the Buddha, or of the early male Buddhist renunciates who were responsible for the compilation of the Pāli Canon. These eight conditions relegate the *bhikkhunī*-s to a secondary status in the *Sangha* and stipulate their dependence on the *bhikkhu*-s. According to these revered conditions, a *bhikkhunī* must pay respect to *bhikkhu*-s (fully ordained male renunciates, not including novices), irrespective of her seniority in the *Sangha*. She may not criticize or reprimand *bhikkhu*-s, while *bhikkhu*-s may reprimand *bhikkhunī*-s. *Bhikkhunī*-s are to invite a *bhikkhu* twice a month to give an exhortation. A *bhikkhunī* must be ordained by both the *Bhikkhu Sangha* and the *Bhikkhunī Sangha*, whereas a *bhikkhu* only needs to be ordained by the *Bhikkhu Sangha*. In the case of grievous offense, a *bhikkhunī* must be disciplined and reinstated by both *Sangha*s. And the *Bhikkhunī Sangha* must hold their rain retreat where a *bhikkhu* is present.[126] If these rules had been prescribed by the Buddha from the beginning of the Buddhist *Sangha*, it seems, they would have considerably curtailed the Buddhist women's activities and their spiritual achievement.

However, textual and archaeological evidence shows that, in the first few centuries of Buddhism, both female renunciates and laywomen were quite active, reputable, and advanced in understanding, preaching, practicing, and realizing the Buddhist *Dhamma*, which suggests a much later origin of the eight revered conditions. Aside from the *Therīgāthā* that recorded and celebrated the spiritual attainments of one hundred and two *bhikkhunī arahant*s, the *Nikāya* texts themselves witnessed the importance and eminence of a number of *bhikkhunī*-s and laywomen followers in early Buddhism. In the *Mahāvacchagotta Sutta* in the *Majjhima Nikāya*, the Buddha said there were far more than five hundred in number in each of the following categories: *bhikkhu*-s who attained arahantship, *bhikkhunī*-s who attained arahantship, male celibate lay followers who became "non-returners," female celibate lay followers who became non-returners, male lay followers who won "stream-entry," and female lay followers who won stream-entry.[127] The *Nandakovāda Sutta* recorded that five hundred *bhikkhunī*-s attained at least stream-entry after one *Dhamma* talk.[128] *Bhikkhunī* Khemā had the reputation of being "wise, competent, intelligent, learned, a splendid speaker, and ingenious;" she was recorded as having expounded the subtlety of liberated existence to King Pasēnadi of Kosala in the exact same way that the Buddha would have, and her exposition had delighted the King so much that he paid homage to her.[129] *Bhikkhunī* Dhammadinnā, likewise, was praised by the Buddha as being wise for having expounded the subtle points of the Buddhist *Dhamma* in the exact same way that he would have.[130] Laywoman Kādigodhā became a stream-enterer after hearing just one *Dhamma* talk by the Buddha.[131] Some laywomen were depicted as having recognized the virtue and wisdom of the Buddha before their male counterparts had, and in fact they were responsible for bringing the latter to the Buddhist path.[132]

Nancy J. Barnes's study of the inscriptions at the ancient Buddhist site of Sanchi in Northcentral India, dated from the second to first centuries BCE, indicates that lay and renunciant Buddhist women remained quite active and prominent for a few centuries after the Buddha's passing. In fact, it seemed that women supporters of Buddhism outnumbered men by three to one.[133] *Bhikkhunī*-s were highly visible in these inscriptions as well, though it seemed that they either did not hold titles equal to those of the *bhikkhu*-s, or they were not remembered by their titles. After the first century BCE, however, inscriptions about and by *bhikkhunī*-s became rarer, which indicated a significant change in their situations.[134] Perhaps not coincidentally, scholars located the interpolation of the eight revered conditions into the orally transmitted Canon during this time.[135] Barnes thinks that the formulations of conditions against the *bhikkhunī*-s in the first century

BCE both indicated the prominence of the *bhikkhunī*-s prior to that time and explained the decline of the *Bhikkhunī Sangha* afterwards:

> Nuns were so prominent that monks kept promulgating rules to keep them in check . . . Monks would have had no need to make special rules to limit nuns' actions and rights if nuns hadn't already shown monks how independent they could be. . . . It seems likely that the nuns lost their impact because the monks asserted their own primacy in the Sangha, and created regulations that would keep the women permanently in their place.[136]

The appearance of the eight revered conditions for the *bhikkhunī*-s in the first century BCE was therefore probably the *bhikkhu*-s' reaction to the active and independent roles that the *bhikkhunī*-s had played in the first few hundred years of Buddhism.

One cannot conclusively attribute all of the discriminatory regulations against women to the male compilers in the first century BCE, though. The Buddha parted with the self-mortifying asceticism that was the norm amongst wandering renunciates at the time, and taught the "middle way" of neither indulgence nor asceticism. This incurred accusations of laxity in discipline from other wandering ascetics as well as from the laity who equated sanctity with the severity of practices.[137] The admission of women among male renunciates would have further subjected the Buddhist *Sangha* to criticisms and attacks, considering that celibacy was the norm amongst the anti-Brāhmanic renunciates at the time of the Buddha, and renunciation was generally seen as a men's preserve. It was therefore possible that the Buddha himself might have chosen to respond to those criticisms by complying with the patriarchal norms and putting more restrictions on women. That is, in his dealings with criticisms, the Buddha himself might have been androcentric and patriarchal in that he followed the patriarchal norms of his time that reflected mainly male concerns and male biases. Being androcentric and patriarchal, however, is not the same as being misogynist, and the Buddha was not misogynist even if one takes the Pāli Canon to be his exact words. To say the least, he did unequivocally affirm the equal potentials of women in reaching *nibbāna*, and he did establish the *Bhikkhunī Sangha*.[138]

Regardless of the Buddha's own stance, which remains unverifiable, it seems that the requirement of celibacy was the main reason for many of the regulations about and against women. Aside from guarding the reputation of the Buddhist *Sangha* consisting of both male and female renunciates, the male compilers of the Canon were also preoccupied with keeping their own sexual desires contained, which was evidenced in the numerous cautions against women's power over men in the *Nikāya* texts. For instance, it was recorded that the Buddha instructed the *bhikkhu*-s to be wary of the sight, sound, scent, taste or touch of a woman.[139] On occasions the caution took a misogynist tone and womankind was compared to a black snake: "she is unclean, bad-smelling, timid, fearful and betrays friends."[140] Noteworthy is that these misogynist tones are found in the *Anguttara Nikāya*, the collection that focused on personal edification and catered to the upper-class males who were most concerned with self-purification.

More importantly, the *bhikkhunī*-s were instructed to be wary of the sight, sound, scent, taste, or touch of a man as well. There were accounts of men seducing or raping *bhikkhunī*-s, just as there were accounts of women tempting *bhikkhu*-s. What was expressed in these passages, then, was not so much that women by nature were temptresses, but that sexual desires could be dangerously powerful. As a result, celibates of both sexes would need repeated cautions and warnings.[141] The fact that the cautions against feminine wiles exceeded the cautions against male temptations both in number and in the severity of language does not prove that early Buddhism as a whole was misogynist. First, as discussed in Chapter 1, the Canon was compiled mostly in male hands and intended mainly for a male audience, and so the messages unsurprisingly betrayed androcentrism. Second, there were (and still are) far more women lay followers than men, and therefore in fulfilling the requirement of maintaining contact with the laity on a daily basis[142] the *bhikkhu*-s might have experienced more temptations than the *bhikkhunī*-s and needed more repeated cautions and warnings.[143]

Furthermore, pro-women and egalitarian statements also existed in the same *Nikāya* texts where anti-women statements appeared. The Buddha was recorded to have assured King Pasēnadi of Kosala, who was dejected over the news of his queen giving birth to a female child, that a girl might turn out to be better than a boy in wisdom and virtue.[144] The *Bhikkhunīsamyutta* recorded ten *bhikkhunī*-s who stood firm in their cultivation of concentration and their pursuit of *nibbāna*; they could not be tempted, distracted, confused, discouraged, intimidated, or terrified by Māra, the delusion personified.[145] Among the ten *bhikkhunī*-s was Somā, who was told by Māra that women were too dim-witted to attain arahantship. She responded that what mattered was concentrated practice and wisdom, not gender.[146] The

Buddha was said to have won *nibbāna* for the sake of both *bhikkhu*-s and *bhikkhunī*-s,[147] and the holy life in the *Sangha* was not considered perfected without all of the four assemblies of male renunciates, female renunciates, laymen, and laywomen.[148] Even amidst the later formulation of the eight revered conditions in the Vinaya text, the Buddha was said to have affirmed that women had equal potential to reach *nibbāna* as men.[149]

With the prevalence of sexist values in that society and the concomitant androcentric editing of the Canon, what begs for explanation is not the existence of misogynist passages, but the existence and preservation of the pro-women or egalitarian statements in the *Nikāya*-s and the *Therīgāthā*, a collection of songs and poems attributed to the early *bhikkhunī*-s.[150] Similarly, with the norm among anti-brāhmanical movements being male ascetics wandering about in isolation and avoiding contact with society, what is puzzling is not the praise and practice of seclusion, but the fact that the Buddha did not recommend it to every renunciant follower. Instead, he instituted communal existence for the renunciates, required them to maintain daily contact with the laity, and encouraged both renunciates and the lay followers to associate with "good friends" who were noble not by birth but by being wholesome. Contradicting the societal norms of the time as these teachings might be, they could not easily be edited away by the compilers of the Canon, for all of these teachings are grounded in the core teachings of the Buddha such as non-Self and *kamma*, both of which have interdependent co-arising as the rationale. Chapters 3 and 4 will delve into the meanings and implications of these core teachings of Buddhism.

3

A Feminist Exegesis of Non-Self

Constitution of Personhood and Identity

Buddhism and feminism appear to be two very different strains of thought. One originated in ancient Northeastern India and the other gained momentum in the modern West. Traditional Buddhist discourses have rarely tended to the issue of gender except in a handful of Mahāyāna scriptures[1] whose authenticity is questioned by some Theravādins, while modern Western feminists often too easily label Buddhism as just another patriarchal religion that is inevitably sexist and oppressive to women. More than twenty years ago, however, Rita M. Gross pointed out three similarities between Buddhism and feminism: both begin with life experiences and stress experiential understanding, both evince the will and courage to go against the grain and see beyond the conventional points of view, and both explore the ways in which habitual and conventional patterns of thinking and behaving operate to block basic well-being of people and cause great suffering.[2] A fourth similarity was added some years later: both speak of liberation, albeit the definitions of liberation may seem different.[3]

Classical Buddhist teachings and recent poststructuralist feminist theories further converge on the constructedness of individual persons and their self-identities. One of the most widely known and possibly the most perplexing teachings of Buddhism is the teaching of non-Self (Pāli: *anattā*; Sanskrit: *anātman*), which seems to negate categorically the existence of individuals and thereby deny the efficacy or necessity of moral actions taken by individuals. Coincidentally, the theory of socio-cultural constructedness of the subject with its concomitant negation of autonomy has drawn much critical attention to

poststructuralist theorists such as Judith Butler. Yet Buddhism, especially Theravāda, places much emphasis on *self*-control and individual
moral responsibility, which is reflected in the Buddhist teachings
regarding *kamma*, and poststructualist feminist theorists argue the
lack of autonomy does not dissolve moral agency. The consonance
between these two strains of thought is more than just intellectually
stimulating. They provide an exegetical framework as well as a basis
of critique for one another. The Buddhist teaching of non-Self may
be easier to comprehend with the assistance of the feminist analysis
of the constructedness of gender identity, which has been curiously
overlooked in the traditional discourses of Buddhism, a tradition "so
dedicated to noticing and reflecting on habitual patterns of conventional ego."[4] The classical Buddhist analysis with regard to the relations between person construction, attachment, identity, and *dukkha*,
along with its emphasis on moral discipline and mental training, in
return, may provide a useful perspective and have much to contribute
to contemporary feminist theories and social practices. This chapter
expounds the teaching of non-Self by employing the analysis of the
five aggregates on the one hand, and the feminist analysis of gender
identity and subject formation on the other.

Five Aggregates: The Constitution of Individual "Self"

Buddhism is well known for its radical assertion of *anattā*, the negation ("*an-*") of "*attā*" (Sanskrit: *ātman*). With the word "*attā*" commonly
translated as "self" or "soul" in English, this core Buddhist teaching,
it seems, reads "no self" or "no soul." The translation of "*attā*" as
"self" or "soul," though not completely incorrect, is highly misleading. In the ancient Indian usage, "*attā*" means neither "self" in the
sense of an individual person with her or his unique combination of
life experience and characteristics, nor "soul" in the sense of mental-
spiritual functioning of an individual person. *Anattā* thus does not
mean that no individual being exists, or that all beings exist only as
bodies with no mental-spiritual dimension left after bodily death. As
a matter of fact, both nihilism (*natthikavāda* or *natthika-diṭṭhi*; the view
that no being exists) and annihilationism (*ucchedavāda* or *uccheda-diṭṭhi*;
the view that a being exists only as a body and perishes completely at
the breakup of the body) are rejected by the historical Buddha. Such
views deny the validity of ethics and are called "pernicious views"
in the *Nikāya* texts.[5]

The Buddhist teaching of *anattā* negates "*attā*" only in the sense of eternal, never-changing, independently-existing innermost "Self-Essence" of all beings. In the *Upaniṣads* this "Self-Essence" is identical with *Brāhman*, the permanently existing Being (Sanskrit: *sat*), Pure Consciousness (Sanskrit: *chit*), and Bliss (Sanskrit: *ananda*). This eternalist view (*sassatavāda*) of "Self" is also called a "pernicious view"[6] in the *Nikāya* texts, and it is this peculiar definition of "Self"—"permanent, stable, eternal, not subject to change"[7]—that the Buddha refutes. Thus the teaching of non-Self is frequently summarized in the *Nikāya*-s in these two succinct sentences: "What is impermanent is *dukkha*. What is *dukkha* is not *attā*."[8] "Self," by the *Upaniṣadic* definition, is never-changing eternal bliss. Individual existence, being subject to change and subject to suffering, simply does not match this definition. Instead, Buddhism teaches that a person and her or his consciousness interdependently co-arises with the surrounding phenomena in the world and therefore cannot be unchanging or stay uninfluenced by life experiences.

The twin central teachings of Buddhism, non-Self and interdependent co-arising, are actually the same concept stated from two different angles. Non-Self is taught in response to "the eternalist view" of "Self," and interdependent co-arising is emphasized in response to nihilism and annihilationism. Individual persons and their consciousness do arise and therefore are not entirely nonexistent, but they exist only in relation to their bodies, to other individuals, and to all non-Self entities in their surroundings.[9] Gier and Kjellberg put it this way: "You wouldn't be the person you are if your family, friends, and acquaintances all weren't the people they are, if you hadn't had the experiences you've had, lived in the society you live in, and so on."[10] Human existence is relational, and this relational existence is subject to change: "the physical bodies change; feelings, beliefs, desires, and intentions all change; consciousness is intermittent; and our selfconceptions change over time. None of the things we can point to as the self remains the same."[11] Individual persons co-arise with, and are contingent on, their surroundings, and therefore do not exist as unchanging, permanent, blissful pure consciousness that is separate from, and independent of, worldly phenomena. There is no eternal, unchanging "Self" because of interdependent co-arising, and nihilism or annihilationism is an incorrect description of reality since beings do arise.

While rejecting both of the extremes of nihilism and eternalism, in the early texts the Buddha seemed to be more concerned with refuting the eternalist view than the nihilist view. The eternalist "Self" was compared to a lump of foam on a river, a water bubble during rain, a mirage, a plantain trunk, and a magical illusion.[12] The counter-eternalist teaching of non-Self is further elaborated through breaking personhood down to the five aggregates and then stating that a person is neither identical with any one of the five aggregates, nor an independent spiritual entity possessing or containing the five aggregates, nor an entity being contained by any one of the five aggregates.[13] All of these views are called "identity views" because they are considered conducive to, and reinforcing, egocentric clinging. They lead to unsatisfactoriness or outright suffering.

The meaning and scope of the five aggregates have to be understood in order to see the subtleties of the teaching of non-Self and the ways in which this teaching is highly morally demanding. In the classical Buddhist understanding, the entity we consider an individual "self" is a socio-psycho-physical compound of material forms (Pāli/Sanskrit: *rūpa*), sensations (Pāli/Sanskrit: *vedanā*), perceptions (Pāli: *saññā*; Sanskrit: *samjñā*), volitional constructions (Pāli: *saṇkhāra*; Sanskrit: *samskāra*), and consciousness (Pāli: *viññāṇa*; Sanskrit: *vijñāṇa*).

What is noteworthy is that in the ancient Indian perspective (orthodox teaching of Brāhmanism as well as the "heterodox" teachings of Buddhism and Jainism) there are six senses, and the term *rūpa* refers to both the sense organs and their respective sense-objects. Mind is treated as one of the sense organs alongside the ordinary five sense organs of eyes, ears, nose, tongue, and skin. Serving as the objects of these six sense organs, also termed "internal sense bases," are the six classes of "external sense bases"[14]: that which can be seen, that which can be heard, that which can be smelled, that which can be tasted, that which can be touched and felt, and that which can be processed by the mind. The words "external" and "internal" here obviously do not indicate absolute demarcation, for they are expediently used only to explain the function of senses, which only occur when the "external sense bases" and the "internal sense bases" are in contact with each other, or, in Gier and Kjellberg's words, when "the inner flows into the outer and the outer flows into the inner."[15] With mind being considered a sense organ, virtually all phenomena in the world can be considered the "external sense bases" for the mind insofar as they can all be processed in one way or another by the mind. Colors, for example, are objects for the eyes, and yet the difference between two colors may be an object for the mind. Thus considered, "external sense bases" encompass not only concrete objects with physical dimensions, but also abstract entities without physical dimensions, such as languages, philosophies, histories, social conventions, cultural norms, political institutions, and the sentiments involved in interpersonal relationships in the past, present, and future. In the Pāli *Abhidhamma*, six kinds of objects are considered mental objects: sensitive matter, subtle matter, consciousness, mental factors, *nibbāna*, and concepts. While the consciousnesses of the other five sense organs pertain only to the present, the mind-consciousness can cognize an object of the past, the present, or the future.[16] Considering that both mind and mind-objects are included in the Pāli/Sanskrit word *rūpa*, it is better rendered "material and socio-cultural forms" or "material and symbolic forces" than simply "material forms," given that the word *rūpa* actually encompasses both the abstract and the concrete, the mental and the physical, the internal and the external, while the word "material" in quotidian English usage does not usually include mind or mind-objects.

Another one of the five aggregates whose complexity is not readily discernible in its English translation is *saṅkhāra*. This term is variously translated as "mental formations," "mental proliferations," "dispositions," "volitions," or "volitional constructions." The various translations themselves are puzzling since in English it is difficult to consider mental formations, dispositions, and volitions to be in the same category. Etymologically, the word *saṅkhāra* means "put together," and Pāli scholar Bhikkhu Bodhi explains, "*saṅkhāras* are both things which put together, construct, and compound other things, *and* the things that are put together, constructed, and compounded."[17] On account of the references to "things that are put together, constructed, and compounded," *saṅkhāra* is translated as "mental formations" or "mental proliferations;" on account of the references to "things which put together, construct, and compound other things," the same word is rendered "dispositions" or "volition." A person's dispositions and volition both result from the things that have been put together, and affect the ways in which things are being put together. In other words, one's dispositions and volition shape the ways in which one's thoughts are formed, and the thoughts formed in turn mold one's dispositions and volition. In this book, when "mental formation" and "disposition" are not discussed separately, *saṅkhāra* will be rendered "volitional construction" since the word "volitional" conveys the *constructive* aspect of *saṅkhāra*, and the word "construction" conveys the *constructed* aspect.

Corresponding to, and co-arising with, the six senses and their respective sense-objects are six classes of sensation, six classes of perception, six classes of volitional construction, and six classes of consciousness: eye-consciousness, ear-consciousness, nose-consciousness, tongue-consciousness, body-consciousness, and mind-consciousness.[18] As fire always burns on fuel, consciousness is always consciousness of some material or symbolic forms. The fire that burns on gasoline is not identical with the fire that burns on a match—they may differ in temperature and color and duration and extension, albeit they are both fire and both burning. In the same way, consciousness varies from one class of *rūpa* to another, from one event to another, from one round of volitional constructions to another, from one individual person to another, albeit different kinds of consciousness are all abstract mental functioning of individual persons.

It says in the *Samyutta Nikāya*: "When there is name-and-form (Pāli/Sanskrit: *nāma-rūpa*), consciousness comes to be; consciousness has name-and-form as its condition."[19] In this passage the term *nāma* is used to refer to the aggregates other than *rūpa* and consciousness, i.e., sensations, perceptions, and volitional constructions. Sometimes, however, it seems that *nāma* encompasses only sensations and perceptions, for in the "Twelve Links of Interdependent Origination" volitional constructions are discussed separately from *nāma-rūpa*: "With ignorance as condition, volitional constructions come to be; with volitional constructions as condition, consciousness comes to be; with consciousness as condition, *nāma-rūpa* comes to be . . ."[20] The discrepancy between the above two usages of *nāma* in *Samyutta Nikāya* shows *saṅkhāra*'s affinity with sensations and perceptions, but at the same time it indicates that *saṅkhāra* functions in a different way than sensations and perceptions and is far more important.

Like sensations and perceptions, *saṅkhāra* is a kind of *nāma*. It is a kind of "internal" mental functioning that depends on the "external" sense-objects to exist. Yet *saṅkhāra*, being constructive as well as constructed, is much more complex than sensations and perceptions. In fact, among the fifty-two "mental factors" (*cetasikas*) enumerated in the Pāli *Abhidhamma*, the aggregates of sensations and perceptions each count as one mental factor, and yet the aggregate of *saṅkhāra* is further divided into fifty mental factors, including greed, delusion, hatred, mindfulness, malleability of consciousness, compassion, altruistic joy, and so on.[21] *Saṅkhāra* can put together existing sense-objects to form new mind-objects that are prior-to-now nonexistent in the socio-cultural realm, and then the newly formed mind-objects are fed to consciousness just as the existing mind-objects are. One's consciousness, in turn, affects the ways in which she or he senses and perceives *rūpa*, thereby also affecting the volitional constructions to come. That is, besides the material and symbolic forces that one is exposed to (*rūpa*), one's consciousness is also influenced by the functioning of one's own *nāma*, especially *saṅkhāra*. David J. Kalupahana expounds,

> *Rūpa* or material form accounts for the function of identification; *vedanā* or feeling and *saññā* or perception represent the function of experience, emotive as well as cognitive; *saṅkhāra* or disposition stands for the function of individuation; *viññāṇa* or consciousness explains the function of continuity in experience.[22]

The constructive aspect of *saṅkhāra* accounts for the process and result of individuation. It accounts for the fact that people exposed to the same *rūpa*, if they ever are, do not necessarily have the same personality or consciousness. Of course it is doubtful that any two persons are ever exposed to the exact same set of *rūpa*. Two siblings growing up in the same family, for example, are not necessarily treated in the same way by their parents, and they certainly do not treat each other in the same way they are treated.

Let me employ a real-life incident as a vehicle to explicate the inter-working of the five aggregates, especially the rather complicated aggregate of *saṅkhāra* that can be variously rendered "dispositions," "volitions," and "mental formations." My older brother is fairly tall and heavy and, according to my parents, he has been bigger than boys of the same age for his whole life. Yet, for a man who may be physically intimidating, he is, as both of my friends and his own friends put it, "surprisingly gentle with his bodily motions and incredibly considerate." One may describe his "disposition" as gentle and considerate, which one may attribute to his "volition"—he is gentle and considerate because he had made a conscious choice to be so. His "disposition" and "volition" as such may have something to do with, although certainly is not determined by, the "volitional constructions" surrounding a childhood experience that happened when he was five-and-a-half years old.

One day he was dragging me upstairs to find my mother, at a rather fast pace, due to something urgent that neither of us can recall now. Being an extraordinarily tall boy for his age, he was more than a foot taller than me even though he was only one-and-a-half years older. As a result of the significant difference in height, I could not catch up with him and fell on the stairs. The upper part of my nose hit the angular edge of a step. Blood immediately gushed out from my face and I was screaming and crying. My mother was not far away and, upon hearing my voice, she rushed over and took me to the hospital while yelling at my brother non-stop for not realizing his steps were much wider than mine and for causing me the injury.

In this incident, the color of blood was an "external sense base" for the "internal sense base" of my brother's eyes, and the contact of the two bases resulted in a "sensation" (*vedanā*) of seeing, which was followed by the "perception" (*saññā*) of seeing red. My screaming and crying was an "external sense base" for the "internal sense base" of his ears, and the contact of the two bases resulted in a sensation of hearing, followed by the perception of hearing a loud and high-pitched voice. The smell of blood was an "external sense base" for the "internal sense base" of his nose, and upon the contact of the two a sensation of smelling was caused, followed by the perception of smelling something pungent. The three perceptions were "put together" (*saṇkhāra*) to cause the "mental formation" (also *saṇkhāra*): "My little sister is hurt." The sound of my mother's yelling was an "external sense base" for the "internal sense base" of his ears, and upon the contact of the two bases a sensation of hearing was caused, followed by the perception of hearing a reprimanding voice, which contributed to the mental formation: "It is my fault." The content of my mother's yelling was an "external sense base" for the "internal sense base" of his mind, which led to another mental formation: "It is because of my size and because I was not careful." Put together, the three mental formations led to the conclusion that "If I am not careful, someone may get hurt because I am bigger than others."

This particular way in which he put those perceptions and mental formations together might have resulted from the life experiences of his infanthood (or of past lives, if one believes in past lives). That is, his disposition and volition was a consequence of his mental formations in the near or distant past, and his existing disposition and volition affected his mental formations at that moment and led him to form that particular thought. What led to his existing disposition and volition at that moment remains unknown to me, and yet it is clear that, as a result of the incident, a new volition was formed, which has affected the ways in which he has been interacting with the "external sense bases" ever since. (Even to this day, from time to time I still find him staring at the dent on my face, which is invariably followed by some caring gestures and/or words.) And the ways in which he has chosen to respond to people and situations have contributed to his current disposition of being gentle and considerate as well as having become part of his self-identity as a big but considerate man.

A person's consciousness does not exist independently or eternally and is subject to change when new phenomena are experienced.

Moreover, a person's consciousness is neither unified nor monolithic, for in response to every situation multiple consciousnesses would co-arise. In the example given above, besides the eye-consciousness and nose-consciousness that co-arose with the blood and the ear-consciousnesses that co-arose with my crying and my mother's yelling, there were multiple mind-consciousnesses that arose in response to the incident: the mind-consciousness of me being hurt, the mind-consciousness of him being blamed, and the mind-consciousness of his size. His volitional constructions further gave rise to the mind-consciousness of taking responsibility and the mind-consciousness of demanding himself to be careful. At the same time, he might also have the mind-consciousness of the fact that he could not change his size and, consequently, the mind-consciousness that the difference in size would always be a factor and so he could not be trusted with his sister's safety.

Multiple mind-consciousnesses co-exist at the same time, and the outlook of one's personality depends on which consciousness is most consistently prompted to her or him by the things and people in the surroundings, as well as by one's own "mental formations" and "dispositions." The preceding and ensuing experiences, together with the concomitant mental formations, may consistently prompt a person to choose to identify with one particular consciousness, or they may support the choice for a while and then lean toward a different choice, or they may feed into multiple possibilities at the same time and allow them to compete with each other. At any rate, it is possible that the choice changes frequently and rapidly, for consciousnesses are constantly arising with every single contact between the "external sense bases" and "internal sense bases," as well as with every single "mental formation." "Just as a monkey roaming through a forest grabs hold of one branch, lets that go and grabs another, then lets that go and grabs still another, so too that which is called 'mind' and 'mentality' and 'consciousness' arises as one thing and ceases as another by day and by night."[23] A person may be consistently prompted with a certain consciousness and identify with it for a certain period of time, and then may choose, or be prompted by other life experiences, to identify with a different consciousness some time later. When my brother was younger, for instance, the consciousness that he could not be trusted with his sister's safety seemed to be held onto more than the consciousness of demanding himself to be careful—for several years he would avoid taking me anywhere by himself.

This Buddhist analysis of the five aggregates points to the conditionality of personhood. An individual person is, and continues to be, a product of socio-cultural conditionings as well as a product of her or his life experiences, the latter being affected by her or his own volitional constructions. A person as such is socially constructed as well as mentally constructed. Traditional Buddhist discourses elaborate abundantly on the process of mental construction but somehow come short in explicating the sociality of existence and its implications. Based on the analysis of the five aggregates, to be a person is to become a person in a matrix of socio-cultural forces. What one holds onto as the identity of the self does not come into existence without the material and symbolic forces (*rūpa*) that have been suggesting and reinforcing it. An identity as such is not permanent and does not stay static. It is subject to change, and it changes when new experiences arise or when new situations prompt new ways of putting together old experiences. The Buddhist teaching of non-Self, at least in its classical sense, merely denies the idea of permanently-existing, never-changing individual Self-Essence that is abstractly defined (by the most privileged stratum in society) and uninfluenced by worldly phenomena or day-to-day experiences. The teaching of non-Self does not negate individual existence, nor does it dismiss social relations and interactions as utterly unimportant. Quite the contrary, it indicates that an individual self is continually being conditioned and reconditioned by "external" social surroundings, as much as by "internal" mental processes such as sensations, perceptions, volitional constructions, and consciousnesses. In the next section, through looking at the constructedness of gender identity as analyzed by constructivist feminists, I will further illustrate the meaning and social implications of the Buddhist teaching of non-Self, of seeing an individual person as an ongoing process rather than a static existence.

Seeing "Non-Self" in the Making of Gender Identity

As Gross observes, there is something curiously illogical in many Buddhists' understanding and acceptance of the central Buddhist teaching of non-Self: "while most Buddhist do not believe in the existence of a permanent, abiding self, their attitudes and actions nevertheless indicate that they do believe in the real existence of gender."[24] Karma Lekshe Tsomo observes that in modern Buddhisms when the issue of gender inequality arises, "The most common attitude is to ignore the problem altogether, dismiss it, deny it, and trivialize it."[25] People often appeal to the idea that the Buddhist *Dhamma* transcends gender, thereby either dismissing gender justice as a petty *saṃsāric* concern that is irrelevant to the ultimate Buddhist goal of *nibbāna* and "unfettered mind,"[26] or defensively denying and willfully ignoring the persistent gender discrimination, gender stereotypes, and rigid assignment of gender roles in both of the voluminous traditional Buddhist texts and the day-to-day operation of Buddhist institutions.[27] With regard to gender discrimination and gender stereotypes in traditional Buddhist texts, Alan Sponberg finds that the "soteriological inclusiveness" in early Buddhism, i.e., everyone can reach *nibbāna*, is compounded with "institutional androcentrism" and "ascetic misogyny."[28] In terms of day-to-day operation of Buddhist institutions, it is in fact quite common for Buddhist communities to divide needed labor and volunteer work along gender lines and, in effect, impose and reinforce stereotypical gender attributes. The central teaching of non-Self, i.e., the lack of eternal, unchanging, self-existing essence, is invoked from time to time in response to various kinds of contentions and disputes, but it is rarely remembered when conventional gender roles are described, expected, and even imposed. Susanne Mrozik notes, for example, that in South Asian Buddhist traditions virtues are still strongly associated with the male body, despite the talk about the "ultimate" irrelevance of bodily distinctions.[29] Similar attitudes can be found in East Asian Buddhist traditions as well. This is true not only of average Buddhists who are not particularly educated in Buddhist thoughts and theories, but also of some Buddhist masters who are respected for their knowledge of the *Dhamma*. Consider, for instances, the three most prominent Buddhist masters in Taiwan, each leading an international organization comprised of 1 million to 4 million members, two-thirds to 88.5 percent of whom are women. When being asked about why there have been many more female than male followers in Buddhism, a male *Dhamma* master whose sangha has many more *bhikṣunī*-s than *bhikṣu*-s said,

> Women are gentler and more fragile . . . Men are tougher and stronger; they think highly of themselves, try to solve everything by themselves, and are unwilling to take advice. . . . Women *by nature* are not as tough or strong, so they are more likely to accept religious teachings and more in need of consolations provided by religion. In addition, women are not as fit and energetic as men, so upon encountering difficulties they get scared and would turn to the Buddhas and Bodhisattvas for protection and blessing. . . . Women are more willing to take religion because it can positively influence their family life.[30] (emphasis added)

Another of the most renowned male Buddhist masters in Taiwan also often typecasts women as soft, nurturing, considerate, patient, compromising, and *helpful to men's careers*. He exhorts women to exert these positive traits of their feminine *nature*, even though he also has consistently advocated for equal rights of women.[31] The largest Taiwan-based philanthropic organization, comprised of 4 million members worldwide, is led by a female Buddhist master. She idealizes the traditional feminine roles in Chinese society as wives and mothers and essentializes women by stating, "consideration, kind-heartedness, and compassion can be seen as being symbolic of women. Steering the husband down a good path is the wife's responsibility. This will benefit humanity, enrich human life, and is also the responsibility of the mother."[32] Scott Pacey observes that the three most influential Buddhist masters in Taiwan, despite their different interpretations of "Buddhism for the Human World," are quite similar in that they take stereotypical gender attributes for granted and expect women to fulfill their traditional feminine roles as wives and mothers, and only as wives and mothers.[33]

Theoretically, the Buddhist *Dhamma* transcends gender. In everyday life, however, it often seems it is gender that transcends the *Dhamma*, for the *Dhamma* is supposed to cover every aspect of Reality/Existence but somehow is hardly ever applied to gender. The reluctance to acknowledging the existence of gender stereotypes and androcentrism within the Buddhist traditions, Gross rightly notes, "is a more destructive and dangerous form of opposition to gender equality than outright opposition to egalitarian reforms,"[34] for it precludes the possibility of reform by making it impossible to even bring up the topic of reform.

Most Buddhists seem to be familiar with the theory of the five aggregates and its relation to the teaching of non-Self: a person is impermanent and subject to change because she or he is constituted of material forms (*rūpa*), sensations, perceptions, volitional constructions, and consciousness. Many also seem to be familiar with the notion that there are six sense organs and mind is considered one of them. Few, however, grasp how much is encompassed within the term *rūpa*, especially when it comes to the sense-objects for the mind. This lack of understanding may have resulted from the common but rather misleading rendering of the term *rūpa* as "material forms" on the one hand, and the unfamiliarity with ancient Indian thought on the other. If the scope of the aggregate *rūpa* were properly understood, there would be no justification for excluding gender from the consideration of identity construction and the concomitant attachment to the identity constructed. After all, the aggregate *rūpa* does include the sense organ of the mind and the sense-objects for the mind, and what, if not sense-objects for the mind, are the social conventions and prescriptions that strongly suggest, support, impose, and reinforce gendered identities and gendered behaviors through gendered colors, toys, chores, career ambitions, postures, uses of language, etc.?

The cultural scripts about genders are certainly a form of *rūpa*, and the Buddhist teaching of an individual identity being constructed and subject to change is consonant with constructivist feminist analysis of gender formation. Drawing on Simone de Beauvoir's claim that one is not born but rather *becomes* a woman under cultural compulsion, poststructuralist feminist philosopher Judith Butler observes,

> Gender is the repeated stylization of the body, a set of repeated acts within a highly rigid regulatory frame that congeal over time to produce the appearance of substance, of a natural sort of being. A political genealogy of gender ontologies, if it is successful, will deconstruct the substantive appearance of gender into its constitutive acts and locate and account for those acts within the compulsory frames set by the various forces that police the social appearance of gender.[35]

Gender is produced through repeated bodily performances of the cultural scripts that define masculinity and femininity. Since the beginning of their existence in human societies, people are systematically inculcated with, and disciplined to perform, certain behaviors and roles that are supposedly appropriate for their anatomical characteristics. The compulsory repetition of bodily performances of gender norms has a materializing effect and can "congeal over time," for the gender norms repeatedly performed by the body are thereby inscribed on the body, which is an integral part of a person's self-identity. Since gender norms are inscribed on the body and thus become part of the person, gender is not like an outfit that can be taken off at will. That is, gender is not something that can be undone or changed with just one alternative act because it is not created once with just one socially-prescribed act. Still, gender "has no ontological status apart from the various acts which constitute its reality,"[36] nor is it a "substance" that is necessitated by anatomical characteristics. It appears to be substantive and "natural" because the body has been compelled by social expectations and cultural conventions to perform the various gender-specific acts over and over, and the very repetition results in the illusion of an abiding "gender core."[37]

The gendered social expectations and cultural conventions are pervasive in everyday life, from gendered colors to gendered toys, from gendered chores to gendered career ambitions, from gendered postures to gendered uses of language. Some colors are associated with and used on girls, while some other colors are associated with and used on boys. It is very common, in the United States at least, for people to put baby boys in blue clothes and bassinets, and baby girls in pink. When I was a child in Taiwan, the warm colors, such as red, pink, and orange, were commonly considered "girly colors," while the cool colors such as green and blue were considered "boyish colors." Children learn from very early on that certain colors are appropriate for their gender and others are not.

Children learn their gendered identities through toys as well. Girls are still commonly given dolls or items of sedentary and domestic nature to play with, while boys are often encouraged to play with toy cars, trains, airplanes, tanks, guns, robots equipped with weapons, and generally items that are mobile and/or destructive. Supposedly girls do not like to move about, and supposedly they *like* to play house, imagining being wives and mothers and *enjoying* the imaginary cleaning, cooking, and taking care of other members in the family.

The assignment of household chores is frequently gendered as well, if boys are expected to do chores at all. In Taiwan and other Chinese societies, many parents expect only girls to help out with chores, while some others train their boys to perform tasks that require a little more physical strength, such as mopping the floor. In the United States, in families that do expect both boys and girls to do household chores, girls are more likely to be assigned with more "domestic" chores such as tasks in the kitchen or tasks related to cleaning and nurturing, while boys are more likely to be expected to take on chores of higher mobility such as taking out the trash, mowing the lawn, shoveling the snow, etc. The gendered assignment of household chores not only suggests the *division* of genders and reinforces gender roles, but also affords the male gender more physical mobility and financial resources since childhood: boys can earn some pocket money by mowing the lawn or shoveling the snow for their neighbors, but no one would really hire girls in the neighborhood to do the dishes. Even when girls and women are hired as maids for household maintenance, their contributions are commonly deemed less valuable and, as a result, they may work longer hours and still earn less money. "A sexual division of labor," Zillah Eisenstein observes, ". . . divides men and women into their respective hierarchical sex roles and structures their related duties in the family domain and within the economy."[38]

As an extension of the gendered assignment of household chores, jobs are frequently gendered, and boys and girls are often encouraged to envision their future careers according to cultural conventions. Some occupations are still strongly associated with the female gender, such as nurses and kindergarten teachers, although the male monopoly of certain occupations, such as doctors, scientists, and politicians, is gradually breaking down.

Boys are expected to take up physical space, running around and sitting with their arms stretching out and legs wide open. If, in the process of using their bodies, they are a little disruptive and destructive, they are "just being boys." Their postures are rarely corrected except when their parents grow concerned with their spinal formation and tell them not to slouch. Girls, on the other hand, are allowed a lesser range of postures and bodily movements, especially in areas where population density has been high for many centuries and space has been quite limited, such as coastal cities in China and Taiwan. They are taught "lady-like" behaviors from very early on, such as sitting with their legs together or crossed.[39] Inasmuch as "lady-like" behaviors involve taking up less space and moving less, girls are often subtly discouraged from physical exercises, and as a result are less likely to engage in sports.

"Lady-like" behavior commonly includes using soft voice and polite wording. Popular books in the field of gender communication, such as *Men Are from Mars, Women Are from Venus*, while having the effect of reinforcing gender stereotypes, are indicative of the extent to which men and women have been socially conditioned to use language differently. Women have generally been socialized to be more polite by using more words and in less direct forms, while men have generally been socialized to use short, direct imperatives. This gendered expectation with respect to language is noticeable in English and Chinese, and particularly salient in Japanese-speaking environment, where for each sentence there are several different forms showing different levels of respect. People of lower status have to use the form(s) showing greater respect, which means that, to be recognized as a person capable of using the Japanese language, one has to accept one's social status in relation to one's interlocutor. Women are generally expected to use the form(s) of the higher respect level, no matter who their interlocutors may be. The forms showing higher respect levels typically involve longer sentence constructions and therefore more syllables, which indirectly forces women to articulate. In many cultures, women have also been socialized to use a wider range of tones and be more dramatic with their intonations. In tonal languages, the social expectation of "feminine tones" generally translates to soft and high-pitched voices. In general, a girl is expected to completely steer away from foul language, and yet a boy is "just being a boy" if he curses or makes a reference to some bodily functions that are conventionally considered "gross." The common tolerance of boys' being "gross" with language and activities is extended to their personal hygiene and appearances. Boys who are neat and clean may even be teased for being "feminine." By contrast, girls are more likely to be expected to maintain a higher level of physical cleanness.

The cultural scripts of gender as discussed above are objects for the sense organ of mind and therefore are encompassed by the term *rūpa*. These various forms of *rūpa* may be "put together" (*saṇkhāra*) and become part of one's "disposition" (*saṇkhāra*), and, further, that which has been put together becomes the fuel for one's mind-consciousness. Through the mind-objects in the forms of subtle hints and explicit injunctions about acceptable and unacceptable behaviors, one learns what it means to be of a certain gender and is socialized to *act* out a certain gender according to the norms in a certain society, such as wearing "feminine" clothes and using courteous language. If these mind-objects are consistently presented to a person, the mind-consciousness of a gendered identity would repeatedly arise and, overtime, she or he is likely to take it for granted and identify with it. Through repetition, the performance of gender norms congeals, resulting in the illusion of substance and becoming a part of the person's identity, which is often clung to and mistaken to be something inherent and "natural." Cultural scripts of genders, being pervasive and repeatedly presented, shape the ways in which people behave and see themselves.

However, as mentioned above, with every situation, multiple consciousnesses may co-arise, some of which may be clashing with each other or dissonant with one's gender identity formed under cultural conventions. It is possible that, upon detecting the incoherence, one would choose to identify with something different and, concomitantly, behave differently. A girl may have been socialized to accept the gendered assignment of chores in the household, but she may also have been inculcated with the modern ideology of equal rights. The common dependence on "women's work" and the simultaneous devaluation of it, once perceived, may ferment doubt about the unequal workload in the family and even stimulate resistance to the gendered division of labor in general. A girl may have learned more dramatic intonation, either through imitation or due to the social expectation and encouragement she experienced. Yet she may also have detected the occasional contempt or ridicule for the "girly" tones coming from boys and adult men. She may decide to continue using the tones that she is familiar with, or she may become more monotonal in the hope of avoiding ridicule or in the hope of placing herself on equal footing with the boys around her. At moments like this, one can see that gender, as a part of a person's self-identity, is socially conditioned rather than an innate precondition. It is a process rather than a substance, a *becoming* through a sequence of culturally sanctioned behaviors rather than a predetermined "natural" state of *being* that one is born with and that stays unaffected by life experiences.

That gender is not "natural" can be seen when one considers the cultural variations of the societal prescriptions for the ways in which genders should be performed. In as early as 1935, Margaret Mead's anthropological work finds that the temperaments between and among sexes to be malleable and culturally variable.[40] Recent European studies also show that, even in a comparatively homogeneous part of the world as Europe, gender constructions and gender relations vary from locality to locality, intertwining with the local community's economy, politics, religion, culture, and even space.[41] The association between a certain gender and a certain group of colors is for sure culturally and historically variable. At earlier times in Chinese culture, the color red was associated with good fortune and was certainly used on wealthy men. My mother, however, gets intensely uncomfortable with my brother wearing red, and so do most of the Taiwanese and Chinese people of her and her parents' generations because the color red had been associated with the female gender. In fact, once in a Buddhist temple in Philadelphia I was chided, by a Chinese woman somewhat older than my mother, that I should wear more pink and red instead of black. "Wearing black makes one look like a boy, and wearing red makes one look like a girl," she said, completely oblivious to the fact that, at that very moment I was sitting right next to a Tibetan monk who, like most Tibetans, favors the color red and wears red all the time. Among the colors that were called "girly colors" when I was little, my brother is comfortable with red and orange, but not pink. The Taiwanese men of an even younger generation, by contrast, no longer consider the color pink off-limits.

The perceptions of "lady-like" postures vary across cultures and generations, too. For instance, Chinese and Taiwanese people of older generations consider it impolite, for both males and females, to sit with their legs crossed. In fact, one of the unwritten but much reinforced internal rules of the Taiwan-based International Tzu-Chi (Compassionate Relief) Foundation, laid down by Master Chengyen herself, is that no volunteer, male or female, may sit with their legs crossed if they are wearing the Tzu-Chi uniform. More Westernized younger generations commonly take sitting with legs crossed to be "lady-like."

That gender is a set of conditioned acts becomes especially salient when two persons of the same biological gender in the same society are conditioned to perceive and perform their gender in different ways due to their different economic or social stations. Some of my wealthy female friends in Taiwan habitually buy clothes that are pleasing to their eyes but may be inconvenient for their everyday bodily movements, and they often attribute that habit of choosing beauty over functionality to the "natural" dictates of their female gender. My mother and some other women who have had to perform physical labor to make a living, by contrast, do not appreciate restrictive clothing that would limit their bodily movements or make them too self-conscious when they toil. Besides, having very limited resources, they have to pick the type of clothing that allows them to function in various situations throughout the whole day. That is, they do not really separate work clothes from fun clothes, or sportswear from sleepwear, for they have neither the money to buy, nor the energy to maintain, all those different clothes for such different occasions.

Like upper-class women, lower-class women may be influenced by the fashion trends as seen in the West-dominated mass media, which all too often broadcast Euro-American beauty standards, including the body type that is used to display those fashions. As a result, women in Taiwan, and in fact in all East Asian countries, may consider white skin to be more feminine and more beautiful, resulting in the plethora of skin-whitening cosmetic products on the market throughout East Asia. For women laborers, however, the demand of functionality and low maintenance usually outweighs the concern for the "feminine beauty" defined by the West-dominated global market culture. After all, for women who live in subtropical areas and who do not work indoors, Caucasian-like white skin is extremely high maintenance, if not utterly unattainable.

Similarly, women laborers in Taiwan would in general conform to societal gender expectations for females, such as soft-speaking and deferring to authority figures, who are often males. But the reality of their working-class life has also trained them to be tough and to tackle most tasks by themselves, including lifting heavy objects. Most of my upper-middle-class female friends, by contrast, would predict-ably enlist help from men for those tasks. Interestingly, in an ethno-graphical study in Montréal that deliberately leaves out the factor of social class, Jean-Sébastien Marcoux finds that gendered division of tasks is developed and reinforced *relationally*. When a family moves from one residence to another, moving heavy objects is often done by men in a paternalistic manner and so in effect becomes a privilege of men and boys. In the presence of men, women either voluntarily stay away from, or are intimidated out of, the heavy-lifting that is much appreciated. With men around, women are typically relegated the under-appreciated tasks of sorting, packing, and cleaning. In the absence of men, however, women, especially younger ones, do not hesitate to handle heavy objects.[42]

Neither the choice of "feminine" clothes nor the habitual reliance on men's help is the inalterable "substance" of the female gender. Females who do not respond to these social pressures may be judged less "feminine" by those whose material surroundings and social upbringing have systematically created a narrow way of perceiving "femininity." For example, a Taiwanese friend of mine, who is from a wealthy, well-connected, and highly Westernized family with both parents speaking fluent English, once expressed her conviction that it was "not feminine" for women to have no pajamas and sleep in T-shirts. She did not consider that, for one thing, women of poor families cannot afford clothes made for sleep only and nothing else, and for another, the idea of pajamas is a Western import. Social sta-tions affect one's cultural exposures, which affect one's perception and definition of gender-appropriate behaviors. Gender consciousnesses, like any other kind of consciousnesses, depend upon the material and socio-cultural *rūpa* to arise.

The Buddhist teachings of interdependent co-arising and non-Self reject the notion of a permanent "Pure Consciousness" or Self-Essence completely detached from worldly phenomena. An individual's ways of perceiving and conducting oneself are shaped by one's life experiences, which are composed of, and conditioned by, one's socio-cultural surroundings, as well as by the functioning of one's *saṇkhāra*. As such, Buddhist thinking does not, and logically cannot, support any claim of inherent superiority of any social group. With regard to the purported inherent caste distinctions related in the last chapter, for example, the Buddha taught that brāhmins were not born supe-rior to all other social classes. It was by means of their definition of nobility, their propaganda of their naturally endowed characteristics, and their privileged upbringings, that they appeared to be superior.

The superiority is the work of their socio-cultural *becoming*, not the inherent state of their *being*. Contained in the Buddha's teaching is a call to reexamine critically the assumptions about the self-existent, unchanging qualities of social groups, especially when those qualities have been defined, prescribed, and propagated by the social group that is currently occupying the uppermost rung of the social hierarchy. The same kind of critical reexamination can and should be applied to the social grouping of genders. Gendered identity, like class identity, is conditioned, subject to change, and lacking Self-Essence.

Subject Formation and Cultural Delimitation

It is worth reiterating that the word *rūpa*, besides denoting mind and mind-objects, does refer to the material circumstances and the physical makeup of individual persons. A person does not exist in the world without the *rūpa* of a physical body. The bodily features and functions may serve as objects for the mind, which means that the physical makeup of a person may affect her or his personality and consciousness (or, more precisely, consciousness-es). In addition, the *rūpa* of socio-cultural conventions has circumscribed the meanings of a body and prescribed the proper ways to interact with such a body. That is, inasmuch as a person's contact with the socio-cultural world is mediated through her or his body, the body can play a crucial role in shaping life experiences and forming consciousness and self-identity. The analysis of the five aggregates acknowledges the body as a constituent of a person, but the body does not determine a person, for each person has developed her or his own way of putting together (*saṅkhāra*) sensory data. Therefore, the same bodily functions do not necessarily fuel the same consciousnesses, and different bodily functions do not necessarily fuel different consciousnesses. In other words, it is the interconditionality of physical existence, social constructs, and mental constructs that accounts for an individual.

It is because of a body that one can live and think and function in a society, and it is because of this particular body that exists in this particular socio-cultural environment at this particular time that one is conditioned to live and think and function in these particular ways. The values and norms of a society often seem natural or normal to its subjects precisely because those values and norms have been inscribed on the bodies of the subjects. In *Discipline and Punish: The Birth of the Prison*, Michél Foucault draws on Jeremy Bentham's concept of panopticon and delineates the ways in which the socio-cultural norms, which vary from culture to culture and greatly depend on the dominating power, become such a seemingly integral part of a person that they are simply considered normal or even "natural." Through a series of apparently innocent subtle arrangements concerning details in life,[43] people's minds as well as bodies are trained to act in conformity with the existing norms in society. Foucault observes that schools, through activities that have to be taken in a certain sequence and through grouping students into different grades, are clearly marking the direction of progress and hence elevating a certain set of norms. School teachers, by making students do seriated exercises repetitively according to a minutely partitioned timetable, by examining their progress and ranking their performances up against one another's, and by punishing them for not moving toward the predesignated direction in a preassigned pace, are serving as the disciplinarians who make the students' bodies accustomed to the regulations imposed, make those imposed regulations appear to be normal and natural, and thereby make students voluntarily continue to be disciplined by the normalized regulations. Students' bodies and minds are thus meticulously programmed, disciplined, and contained in a pre-drawn frame so that they are useful to the administrative power and can be used by it. Social workers, doctors and nurses, factory supervisors and company managers, and police and soldiers, are all similarly using the instruments of hierarchical observations, normalizing judgments, and examinations[44] to exert their disciplinary powers in different aspects of people's lives. Individuals are incessantly watched and disciplined to conform to the norms that, once recognized as such, make further societal disciplines easy and invisible. Thus the gazes of power are internalized, social norms are inscribed on the bodies, "automatic docility"[45] is achieved, and possibilities of rebellions and dissent are largely checked before they can even emerge. The network of disciplinarians, which Foucault associates with modern states, domesticates the masses and hides domination behind the pursuit of what seems to be normal and natural.

According to Judith Butler, however, the uniformity-creating constraints did not just start with modern state, and people had been conditioned to discipline themselves unreflectively long before the emergence of what Foucault saw as modern disciplinary institutions. Rather, social existence itself exerts the conditioning and disciplinary effects upon any individual born into it. Various cultural discourses and tropes have conditioned individual subjects to think, speak, and act in certain ways. Take language for example, "the subject has its own 'existence' implicated in a language that precedes and exceeds the subject, a language whose historicity includes a past and future that exceeds that of the subject who speaks."[46] Any individual, from the beginning of her or his life, is configured by the language that carries conventionally-established concepts and collectively-recognized meanings, by the historical usages of that language, and by the socio-cultural circumstances in which that language has been used.[47]

The concepts, meanings, usages, and socio-cultural circumstances reflected in that language are formed as a result of, in Butler's word, sedimentation. In the same way that sediments of earth are formed because a large amount of sand is repeatedly brought over by water to the same place and allowed to accumulate and solidify, socio-cultural conventions are formed because people are acting and reacting in certain ways over and over again. A particular social convention, such as dressing baby girls in pink or allowing boys to be disruptive and aggressive, is in place because people repeat it, generation after generation, though not entirely without variations. Being able to function and to be recognized as a functioning subject in any society necessarily means carrying the weight of the tradition and internalizing to a large extent the cultural sediments of that society. By the same token, cultural contours and social institutions, as sediments of what people have spoken and done prior to the present moment, also precede, exceed, constitute, and condition the subject.

As a means of appreciating and further unpacking Butler's insight with regard to social sedimentation, I would like to provide some observations on the differences between the conventions of the English language and those of the Chinese language, in conjunction with the manifested differences in terms of assumptions and behaviors in the respective social groups. To denote a time or a place in the English language, one moves from the smaller units to the larger ones. The building that houses the Religion Department of Temple University, for example, is located in 1114 West Berks Street, Philadelphia, Pennsylvania, USA. In this sequence, one first identifies the smallest unit, i.e., the street number "1114," and then moves up to the next smallest unit, the "west" segment of the street, which is a part of a bigger unit, i.e., the whole "Berks Street." One then identifies the city of Philadelphia, in which the street is located, and then the state of Pennsylvania, in which the city is located, and then finally reaches the largest unit in this sequence, the country in which the state is located. In the Chinese language (in fact, in most East Asian languages), to denote the same location one would identify the country first, and then the state, and move down to the city, the street name, the segment of the street, and finally the street number. That is, one moves from the larger units to the smaller ones. The contrast also appears in personal names: in East Asian cultures the family name, which encompasses the larger unit, takes precedence over the individual given name, whereas in English-speaking societies the individual given name is the "first name."

The linguistic conventions in Chinese and other East Asian cultures embed an individual person (smaller unit) in a larger social unit and encourage a certain level of self-effacement vis-à-vis that larger social unit in question. By contrast, the conventions of the English language suggest the importance of individuals as the fundamental unit that requires attention. Individual subjects are so important in the English-speaking environment that they form an indispensable part of sentences, and situations are created for their names to be repeated by as many people as possible. A common way to honor someone in the English language, for example, is to name a thing or a person after her or him. To show respect for someone in the Chinese language, one avoids directly speaking her or his name. Most Chinese people do not name their children after their parents, contrary to the common practice of English-speaking people. Most streets and shops in the United States are named after individuals. In conventional Chinese usage (in fact, in the usage of most East Asian countries), by contrast, only a minority of streets and shops are named after individuals. With the exception of modern-day dictators, sycophantic politicians, and some self-absorbed individuals, Chinese people generally do not find it favorable for individual names to be repeated over and over, and the proper names that bear significance for the larger units (the whole town, the whole village, the whole clan, etc.) are preferred over the given names of individuals. The majority of streets and shops are so named that they either signal some common goals (such as "success," "peace," "universal love," etc.), or describe the features of the locality (such as its historical significance, its natural attraction, or its most well-known produce), or commemorate the shop owner's ancestry or the common origin of the people on the same street.

In the Chinese language the grammatical subjects, especially in the forms of pronouns, are often dropped; in the English language the grammatical subjects cannot be dropped, and the first person singular pronoun "I" even has to be capitalized. By contrast, many Chinese do not use the pronoun "you" at all when speaking to people of higher social status. In the late imperial period, one would even have to drop a stroke from a character if that character was also part of the name of an honorable person, such as one's own parents or the emperor. Namelessness, however, does not necessarily signify high social status. Namelessness indicates either that the individual is identified with the larger social unit due to her or his power position, or that the person is completely absorbable to the larger social unit. Before modern times, for example, Chinese girls were generally not given individual names but were simply referred to by their family names. My grandmother on my father's side was simply referred to as "[the one] of the family name Yao" in official documents as well as on my paternal family's ancestral tablet. Honorable persons were not directly named because they *were* their larger social units—the emperor represented the whole state, and the patriarch represented his whole family. Individuals at the very top and the very bottom were both absorbed into their larger social units and rendered nameless.

Positional and relational terms, rather than individual names, are often used to address relatives in the Chinese language. In some less urbanized and less Westernized areas in China, people still conventionally refer to individual children and their own siblings ("smaller units") by their positions in their respective families ("larger units"), such as "the third boy of the Yang family," "the second one in my family," and "my oldest sister." There are at least twelve different Chinese terms for the English word "cousin." A cousin on one's maternal side of the family is termed differently from a cousin on one's paternal side, and a cousin born to a brother of one's father is termed differently from a cousin born to a sister of one's father. One would also need to know if the cousin is male or female, younger or older than oneself. One needs to correctly identify a cousin's age, gender, and position in the extended family before one can correctly address the cousin. And by being told to address any cousin in a particular way, a child is also learning to position oneself in relation to that cousin. Knowing the relation and position is far more important than knowing the individual's given name.

With the linguistic conventions mentioned above, it is not difficult to understand why (individual) humility is often extolled as a virtue in Chinese cultures, while (individual) pride seems to be very important part of life in the modern-day English-speaking cultures, as reflected in the frequently used expressions, "I am proud of you" or "you must be proud." Also, instead of being told to "Be yourself" when entering an unfamiliar social circle as in an English-speaking environment, Chinese youngsters are much more likely to be advised to be unobstrusive and to keep the need of the larger social unit in mind. Sallie King remarks that the contrast between American hyperindividualism and Asian communitarian values can also be seen in the instructions and messages children receive at school: American kids have been told they are special since preschool, while kids in Asian schools are expected to pitch in together to clean the classroom from day one.[48]

Language constitutes the persons who use it in the sense that it suggests and promotes a certain way of thinking of the self and relating to each other as well as to the larger society. The East Asian linguistic principle of larger units enveloping and taking precedence over smaller units is also mirrored in people's communication patterns. Researchers of speech communication and business negotiation have long described East Asian communication pattern as "high-context," "collectivist," characterized by the interdependent view of the self, and oriented toward social relationships and nebulous general atmosphere. American communication pattern, by comparison, is "low-context," "individualistic," characterized by the independent view of the self, and focusing on specific personal goals.[49] Scholars of business communication Kam-hon Lee, Guang Yang, and John L. Graham observe, "Americans tend to reduce a complex negotiation problem into its several parts or issues, then discuss one at a time, settling each before moving on to the next. . . . Alternatively, the normative Chinese approach is to discuss all issues at once without apparent focus or order."[50] Literature abounds in the correlation between cultural values and communication patterns, but few researchers have specifically linked cultural values to linguistic principles.

In Buddhist terms, as the *rūpa* for the mind, socio-cultural conventions supply the raw materials from which the consciousnesses of the individuals who are embedded in those conventions are made. Different people may "put together" (*saṇkhāra*) the *rūpa* in different ways and thus may have different dispositions and may further choose to continue putting things together in those ways. That is, various forms of *rūpa* do not determine the individual consciousnesses, and socio-cultural conventions do not determine the ways in which people think and perceive their environment and relate to each other. Yet those forms of *rūpa* do limit the possibilities of the ways in which individual consciousnesses take shape. With the raw material of iron, one may make a chair or a weapon, but the possibility of making ceramics is precluded. Thus Butler contends, "The one who acts . . . acts precisely to the extent that he or she is constituted as an actor and, hence, operating within a linguistic field of enabling constraints from the outset."[51] Likewise, albeit on a different topic, feminist scholar Linda Martín Alcoff remarks, "the options available to us are socially constructed, and the practices we engage in cannot be understood as simply the results of autonomous individual choice."[52] Take language for example again, in order to be understood as a speaker of a certain language, not only does one have to follow the grammatical rules of that language, but one has to conform to the cultural assumptions and values carried in the customary usages of that language. One would not be considered as being able to use the English language if one constantly "forgets" to put the grammatical subjects in place, and one may appear to be awkward, strange, or even adversarial and rude, if one always uses the subjective nouns and pronouns when speaking Chinese. In the same way, one has to incorporate the conventions and norms in one's society and manifest them in one's actions in order to be recognized as a part of that society, to be considered culturally competent. "[T]o become subject to a regulation is also to become subjectivated by it, that is, to be brought into being as a subject precisely through being regulated."[53] To survive in a certain culture, one has to be socialized with, and constrained by, that which the culture takes for granted and renders normal, which also means that one is never really completely autonomous but has to operate within the parameters of cultural norms. One's speeches are citations of what has been conventionally said, and one's actions are performances of what has been conventionally scripted in the socio-cultural milieu.

Nevertheless, neither society nor culture stands unchanged. "[T]he norm only persists as a norm to the extent that it is acted out in social practice and reidealized and reinstituted in and through the daily social rituals of bodily life. The norm has no independent onto-logical status."[54] For example, the spreading of English as the most widely acquired second language in the world has contributed much to the change of cultural contours in East Asian societies. As a result, the issue of individual human rights is receiving greater attention. At the same time, the older generations of East Asians are commonly complaining that the younger generations are growing more self-absorbed and more individualistic. In urban and more Westernized areas in the Chinese societies, people rarely address their siblings by their positions in the family any more, and more and more brands and buildings bear individual names. Perhaps soon one will not be able to characterize East Asian cultures in the same way that I just did, for collectively East Asians are acting differently, which will make their cultural contours different. The ways people act are conditioned by the cultures with which they co-arise, and at the same time people's actions are conditioning their cultures and conditioning each other.

"In order to understand Buddhist ethics," David R. Loy asserts, "we must consider its foundation in the Buddhist understanding of the self—or, more precisely, the Buddhist deconstruction of the self."[55] In line with the logic of interdependent co-arising, Buddhism "does not presuppose a unitary soul or self-determining subject."[56] A person and a person's identity are constituted through the surrounding material and symbolic forces to which she or he is repeatedly exposed, including gender norms. Likened to food in many early Buddhist texts, the material and socio-cultural reality is not "something 'out there,' cleanly and neatly separable from our observing consciousness. Rather it is in us, of us," shaping and limiting our existence.[57] "Social forces . . . mold the ways we think, feel, and act."[58] The ways in which one thinks, speaks, and acts are, and always will be, conditioned by the material and symbolic forces, and thus one does not have an eternal, changeless "Self" that is above, or operating independently of, the matrix of *rūpa* in which one is embedded. Both personhood and identity are in continuous construction and reconstruction, as a result of their continuous interaction with the society and the culture.

With the language of recent feminist theories informed by poststructuralism and Foucault, it can be clearly seen that the classical Buddhist teachings do not categorically negate the existence of individual persons, nor do they deny the efficacy of actions. Rather, with interdependent co-arising as the rationale, classical Buddhist discourses simply point out the extent to which we are social animals: persons co-arise with, and are conditioned and circumscribed by, the material and socio-cultural forces in their surroundings, which in turn have been produced and maintained through people's repeated actions. Buddhist deconstruction of "Self" is that all selves are processes interacting with and interconditioning one another in a web of co-existence, each is reflecting and reflected by the actions of others, many of which have been sedimented as cultural norms and social structures. At the same time, just as individuals do not have any permanent, independent, unchanging Self-Essence, cultural norms and social structures are constructed and subject to change as well. The twin teachings of interdependent co-arising and non-Self thus do not negate the efficacy of actions. In fact, they accentuate the primacy of volitional actions, *kamma*. Just as individual selves can be consciously transformed through repeated volitional actions, so can cultural norms and social structures. Buddhist ethics rests on this perspective of interdependent co-arising and this interconditionality of life: *once seeing oneself in others and others in oneself, once seeing individuals shaping society and society shaping individuals, the sane and socially responsible response cannot but be volitionally disciplining oneself and dedicating oneself to the transformation of society for the well-being of*

ncluded. Since both individual transformation and social
ion depend on volitional actions, a Buddhist social ethic
in an exposition of *kamma,* which will be the subject of
r.

4

Person-in-*Kammic*-Network[1]

Moral Agency and Social Responsibility

Within the tradition of Buddhism, the term *kamma* has been used and misused in multiple ways. Many Buddhists and non-Buddhists alike have believed it to be a fatalistic doctrine that everything one experiences in life has already been determined by previous lives. A look at the *Nikāya* texts in the Pāli Canon, however, will reveal that the Buddha's teaching regarding *kamma* was by no means deterministic, especially in the light of the teaching of non-Self. Poststructuralist constructivist feminist analyses on gender construction and subject formation provide a more nuanced language with which the seeming paradox between non-Self and five aggregates in classical Buddhist teachings can be clearly expounded. Judith Butler's concept of sedimentation, in particular, is useful in explicating the classical Buddhist concept of *kamma*. What people actually do invariably deposits something in the cultural context, and if a large enough number of people, and for a long enough period of time, keep acting the same way, it will gradually be sedimented and become a norm, to which people living in that culture will in turn be conditioned to conform. That is, what every person chooses to do at every moment has an accumulative effect both on the person's own character and on the culture at large. On the other hand, the choices available to an individual person are already limited by the existing material and socio-cultural *rūpa* that have been constituted by what people have chosen to do prior to the present moment. Understanding the relation between socio-cultural conventions and people's actions, one can see one's role in constituting and reconstituting oneself, as well as in constituting and reconstituting the socio-cultural conventions. At the same time that one owes one's very existence to the cultural sediments in the society, one's actions can perpetuate the socio-cultural conditions or effect changes. The Buddha therefore repeatedly urged that his followers be careful with, and take responsibility for, their *kamma*. The teaching of interdependent co-arising thus conveys the interdependence of all beings on a profound level. What we are and what we do are conditioned by, and are conditioning, each other's being and doing.

In Buddhism, this concept of the interconditionality between all beings and their actions is best depicted by the image of the Indra's Net in the *Avatamsaka Sūtra*, even though it is a Mahāyāna text and not a text of early Buddhism. Indra, one of the supreme gods in the Vedic pantheon, has a net that stretches infinitely in all directions. At each node of the Net there is a jewel that reflects all other jewels in the Net, and if one looks closely, one can see that any of the jewels is reflected on all other jewels that are reflecting and reflected in one another. Loy succinctly expounds the significance of the imagery as such: "In this cosmos each phenomenon is at the same time the effect of the whole and the cause of the whole, the totality being a vast, infinite body of members, each sustaining and defining all the others."[2] As Indra's Net stretches infinitely in all directions, so is the scope of the repercussions of any action. And as the shape and color of one jewel at one node of Indra's Net are reflected by all other jewels on the Net, and then will be reflected back and seen in its reflections of other jewels, so are a person's thinking, feeling, and behavioral patterns reflected in others' patterns and further reflected back on oneself. In the past, the interconditionality as implied by the metaphor of the Indra's Net might be difficult to grasp, but it is no longer a difficult concept in an age when people at the opposite sides of the world can communicate with one another within seconds through the use of the World Wide Web. An Internet user's day could be ruined if she or he is a recipient of hundreds of junk e-mails or even viruses. And yet this recipient is simultaneously a giver over the Internet; one can easily spread negativity as well as positivity in the same way one has received it. The difference between the Internet and the net of interpersonal relationships is that one can sign off from the Internet and still has a life, but it is impossible to drop off from the social network of relationships.

With the rapid globalization through military, economic, and technological means, now more than ever we can see the extent of the interdependence of all people and the extent to which people's actions impact each other. Latin American liberation theologians, as well as some economists and social theorists, have long attested to the layers of insidious aftermaths of colonialism and imperialism that are still vividly felt today. The capitalistic expansion and the pursuit of material goods in the wealthy countries further take their toll on the lives of people in the so-called "third world" countries. When the "underdeveloped" countries are "developed" and become a part of the capitalistic global economic system that has been established and dominated by the élite of the "first world," the gap between the rich and the poor, and between men and women, widens rapidly; and the Earth is further polluted and becoming increasingly uninhabitable, especially in the poverty-stricken areas. Thus viewed, the seemingly "individual" decisions and actions, such as buying bottled water, driving gasoline-guzzling automobiles, reproducing and overindulging one's offspring, or raising one's children to conform to the rigid binary gender roles, are not so "individual" after all. Individual persons are participating in the global co-arising of *dukkha*, whether or not they are aware of their complicity.

Kamma as Taught by the Buddha: Volitional Actions Here and Now

The Sanskrit term *karma* had been a multivalent word long before the time of the Buddha. In the Vedic texts it was said that, by performing sacrificial rituals, one would be brought to the heaven in the afterlife. If a sacrificial ritual performed when one was alive really had the power to bring the ritual performer to heaven when his body was dead, the ritual had to produce some kind of effect, which had to last from the time of ritual performance to the time of the ritual performer's physical death. The term *karma* was initially used in pre-Buddhist Brāhmanical texts to refer to such long lasting effect produced by ritual actions.[3] In fact, the main focus of discussion in pre-Buddhist Brāhmanical texts was the negative leftovers (*karmaphalasesa*) of incorrect rituals or imprecise performances of sacrifices. In the *Śatapatha* and *Jaiminiya Brāhmaṇas*, for instance, those who were confined to hell were said to be those who killed and ate animals and even herbs without performing the correct rituals.[4] In the pre-Buddhist *Upaniṣads*, such as the *Bṛhadāraṇyaka Upaniṣad* and the *Chāndogya Upaniṣad*, the term *karma* was broadened to refer to all actions, and yet the focus was still the effects of actions (*karmaphalasesa*). In the *Bṛhadāraṇyaka Upaniṣad*, for example, it was stated that "[a] man turns into something good by good action and into something bad by bad action."[5] In the *Chāndogya*

Upaniṣad, the effects of actions were more explicitly linked to the destination of one's rebirth: "People whose behavior is pleasant can expect to enter a pleasant womb, like that of the Brahmin, the Kṣatriya or Vaiśya class. But people of foul behavior can expect to enter a foul womb, like that of a dog, a pig, or an outcaste woman."[6] In Jainism, which probably arose as an anti-brahmanic ascetic movement not long before Buddhism, *karma* was conceived as fine material particles that would be accumulated with every bodily, verbal, and mental action, regardless of intentions.[7] It was through exhausting the karmic particles already accumulated by means of severe austerities that one might liberate one's originally pure soul (*jīva*). In other words, *karma* was considered by Jainas as the material results of actions instead of actions themselves. In short, in all of these pre-Buddhist usages, *karma* was discussed in the passive sense as the effects of actions, and the actions in question were those already taken instead of those about to be taken.

In analyzing the discourses on *kamma* in Buddhism, James R. Egge contends that, although the Buddha adopted the category of sacrifice from Brahmanism, he however completely dispensed with the word's original reference of sacrifices. Instead, the Buddha used the word *kamma* to refer to ethically accountable acts,[8] and thereby shifted people's attention from sacrificial rituals to the actions that have impact on others and, broadly, on the mode of co-existence of all beings. More importantly, he consistently discussed *kamma* in the active sense as the actions to be taken here and now.

With regard to the actions that supposedly had been done in past lives, the Buddha's attitude was consistent with his attitude toward metaphysical speculations, as discussed in Chapter 2. In a conversation with the Niganṭhas (i.e., Jainas), who believed that they had to perform austerities in order to exhaust the bad *kammic* particles they had accrued to their souls in past lives, the Buddha asked:

> But, friends, do you know that you existed in the past . . . that you did evil actions in the past . . . that you did such and such evil actions . . . that so much suffering has already been exhausted, or that so much suffering has still to be exhausted, or that when so much suffering has been exhausted all suffering will have been exhausted?[9]

After the Niganṭhas answered "No" to all of the above questions, the Buddha then asked, "Do you know what the abandoning of unwholesome states is and what the cultivation of wholesome states is here and now?"[10] Noteworthily, the Buddha did not say past lives were completely unknowable to all people; the *Nikāya* texts indicate that one of the kinds of "direct knowledge" (Pāli: *abhiññā*; Sanskrit: *abhijñā*) accompanying the experience of *nibbāna* is recollection of past lives.[11] Nevertheless, instead of discussing and speculating about the actions already taken in past lives, which remained unknowable to most people and could not be undone anyway, the Buddha taught it was far more important and far more urgent to abandon unwholesome states and cultivate wholesome states at the present moment. In this spirit he urged his mostly privileged followers to contemplate their responsibilities for the actions they were about to take.[12] With the notion of *kamma* discussed in the active sense, the focal point is the intentional undertaking of ethical behaviors right here and right now, rather than the passive dealing with the consequences of past actions that may or may not be verifiable.

Moreover, in the *Samyutta Nikāya* the Buddha was recorded to have specifically refuted *pubbekatahetuvāda*, the deterministic theory that "whatever a person experiences . . . is caused by what was done in the past."[13] He rejected attributing every occurrence to past *kamma* because, in addition to physiological disorders and imbalances, some experiences could be caused by "change of climate . . . careless behaviour . . . assault."[14] Attributing every experience to *kamma* accumulated in the past not only has the effect of blaming the victims of illness and natural disaster, but also allows people not to take responsibility for their carelessness or even aggressiveness at the present moment. It may even lead to the following difficulty for the Niganthas/Jainas who voluntarily take on extreme ascetic practices and inflict pain on themselves: "If the pleasure and pain that beings feel are caused by what was done in the past, then the Niganthas surely must have done bad deeds in the past, since they now feel such painful, racking, piercing feelings."[15] Following the same reasoning, attributing gender discrimination to women's negative *kamma* in the past not only blames women for the mistreatments they receive, but also allows men to treat the other half of the population in an inhumane way.

This is not to say that in the Buddha's teachings past actions do not affect the present experience. As a matter of fact, so many passages in the *Nikāya*-s attribute a person's present experience to past actions that a reader may be convinced that the Buddha taught determinism. On occasion, in the *Nikāya* texts the consequences of actions taken in the past, including one's bodily existence and bodily features in the current life, were referred to as the "old *kamma*," while the actions about to be taken were referred to as the "new *kamma*."[16]

As "old *kamma*," the consequences of past actions do affect the current situations in which one finds oneself. In the *Cūlakammavibhanga Sutta* (The Shorter Exposition of Action), for example, the Buddha is said to have taught that "beings are owners of their actions, heirs of their actions," and for this reason people are reborn to be "short-lived and long-lived, sickly and healthy, ugly and beautiful, uninfluential and influential, poor and wealthy, low-born and high-born, stupid and wise."[17] One might find oneself being born with a body-mind that is particularly gifted or impeded in a certain regard. In the *Lakkhaṇa Sutta*, the characteristics of the Buddha's body-mind, such as his ability to tolerate physical exertion and his ability to learn quickly, were said to be the results of his past actions.[18] K. N. Jayatilleke suggests that, as a person gets genetic influences from one's parents, one gets one's parents from one's past *kamma*.[19]

That influence from actions in past lives, however, is by no means an excuse for anyone to mistreat anyone else in the name of kammic retribution, for one cannot be certain of what exactly others and one's self have done in past lives. In the *Mahākammavibhanga Sutta* (The Greater Exposition of Action), the Buddha taught that people reborn to happy destinations may still have done harm; it is just that the good deeds they had done come to fruition first, but the misdeeds will eventually ripen as well. Likewise, people reborn to states of deprivation may also have done good deeds but are simply experiencing the fruit of their misdeeds first.[20] That is to say, people who find their current selves in privileges are not inherently "better" than those who are born in unfavorable conditions. People who have suffered much do not necessarily deserve more suffering than people who are born into wealth and high social status, or people who are born with socially favored sex, skin color, facial features, or bone structure. They certainly do not deserve to suffer more if the suffering they are experiencing is a direct result of privileged people's exploitation and abuse. It is a misunderstanding that "the doctrine of karma must affirm that people's circumstances are ultimately the results of their own past actions, even if the vehicles of bringing those circumstances about might be the unmeritorious actions of others."[21]

Actions in past lives may also influence one's current self in terms of one's behavioral pattern. One might be prone to a certain pattern of behavior due to the habits that one might have formed through repeated actions in past lives. That, however, is no excuse for the current self to continue misconduct now. After all, there is no way of saving people from evil deeds if they continue to find excuses to justify their own deeds. The Buddha taught that the way to overcome "evil" is simply to stop evil conduct:

A person given to cruelty has non-cruelty by which to
  avoid it.
One given to killing living beings has abstention from kill-
  ing living beings by which to avoid it.
. . .
One given to avarice has non-avarice by which to avoid it.
One given to fraud has non-fraud by which to avoid it.[22]

In other words, he taught that the way to overcome the influence of
repeated actions in the past is simply to stop repeating those actions
and to discontinue those behavioral patterns.

Unlike Jainism, however, the Buddha did not teach people to
cease all actions for the goal of liberating the soul encased in *kammic* dusts. Seeing *kamma* as material particles and focusing on the
passive sense of *kamma* as the consequences of actions, the Jainas at
the time of the Buddha upheld the ideal of refraining from all kinds
of actions for the fear of the accumulation of new *kammic* particles
on the soul (albeit it probably remained an ideal instead of a reality
for most Jainas since living necessarily involves taking actions). The
Buddha, by contrast, differentiated between wholesome conduct and
unwholesome conduct on the issue of inactivity:

> I do teach people to be inactive in regard to evil conduct
> in deeds, words, and thoughts; I teach inaction in regard
> to the multitude of evil, unwholesome qualities. But I
> also teach people to be active by way of good conduct in
> deeds, words, and thoughts; I teach action in regard to the
> multitude of wholesome qualities.[23]

Recasting *kamma* into the active sense, the Buddha taught people to
be reflective and watchful of the actions they were about to take, to
see danger in the slightest faults, and to dedicate themselves to ethical
behaviors.[24] In accordance with the Buddha's practical and this-worldly
concerns, what is important is not what one might or might not have
done in the past, but what one needs to do at every present moment.
In contrast to the previous tendencies of considering *kamma* to be the
consequences of actions in the past, the historical Buddha taught *kamma*
in the active sense as actions in the present, thereby emphasizing the
possibility of making positive changes even though one may be under
the influences of negative past actions in multiple forms.

Understood in the active sense, *kamma* is not at all incompatible
with the teaching of non-Self. On the contrary, *kamma* fully supports
the Buddha's refutation of the permanent, unchanging Self, for *kamma*

as intentional action denotes the possibility of volitionally changing one's current "self" despite what one might have been in the past. The Buddha's usage of *kamma* points to the fact that the making of one's being is an ongoing process, even though one is inevitably influenced by what has been done by both oneself and others up to the present moment. Thus regarded, one's "self" is neither entirely determined by preceding events and actions, nor a product of one's own unadulterated "free will."

The active sense of *kamma* has much to do with the exercise of one's volition (*cetanā*, part of the aggregate *saṇkhāra*; see Chapter 3), so much so that it is generally understood by scholars of Buddhism that Buddhist *kamma* refers to volitional actions only.[25] *Anguttara Nikāya* III.415 and VI.63 read, "It is volition (*cetanā*), O monks, that I call *kamma*; having willed, one performs an action through body, speech or mind." Even the aforementioned "old *kamma*" was said to have been "generated and fashioned by volition."[26] U Rewata Dhamma and Bhikkhu Bodhi explain that volition organizes its associated mental factors in acting upon the object, and as such it determines the ethical quality of the action. It is therefore the most significant mental factor in generating *kamma*.[27] Truly, *kamma* can be active only when volition is put into the equation—one cannot be said to have taken any real action without some qualified kind of "free will;" otherwise one's actions would be, borrowing Butler's words, merely citations of existing socio-cultural sediments. Without the exercise of volition, one is not really *taking* any action but is simply propelled by the socio-cultural conventions and/or personal habits.

More importantly, without the exercise of volition that makes it possible for people to do things differently at the present moment, what had been done in the past would have a determinant hold on what would be done now and in the future, both on the individual level and on the socio-political level. Without volition that would allow different ways of doing things, there would be no way out of the existing social norms and self-identities that induce *dukkha*, the unsatisfactoriness and sufferings created and perpetuated through habitual misapprehension and misbehaviors. Without the exercise of volition, that is, all would be predetermined and there would be no possibility of change and no point in trying to make a difference. Contrary to the popular (mis-)understanding that links the concept of *kamma* with determinism or fatalism, then, it is the account of *kamma* in the active sense as volitional actions that makes the Buddhist *Dhamma* non-deterministic. What the Buddhist *kamma* teaches, Rita Gross suggests, is: "in each present moment, no matter how strong habitual patterns and familiar ways of reacting may be, Buddhist teachings about karma claim that I have some tiny opening of freedom. . . . Likewise, each person who is implicated in my present matrix has similar freedom."[28] For the above reason, Kalupahana considers the Buddhist *Dhamma* the "middle way" between determinism and indeterminism.[29] The terms "determinism" and "indeterminism" were renderings of the Sanskrit words *kriyāvāda* and *akriyāvāda*, with the former referring to the belief that deeds bear consequences and the latter to the belief that deeds are fruitless. In the early texts, Buddhists referred to the teachings of the Buddha as *kriyāvāda* or *karmavāda* since the Buddha did teach that deeds/actions brought results. The Jainas, however, classified Buddhism under *akriyāvāda*, for the Buddha did not teach one-to-one correspondence between action (*karma*) and fruit of action (*karmaphala*). Gómez therefore describes Buddhism as "weak" or modified *kriyāvāda*.[30]

While Gómez's description is appropriate, it is misleading to render "modified *kriyāvāda*" as "qualified determinism" or "soft determinism" as Gier and Kjellberg do, for in the Buddha's teachings past deeds do not *determine* current experiences but only *condition* them. Besides, the use of the word "determinism" defeats the purpose of Gier and Kjellberg's own discussion of Kalupahana's distinction between conditionality and causality:

> The language of causality tends to simplify the explanation of an effect, while the language of conditionality makes it much more complex. The doctrine of interdependent coorigination compels the Buddhist to take a much more comprehensive view of causality. . . . [W]e are morally responsible for our own character and intentions, which although completely conditioned by antecedent events, are nonetheless what we truly want and should do.[31]

In the Buddha's teachings, past deeds do condition the present, but they do not determine the present. For example, the type of body and abilities that one was born with might have been a result of past actions according to traditional Buddhist understanding, but the ways in which one uses her body and abilities and the ways in which others treat her body and abilities are not predetermined. Besides the material and symbolic forces to which one is exposed and within which one has to operate, the exercise of volition is another crucial factor that has been shaping one's consciousnesses and directing one's conduct. Similar to my analysis here and well in accordance with the teaching of five aggregates, Peter Harvey breaks down the conditioning factors of actions into biological influences, social influence, personal history, general history, and psychological influences.[32] People who are subject to the same conditioning do not necessarily think and act in the same way due to the working of their *saṅkhāra*. The aggregate of *saṅkhāra*, which includes mental construction, disposition, and volition, on the one hand accounts for the process of individuation and the reality of individual differences, and on the other hand holds individual persons accountable for what they intend to do. The Buddha's teaching about *kamma* thus affirms the possibility for individuals to exercise their volition and make a conscious choice with regard to the ways in which they act and react under the given socio-cultural conditioning.

Also contrary to the popular (mis-)understanding that associates the teaching of non-Self with the negation of moral agency, non-Self actually affirms the efficacy of volitional moral actions. It indicates that the individual self is not predestined to be in its current mode of being for eternity and can be changed with the exercise of volition. Quite consonant with this implication of the Buddhist teaching of non-Self, Butler reasons,

> Paradoxically, the reconceptualization of identity as an *effect*, that is, as *produced* or *generated*, opens up possibilities of "agency" that are insidiously foreclosed by positions that take identity categories as foundational and fixed. For an identity to be an effect means that it is neither fatally determined nor fully artificial and arbitrary. . . . Construction is not opposed to agency; it is the necessary scene of agency.[33]

Butler understands one's identity to be an effect produced through the repetition of certain kinds of performances that have been culturally prescribed, which she calls performatives, such as the kind of behavior that is supposedly appropriate for women and girls. The culturally prescribed behaviors, being performed by the body, are inscribed on the body and becoming part of one's self-identity. In terms of gender identity, when a girl has been consistently expected to perform a certain kind of "feminine" behavior and has been performing it repeatedly, then that kind of behavior becomes part of her bodily existence and defines her understanding of what it means to be a girl and what it means to be her "self." If one's identity, such as gender identity, is an effect produced through the repetition of certain kinds of performances that have been socially sanctioned, then it can be changed through the repetition of an alternative kind of performances, even though those alternative performances still are delimited and limited by the sedimentation in society.

Counterintuitively, it is the assertion of "Self," the abiding ontological core that exists prior to, and remains outside of, material and socio-cultural forces, that precludes the possibility of change and renders agency in the phenomenal world meaningless. If there is such a thing as an everlasting and unchanging ontological essence that exists regardless of the actions one takes, then whatever one strives to do or to be cannot affect that preexisting essence. If there is an unchangeable essence of women that every female fetus has (and the essence of females is frequently characterized in unflattering ways), then a woman cannot help but embody that essence, no matter what she actually does and no matter if and to what extent she strives to be a different person. Only when identity is understood to be a social and mental construct can a person's volitional actions be understood to have the power to make a difference. This is why Butler asserts that construction is the necessary scene of agency, and this is why the Buddha emphasized *kamma* in the active sense and taught there is no permanent, independently existing, unchanging Self. In both strains of thought, there is no unchanging doer behind the deeds. The doer, in fact, is constructed through the deeds.[34]

As spatially and temporally apart as they may be, the classical Buddhist teaching of non-Self and the poststructuralist theory on subject formation both point out the constructedness of individual persons and the role that repeated actions play in the construction. What a person is depends very much on the *rūpa* in which she or he is embedded. A person as such is neither above nor separate from her or his socio-cultural contexts. This embeddedness, however, does not absolve individuals of responsibilities. For one thing, as argued above, individual persons are only *conditioned* and *constrained*, but *not determined*,[35] by the surrounding material forces and socio-cultural conventions. For another, just as an individual person is socially constructed and not self-existent, a convention is also socially constructed and not self-existent. Socio-cultural conventions do not just come into existence out of nowhere; they are sediments of people's past actions, and they must be continuously repeated in order to work.[36] Likewise, in a Buddhist understanding, social conventions are the precipitates of the repeated actions of the socially-conditioned persons, in the same way that persons are precipitates of social conventions on the one hand, and their volitional actions on the other.[37] David Loy puts it succinctly, "People create the social system, but the system creates people."[38] Nhât Hanh expresses the same idea in his characteristically

simple words: "We are all children of society, but we are also mothers."[39] Both classical Buddhism and poststructuralist constructivist
feminism recognize that an individual constructs his or her identity
through repeated actions, but at the same time both also acknowledge social factors in the process of construction and indicate that the
construction of an individual is never *merely* her or his own doing.
In Butler's theory, the social factors are indicated with the concept
of "sedimentation," while in classical Buddhism the same concept
is encompassed in the analysis of the five aggregates and the social
dimension of *kamma*.

In Buddhism as well as in other ancient Indian traditions, there
are three kinds of actions: bodily, verbal, and mental. In other words,
volitional actions can take the forms of physical activities, speeches,
and thoughts. Among the three kinds of actions and along the line of
poststructuralist feminist analysis, speech provides a rich illustration
of the space between social sedimentation and self-construction. As
Butler maintains, although "[t]he speaking subject makes his or her
decision only in the context of an already circumscribed field of linguistic possibilities, this repetition does not constitute the decision of
the speaking subject as a redundancy. The gap between redundancy
and repetition is the space of agency."[40] Individual persons, albeit
socially constrained and operating within limited possibilities, have
agency and are responsible because they are making decisions and
contributing to the sedimentation process via their actions. Individual
persons can cite the conventions in the same way, or they can exercise
their volition in such ways that their citation breaks away from ordinary usage and leads to the reconfiguration of the conventions. For
example, not very long ago it was the norm in the English language
to use masculine nouns and pronouns to represent all of humanity,
and the practice both reflected male dominance in society and naturalized androcentrism. With the word "man" standing for "human,"
the respect that was supposed to be paid to all humans would be
only paid to man. On the other hand, when more and more people
exercise their volition in such a way that they use gender-neutral or
gender-inclusive language, gradually the use of the masculine-generic
may incur suspicion and criticism because it excludes more than a
half of the human population in the world. In Butler's words, "To
the extent that gender norms are *reproduced*, they are invoked and
cited by bodily practices that also have the capacity to alter norms
in the course of their citation."[41] Individual persons can reinforce and
perpetuate what has become normalized and naturalized, or they can
unsettle or even subvert it. The effects of one single action may not

be discernible, but the existing *rūpa* will change when enough people take the same or similar actions for a long enough time. It is along this line that the Dalai Lama states, "our every action, our every deed, word, and thought, no matter how slight or inconsequential it may seem, has an implication not only for ourselves but for all others, too."[42] People's volitional actions will condition all those who are embedded in the socio-cultural conventions, which have been formed through repeated actions.

It is worth bearing in mind that volition is one aspect of the aggregate *saṅkhāra*. Like the rest of the five aggregates, *saṅkhāra* is culturally conditioned and circumscribed, and like the rest of the five aggregates, *saṅkhāra* is not substantive and does not have an eternal "Self" that is above, and unaffected by, the material and socio-cultural *rūpa*. The word *saṅkhāra* denotes the *constructed* as well as the *constructive*, but it does not denote an abiding, self-existing, unchanging *constructor*. Volition, as a part of *saṅkhāra*, is constructed, though it also constructs; it can be exercised and is a crucial factor in the Buddhist ethical discipline, but it is still embedded in the matrix of material and socio-cultural forces and confined by them. Thus, though Buddhist teachings do value the function of volition and demand the exercise of it, Walpola Rāhula points out that "free will" in Buddhism is conditioned and only relatively "free." In Buddhist thinking, "There can be nothing absolutely free, physical or mental, as everything is interdependent and relative."[43] As King puts it, "From a Buddhist point of view, free will and determinism are the poles of a false dichotomy."[44] Volition is not predetermined. It is relatively free, but it is still interdependently co-arisen and is still constrained and confined by that with which it co-arises.

If volition is conditioned by the socio-cultural *rūpa* that is sedimented through people's repeated actions and thus has not been made by oneself alone, it follows that *kamma*, being *volitional* actions, cannot possibly be a "single-channel, closed circuit course" as some Buddhists and scholars of Buddhism make it out to be.[45] In a conversation with a disciple named Kassapa in the *Samyutta Nikāya*, the Buddha taught,

> Kassapa, [if one thinks,] "The one who acts is the same as the one who experiences [the result,]" [then one asserts] with reference to one existing from the beginning: "Suffering is created by oneself." When one asserts thus, this amounts to eternalism. But, Kassapa, [if one thinks,] "The one who acts is one, the one who experiences [the result] is another," [then one asserts] with reference to one stricken by feeling:

"Suffering is created by another." When one asserts thus, this amounts to annihilationism. Without veering towards either of these extremes, the Tathāgata teaches the Dhamma by the middle.[46]

To assert that a person is *fully* responsible for her or his own actions is to neglect the fact that *rūpa* (with which a person's consciousnesses and self-identities co-arise) includes the socio-cultural conventions that have not been constructed and maintained by oneself alone. To assert that a person is responsible *only* for her or his own actions (and not for other people's actions) is to neglect the fact that one's actions create new *rūpa*, with which other people's consciousnesses and self-identities co-arise. Either assertion presumes complete autonomy, as if volition has a "Self" that can exist independently above the matrix of material and socio-cultural forces. That is tantamount to asserting a form of eternalism that contradicts the core Buddhist teachings of non-Self and interdependent co-arising. In Rita Gross's words, "to claim that how well or poorly I manifest myself as a human being as completely independent of the matrix or container within which I find myself, is to come dangerously close to positing the independent self that Buddhism so carefully dismantles."[47] Saying that one is neither fully nor solely responsible for one's actions, however, is not the same as saying that one is innocently bearing the consequences of others' actions or that one does not need to take responsibility for one's own actions. To make either of these latter two statements, in the eyes of the Buddha, is to annihilate ethically accountable individual selves, thereby asserting a form of annihilationism. Neither eternalism nor annihilationism was countenanced by the Buddha.

Kalupahana is right in considering that the Buddhist *Dhamma*, generally referred to as the "Middle Way," is, *inter alia*, the middle way between determinism and "free will." It is also the middle way between placing moral responsibility entirely on society and placing it entirely on each individual. To place moral responsibility entirely on society is to see the individual as a helpless victim under social institutions and to absolve the individual of all possible wrongdoings. To place moral responsibility entirely on each individual is to see the individual as either a self-made hero or a loser who has no one but herself or himself to blame. Considering that individual subjects are constructed through the socio-cultural conventions, society as a whole is at least partially responsible for the misdeeds and crimes that are seemingly committed by its individual subjects. For this reason, Judith Butler considers the culpable subject to be retrospectively "resurrected" in order to meet the legal demand of accountability.[48] In a similar vein, David Loy comments that "there is the uncomfortable possibility that offenders today have become our scapegoats for larger social problems."[49] The XVI Dalai Lama and Thích Nhât Hanh have the same understanding: the Dalai Lama states, "A child brought up in a violent environment may not know any other way to behave. As a result, the question of blame is rendered largely redundant,"[50] and Nhât Hanh says, "In my meditation I saw that if I had been born in the village of the pirate and raised in the same conditions as he was, I am now the pirate. There is a great likelihood that I would become a pirate."[51] This recognition of social conditioning and shared responsibility is correlated with the fact that most contemporary Engaged Buddhists thinkers seem to think along the line of rehabilitative or restorative justice rather than retributive justice.[52]

Some Buddhists and scholars of Buddhism attribute the "invention" of the social dimension of *kamma* to the great Mahāyāna theorist and synthesizer Nāgārjuna.[53] Some others believe the concept of social *kamma* is influenced by modern Western Protestant values and brought about by Western Buddhists or Western-educated Asian Buddhists.[54] Based on the discussion above, it is inaccurate to attribute the "invention" of the concept of social *kamma* to either Mahāyānists, Western Buddhists, or modern Buddhists, for the Buddha specifically refuted the understanding of *kamma* as a mechanism of retribution in which each person stands alone and is responsible fully, and solely, for her or his own actions.[55] It should be clear by now, and will be made explicit in the following pages, that by "social *kamma*" I do not mean "collective *kamma*" that is basically the same mechanism of retribution applied to a group of people rather than a person. It is true that the Buddha taught his disciples to watch and take responsibility for their volitional actions, and it is true that he was recorded to have said,

> The killer begets a killer
> One who conquers, a conqueror
> The abuser begets abuse
> The reviler, one who reviles
> Thus by the unfolding of kamma
> The plunderer is plundered.[56]

However, considering the interconditionality of people embedded in the same socio-cultural context, the phrase "The abuser begets abuse" does not necessarily mean that the abuser herself or himself will be the very next recipient of abuse. Rather, with the aid of Butler's concepts of performativity and sedimentation, it can be understood to mean that, with every abusive behavior, a person deposits something into the social context and makes it a little more acceptable, in some people's minds, to be abusive. And it gets more and more acceptable with every action of abuse, with every person who initiates or imitates abusive behaviors. The same holds true for all forms of discrimination, domination, aggression, and violence. It is therefore "by the *unfolding* of kamma" (emphasis added) that "the plunderer is plundered." Likewise, the following passage does not necessarily suggest an individualistic mechanism of retribution and can be equally meaningful, if not much more so, with the concept of social *kamma*: "I declare, Monks, that actions willed, performed, and accumulated will not become extinct as long as their results have not been experienced, be it in this life, in the next life, or in subsequent future lives."[57] The results of actions will be experienced without fail, the passage proclaims. It does not indicate that the results will be experienced in the exact same forms by the initial agents of those actions. Understood socially, actions will produce results that will be experienced by people in the same socio-cultural environment and will eventually affect the initial agents of those actions.

The social understanding of *kamma* also provides a "middle way" answer to the question whether or not *kamma* can be counteracted. The Pāli commentarial tradition suggested that *kamma* could be counteracted, while contemporary scholar Jayarava Michael Attwood maintains that, based on the quote above, the results of *kamma* cannot be "counteracted" in the sense of being canceled out, but only mitigated.[58] Attwood clearly understand *kamma* in individualistic terms. Understood in social terms, however, *kamma* can be "counteracted," both in the sense of being canceled out and in the sense of being mitigated—an action will be sedimented and thus experienced, but it will be sedimented together with numerous other actions, some of which may produce the opposite effects and ramifications. Depending on the number and fortitude of those actions that have counteracting effects, in the long run an action may still be significant in terms of its social impact, or relatively insignificant, or not significant at all. In a society where most people have been socialized to hold the door open for the next person, one person not doing the same will not result in much difference. The effect of this not-holding-the-door-open *kamma* by this one person is fairly insignificant and can be canceled out by other people's opposite *kamma* of holding the door open. By contrast, in a society that associates masculinity with dominance through physical power, every wife battering is further solidifying the behavioral pattern for future generations of men. With the socio-cultural sedimentation of dominant masculinity already in place, the effect of one wife-battering *kamma* by one man cannot be mitigated very easily, even though the majority of men do not hit their wives.

Thai Buddhist scholar Roongraung Boonyoros, holding a rather individualistic view of *kamma*, comments that it is by the sugges-tive power of sympathy that others' feelings and thoughts "may be regarded" as those of oneself.[59] Based on the discussion above, however, others' feelings and thoughts can still very much influence oneself even if one has no sympathy. Feelings and thoughts can manifest themselves in actions, and others' feelings and thoughts, through their manifestations in actions, will find their ways to be the constituents of the feelings and thoughts of the "self" through socio-cultural sedimentation. In return, the feelings and thoughts of the "self," through their manifestations in actions, are becoming the constituents of those of others, which as socio-cultural *rūpa* will again come back at oneself. Individual persons' interconnections with one another are by no means external, dispensable, or propped up *only* by the sugges-tive power of sympathy. Rather, they are *internally* and dynamically related to one another.[60] It is important to note that the internal yet dynamic interconnection is radically different from the "ontological unity" or "expansion of self through a process of identification with the world" asserted by some modern Buddhists. Co-arising does not at all convey the fuzzy sentiment, "We are all one." David McMahan and Mark Blum rightly criticize it as contradicting original Buddhist doctrine, which does not picture any static ontological unity by way of an expansion of self.[61] However, neither does the Pāli Canon support an understanding of completely separated individuals, each existing in her or his own closed-circuit mechanism of retribution. The worldview offered by the Pāli Canon is dynamic coexistence, in which people's *kamma* shape the socio-cultural *rūpa*, which in turn affects people's consciousnesses and dispositions, which then manifest in further *kamma*. It is true that many traditional Buddhists have misunderstood and misused the concept of *kamma* to justify the *status quo* and blame individual victims, particularly women, for their own sufferings. The misunderstanding and misuse, however, should not be equated with "authentic" Buddhism or early Buddhism.

Following the logic of interdependent co-arising, each "internal" volitional construction, though individuated and not predetermined, is socially conditioned and constrained. At the same time, each *kamma* (i.e., each volitional action that a person takes) has a social and political dimension. To say that we interdependently co-arise is also to acknowledge that our actions condition each other's actions, and that we make and remake ourselves as well as our world together. It is the sedimentation of people's actions that makes the culture and society the way they are, and it is due to people's repeated conformity and participation that socio-cultural conventions are naturalized and normalized. Peter D. Hershock asserts,

> In combination, the teaching of karma and no-self direct us to see ourselves—and so what is happening in our worlds—as an ever-dynamic expression of dramatic interdependence. In such worlds, causation is not a linear process, but a coalescent one. It is not that our intentions literally influence the world, but rather that they are an occasion for revised confluence or "flowing together" with it. As we revise our intentional activity, we effectively elicit new lived worlds, new patterns of dramatic affinity, aligning ourselves with different constellations of meaning, different patterns of narration. But because persons are understood in a Buddhist context as functions of patterned relationship, neither "you" nor "I" can remain the same in doing so. We are not fundamentally individuals remaining self-identical over time, but *characters* in continuous development.
>   . . . That is, karma is not a projection or transmission of effects of information from life to life. . . .
>   . . . Our past lives are *ours*, not because we are abiding entities or souls that possess or link them, but because the narrative movements—the patterns of conduct—evident within them are most meaningfully aligned with who we have been and are becoming. The continuity among lives is not a result of material or spiritual permanence, but a matter of dramatic affinities among patterns of narrative movement.[62]

The Buddhist discourse on *kamma* is a discourse on the fundamental sociality of human existence and the interconditionality of individual beings. Being fundamentally social and interdependently co-arisen, in Joanna Macy's words, "we are, quite literally, part of each other—free neither from indebtedness to our fellow-beings nor responsibility for them."[63] One comes into being in the matrix of material and socio-cultural forces and has been conditioned by them, and those material and socio-cultural forces are in place as a result of people's actions up to this moment.

Together, the Buddhist teachings of non-Self and *kamma* as volitional actions can be as empowering to individuals as they are morally
demanding. Recognizing that no one and nothing is predetermined to
exist in a certain way and stay unchanged for eternity, one knows that
one does not have to accept the kind of existence defined by culture
(or by oneself, for that matter). Then one can take one's volitional
actions seriously and intentionally remake oneself (and remake the
culture, if a large enough number of people are repeatedly acting in
the same way for a long enough period of time) by taking courses of
actions that are as wholesome as possible, even though those actions
are not necessarily in accordance with socio-cultural conventions or
with one's own habitual patterns of acting and reacting. Community
psychologist Kathleen H. Dockett finds that understanding *kamma*
as an ongoing process is enough to empower people to locate the
"locus of control" internally and to motivate them to actively make
changes.[64] No matter what may or may not have been done in the
past, one can start a series of trainings that can, through repetition,
change the outlook of one's personality, the course of one's life, and
even the socio-cultural norms.

In terms of gender roles and gender stereotypes, the teaching
of non-Self can enable a woman to understand, for example, that it
is not her essence or her inherent nature or her permanent "Self" to
be subordinated and treated as mere appendages to men. Neither is
it the essence or nature of the culture, or the permanent "Self" of the
whole human society for that matter, to sanction or demand such sub-
ordination and mistreatment. It may seem "natural" for women to act
weak and subservient, and for men to exercise dominance even if that
means resorting to violence, but it is largely because, from generation
to generation, women and men have been socialized to replicate those
behavioral patterns and, in turn, expect and even demand others to
act in the same ways. What has been done collectively and continuously, then, appears to be the permanent "Self" of things.

The concept of *kamma* as taught by the Buddha, however, urges
people to take responsibility for their actions and exercise their volition
in order to recondition themselves for the well-being of all beings who
are implicated in the interconnected web of life, instead of passively
allowing what has been done to determine what will happen. Women
can exercise their volition in such ways that they do not assume the
culturally-prescribed role of pleasing the men in their lives by beautifying themselves and being subservient. Men can exercise their volition
in such ways that they do not adopt the culturally reinforced role
that is tough, aggressive, and seeking domination, if not over other

men then at least over "their" women. By exercising their volition as such, women and men are liberating themselves from stereotypes that have been causing *dukkha* for others as well as for themselves. Simultaneously, by doing so they are reconfiguring the cultural norms that define masculinity and femininity, or at least resetting the cultural parameters that delimit what is acceptable and what is not in terms of gender roles. The arising and growth of "Mister Mom," the father taking care of children in the way traditional mothers usually do, is an example of the adjustability of gender roles and the *dukkha*-alleviating benefit of dismantling rigid gender binary. "Mister Mom" allows himself to connect with his own children better, contributes to the children's well-being, and eases the burden on the mother who, in today's society, very often has a full-time job. The Buddhist goal of the cessation of *dukkha* demands that people carefully examine what they have been conditioned to take as their "selves," to actively monitor their actions and reactions, and to exercise their volition to reconstruct themselves and the *dukkha*-producing social norms for the benefits of all sentient beings.

In the "interlocking system" of Buddhism, Herbert Guenther writes, "[i]t is he who as 'causal agent' creates his world which, in turn, is a 'causal agent' creating him."[65] No one lives without taking actions, and the actions one takes in turn become part of the socio-cultural forces that condition all people in that matrix, including oneself. As the feminist slogan puts it, the personal is political. Individual feelings and thoughts and actions are ramifications of what is happening on the political level. And they have ramifications on the political level, too. Through our actions, we make meanings together, write our cultural scripts together, and make and remake ourselves in the process. Paradoxically, the Buddhist *Dhamma* that is known for its teaching of non-Self also emphasizes individuals' moral agency and instructs individual "selves" to take social responsibility. We have responsibility for each other and need to be mindful with the actions we take because, with our actions, we are constructing and reconstructing our world and conditioning people within it. The human society, as a whole, reaps what people sow. We are all implicated in the *kammic* network.

Global Co-Arising of *Dukkha*

Co-arising or interdependence, the rationale behind the teachings of non-Self and *kamma*, is a pragmatic view of the reality of human existence and has profound socio-ethical implications. It reveals the intricate interrelations among individual persons, as well as between individuals and society. It also highlights the social dimension of *kamma*, demanding individual persons exercise their volition in socially conscionable ways to reduce and alleviate *dukkha*. Following the perspective and reasoning provided by interdependent co-arising, to state that existence is fraught with *dukkha*, as the First Noble Truth in Buddhism does, is also to say that all on the interconnected web of existence are complicit in the production and perpetuation of the *dukkha* in the world with their *kamma*, whether directly or indirectly. That, however, does not mean everyone is equally responsible. Interdependent co-arising does not mean that all factors, though interconnected, contributed equally to the arising of something. Some factors are direct, primary causes while others are mere conditions, i.e., indirect and auxiliary factors. Given different positions on the interconnected web, some people's *kamma* carries more weight in the generation and maintenance of certain *dukkha*-inducing situations than others'.

Wars, for example, are fought due to a number of factors: able-bodied persons who have the propensity or ability to fight and are willing or compelled to follow orders, inventors and scientists that design and improve weapons, manufacturers and businesspeople that produce and sell weapons for monetary gain, uneven and/or unfair distribution of social resources, concentration of natural resources in certain geographical areas that incurs covetousness from people not living in those areas, greed and aggression on the part of political and/or military leaders, propagated theories and beliefs about the righteousness of the self-group and the evil of the other-group, ideological conflicts that are more often than not rooted in egocentric assessments of situations and in the attachments to those assessments, anger and hostility on the part of perhaps all parties involved, and so forth. All of the above are conducive to the arising and continuing of wars, and all of the above are responsible. Yet all are not equally so. A soldier does not play the same role in initiating and continuing a war as the political and/or military leaders. A truck driver who transports weapons from the factory to the battlefield is not equally responsible as the Chief Executive Officer of a weapon-manufacturing corporation who reaps profits from the prolongation of wars.

In classical Buddhist discourses, the currently more privileged and more powerful were clearly considered to be more responsible for the arising of *dukkha*. For this reason, historically Buddhist masters have been rather close to the élite. Aside from the fact that the upper-class men were more likely to have the leisure and access to receive education of the complicated Buddhist texts and philosophies, Buddhism is also close to the political élite for the reason that it is dedicated to "conscientize" rulers. In Latin American Liberation Theology, it is the poor that need to be conscientized, that is, to be educated so that they can be critically aware of the structural injustice imposed on them, of their right to life and dignity, and of their agency in liberating themselves.[66] Here I am borrowing the term but using it in a slightly different way: in classical Buddhist thought, that is, it is the privileged that need to be educated so that they would be conscious and conscientious when they enact their decisions that inevitably have tremendous social ramifications. In Buddhist texts and traditions, rulers would be urged by Buddhist masters to play the role of *cakkavatti* (Sanskrit: *cakravartin*) who implements policies in accordance with the Buddhist *Dhamma* in order to safeguard the wellbeing of all subjects and prevent *dukkha* from arising. In the *Cakkavatti-Sīhanāda Sutta*, for instance, the king was said to be responsible for the arising of theft: it was after the king failed to lay down conditions for *all* people to prosper that life became difficult for some; it was after the king failed to implement welfare policies meeting the basic needs of the less privileged that poverty became rampant; and it was after the king did not remedy the situation that some in dire poverty were driven to theft.[67] This text demonstrates that the Buddha recognized a comfortable material life to be "an important factor contributing toward a harmonious social life."[68] He considered it the government's responsibility to safeguard and maintain the welfare of its individual subjects. That is, classical Buddhism recognized that those in power were responsible for the social structures that produced *dukkha*.

Besides recognizing the "external" factor of social structures, classical Buddhist discourses also identified "internal" mental or emotive factors that accounted for the arising of crime and suffering. In the *Aggañña Sutta*, greed was depicted as *the* reason that possessive individualism, crimes and punishments, and differentiation of social classes came into existence.[69] David Kalupahana points out that the Buddha "carefully distinguished between human need and human greed."[70] While the Buddha did consider it the responsibility of the incumbent ruler to implement fair social policies to fulfill the basic needs of the masses because "there cannot be harmony when the belly is empty,"[71] he also saw greed and egocentric concerns as the propeller of *dukkha*-inducing situations.

Greed on the part of those who are currently powerful and privileged, in particular, is detrimental to social well-being, for they are far more likely to influence social policies and further develop theories based on the privileged life in their élite enclave. They are far more likely to have the administrative, financial, and educational resources to propagate ideologies that justify their imposition of unfair structures and regulations. Therefore, since its inception Buddhism has maintained a tradition of attempting to "conscientize" the dominant classes. The *Sigālaka Sutta*, discussed in Chapter 2, is commonly (mis-)taken to be a discourse conveying Buddhist expectations of *all* laypeople, but it was in fact directed at the privileged, property-owning, slave-holding male "householders," urging them to be humane, generous, and socially responsible. While some have taken this text to be evidence of the élitist and androcentric orientation of Buddhism as a whole, I would like to contend that classical Buddhist scriptures addressed mainly upper-class men partly because it was the upper-class men who needed to be "conscientized" the most, given their greater social power over so many others. The Buddhist teaching of interdependent co-arising, throughout history, has always distinguished primary causes from auxiliary conditions while emphasizing interconnectedness and socio-ethical responsibilities. Those in power are clearly the primary causes of *dukkha*-inducing situations, even though all others in the interconnected web may also be somewhat responsible for the perpetuation of those situations. "Conscientizing" the privileged and powerful, then, can potentially alleviate more *dukkha* faster. Given the Buddhist goal of the cessation of *dukkha*, it is understandable that Buddhist masters and philosophers spend much time trying to convince upper-class men to practice the Buddhist *Dharma*.

Keeping in mind the impacts of colonialism and neo-colonialism, we can see the ways in which the greed and aggression on the part of the currently powerful have been creating tremendous *dukkha* for many. Quite a few social critics, economists, and Latin American liberation theologians have related the ways in which the colonial and neo-colonial policies and ideologies, which were first formulated by the (male) élite of the "first world" countries, have undermined the basic welfare of women and men in the formerly colonized areas. Rebecca Todd Peters' account is one of the most succinct:

> First, the colonial governments and their corporations had used their colonies as sources of raw materials, labor, and trade. These policies and practices served an extractive function for the colonial governments and as such they did not emphasize or enable a productive independent economy to develop in most of these countries. Second, decades of "foreign" political control and the imbalance of

trade in the direction of selling raw materials and buying goods from the colonial master had prevented indigenous development of industry or trade that was capable of facilitating the move to self-determination and independent statehood. Consequently, these former colonial states now had formal political recognition of their independence by the international community but were unable to interact on a par with their former colonizers in the political and economic realm.

In the 1950s and '60s "development" became the name of the game in international finance, and billions of dollars were lent to countries in African, Asia, and Latin America to assist them in becoming more "like" Western Economies. . . . The perspectives of capitalist economic activity that shaped the practices of business and industries developed during this period of global economic integration made them unable to ignore the trade potential (and billions of consumers) represented by the "two-thirds" world. To the neoclassically trained economic mind, the continued economic dependence of many of these countries on their formal colonizers could most readily be "solved" by helping these countries develop market economies, like the economies of the nations that colonized them, that could ensure their prosperity.

. . .

In the early Reagan years, there was often talk of "trickle down" economics as a way of justifying continued economic benefits for the wealthy. The new ideology coincided with increased direct foreign investment from the corporate world and a growing capitalist elite within countries now drawn into this growing global network of transnational capitalism. . . . To these folks the profitability of the market was sufficient proof that neoliberalism was working. In contrast, those who had only their labor to sell in the economic arena were to discover that what had actually trickled down was a longer work week for less real wages for many of the world's workers. . . . Simultaneously in the 1980s the IMF and the World Bank imposed strict structural adjustment policies on debtor nations in the "two-thirds" world . . . These structural adjustments were aimed towards making these economies more "efficient," which translated into cutting back on expenditures in the

social serve and educational sectors as a way to "trim fat"
out of budgets and promoting export-oriented programs
of growth.[72]

With the design and manufacture of superior weaponry, the wealthy
and powerful from the "first-world" countries conquered and colonized
much of the rest of the world, stole and exported the latter's natural
resources as well as cultural artifacts, and implemented exploitive
rules that resulted in the colonized countries' economic dependency
on their colonizers.[73] David R. Loy termed the royally chartered corporations, self-aggrandizing nation-states, and modern militaries, the
"unholy trinity" that has fed on colonial exploitations.[74]

This history also resulted in the colonized countries' cultural
dependency on the colonizers. As Joseph M. Kitagawa states in his
introduction to *The Religious Traditions of Asia*, the presence of the overwhelming power of the "West" in Asia during colonialism prompted
many intellectuals in Asia to accept naïvely Western interpretations of
their own cultures and Western scholars' claims of objectivity, neu-
trality, and universality. "In those days, it was fairly fashionable to
appropriate things Western in conformity with the program of westernization of Asia promoted by colonial regimes. To adopt Western
modes of scholarship, moreover, was the only *entrée* into the global
academy."[75] More generally, Western culture is deemed superior,
and traditional non-Western cultures are considered impediments to
"development." The later are therefore supposed to abandon their
traditions and westernize themselves.[76] The colonial past has also
rendered Latin America dependent on Europe religiously in that most
of the Catholic clergy are foreign.[77]

Meanwhile, the wealth furnished and fueled by the colonized
countries further enhanced the colonizers' dominance of the world
economy and lent credence to the economic theories and institutions
they constructed and propagated, even though under the economic
system constructed by the wealthy countries the poor have gotten
poorer, both among nations and within nations, and even though most
projects of the U.S.-dominated World Bank are failures.[78] According
to the report issued by the United Nations Development Programme
in 1999, by the late 1990s the one-fifth highest-income population of
the world had 86 percent of world GDP, while the bottom fifth had
just 1 percent; the three wealthiest people had more assets than the
combined GNP of the 48 least developed countries, while 1.3 billion
people live on less than one U.S. dollar a day.[79] In its 2007/2008
report, the United Nations Development Programme estimated that

the poorest 40 percent of the world's population (approximately 2.6 billion people) lives on less than US $2 a day and accounts for 5 percent of global income, and the richest 20 percent of the world's population accounts for 75 percent of global income. More than 80 percent of the world's population lives in countries where the income gap is widening.[80] The enormous economic inequalities existing in the world today, applied philosophy and public ethics scholar Thomas Pogge points out, "have evolved in the course of *one* historical process that was pervaded by monumental crimes of slavery, colonialism, and genocide—crimes that have devastated the populations, cultures, and social institutions of four continents."[81] In other words, the "underdevelopment" of the poor countries, as Latin American liberation theologian Gustavo Gutiérrez puts it, is "the historical by-product of the development of other countries."[82] Economist Michael Yates puts it bluntly: "the poor countries are poor because they have been exploited by the rich nations."[83]

For poor people living in the "underdeveloped" countries, what the colonial history of exploitations has brought is not so much the numbers describing the widening income gap, but dire poverty that has gotten more and more life-threatening. As of 2003, the United Nations Development Programme estimated that 1 billion people in the world lack access to safe drinking water and 2.4 billion lack basic sanitation.[84] In the 2007/2008 report, the estimates were still that 28 percent of all children are underweight or stunted, 10 million children die of poverty and malnutrition each year before the age of five, 3 million die of AIDS, and 1 million die of malaria every year.[85]

On the global scale, affluent countries and their citizens have been more responsible for the life-threatening poverty in the world than those in the poor or less affluent countries. Within each country, the ruling, policy-making élite have been more responsible than average citizens. In poor countries, the ruling élite often resort to exploiting and mistreating their workforces in order to compete with other poor countries for foreign investment.[86] Compounding the entrenched hierarchical gender relations, moreover, the male-dominated globalized economy has in particular impoverished and exploited women and girls across nations.[87] Of the people living below the poverty line, about 70 percent are women, and the deprivations caused by poverty fall disproportionately on them,[88] both due to global economic inequalities and to local hierarchical gender structures.[89] Without consciously dealing with the existing hierarchies, various non-governmental organizations' programs that seek to empower "the oppressed" or aid the local "community" often end up empowering only the oppressed men and the male community.[90] Even in affluent countries women typically earn only a fraction of what men earn.[91] Women make up the majority of the cheap, skilled labor and therefore are the foundation of world economy in a very real sense. Yet they are the ones who are harmed the most in the economic globalization and are hardly among the ones who receive benefits from it.

Modernity has made the co-arising of *dukkha* global and has made the fact of interconnectedness readily observable. In the area of global ecological crisis, we can most vividly see how the privileged have been far more responsible in creating *dukkha*, and how the poor and powerless are the ones who bear the brunt. While "People in the rich world are increasingly concerned about emissions of greenhouse gases from developing countries," the *UNDP Human Development Report 2007/2008* states, "They tend to be less aware of their own place in the global distribution of CO_2 emissions."[92] Yet the 60 million people living in the United Kingdom emit more CO_2 than the 472 million people living in Egypt, Nigeria, Pakistan, and Vietnam combined. The 23 million people living in the state of Texas leave a larger CO_2 footprint than the 720 million people in sub-Saharan Africa. The 19 million people in the state of New York generate more carbon emissions than the 766 million people living in the 50 least developed countries. An average air-conditioner in Florida emits more CO_2 in a year than a person in Afghanistan or Cambodia in his or her whole lifetime. The *increase* of per capita carbon emissions in Canada since 1990 (5 tons) is greater than the per capita carbon emissions in China in 2004 (3.8 tons). The poorest 1 billion people leave about 3 percent of the world's total carbon footprint.[93]

Yet the climate change resulting from the increase of CO_2 emissions has been far more life-threatening to the poor than to the rich. Climate disasters such as severe tropical storms and floods, are clearly on the rise. Between 2000 and 2004, an average of 326 climate disasters were reported each year, doubling the yearly average between 1980 and 1984. Around 262 million people were affected by such extreme weather events each year, with over 98 percent of them living in developing countries. Countries with high levels of income inequalities experienced the effects of climate disasters more profoundly than more equal societies. Whereas the rich can cope with climate shocks by drawing on savings or selling off assets, the poor may have to cut nutrition and pull children, especially girls, out of school. Malnutrition and educational deprivation have long-term consequences and further lock the already disadvantaged people into poor health and poor earning potential. It is estimated that, by 2080, the climate change could increase the number of people facing acute malnutrition by 600 million, the number of people facing water scarcity by 1.8 billion, and the number of people at risk of malaria by 220 to 400 million.[94]

Among the poor, women are more likely to be affected by extreme weather events than men. "Women's historic disadvantages—their limited access to resources, restricted rights, and a muted voice in shaping decisions—make them highly vulnerable to climate change."[95] In countries where women are the primary producers of staple food, drought and uncertain rainfall mean that women and young girls have to walk farther to collect water. Floods typically claim more women's lives than men's since women's mobility is more restricted and they are less likely to have been taught how to swim. When Bangladesh was hit by a cyclone and a flood in 1991, for example, the death rate of women was five times higher than that of men.[96] Moreover, when the poor affected by climate shocks have no alternative but to reduce consumption, it is girls' nutrition that suffers the most.[97] In the same way that the fathers and mothers are more responsible for the malnutrition of their daughters than the girls themselves, the policy-making élite of the poor countries are more responsible for the plight of their poor citizens than the poor women and men themselves. And those who create, sustain, justify, and benefit from the current global economic and consumption system are more responsible for the rampant economic injustice and drastic climate change than those in the poor countries.[98]

In Buddhism, the discernment of the more responsible party in the generation and maintenance of *dukkha*, however, does not (or rather, should not) lead to animosity toward those who are more responsible. For one thing, wisdom in Buddhist discourses includes seeing things as they really are and taking actions for the well-being of all. Seeing the interconditionality, one is dedicated to cultivating loving-kindness, compassion, altruistic joy, and equanimity toward all and working for their well-being, which will be discussed further in the next chapter. Emotively, naming the oppressors breeds resentment, and the resentment truncates one's capacity of maintaining loving-kindness and seeking out the solutions that are the most beneficial or least harmful for all involved. Cognitively, identifying the enemy reinforces oppositional thinking and makes it even more difficult to maintain the clarity that allows one to see the intricate and dynamic interconditionality of phenomena. Animosity and antagonism easily aggravate the given situation.

For another, given the perspective of interdependent co-arising, no group of people are simply the objects upon which the social forces act. As explicated in the above section on the social dimension of *kamma*, the prevalence of a certain ideology or behavioral pattern is not the doing of a single person or a few persons. And as discussed in the last chapter on the five aggregates, the prevalent ideology or behavioral norm, being a form of cultural *rūpa*, can easily find its way into the consciousnesses of all those who are living in, and being conditioned by, that socio-cultural context. One may or may not currently occupy a power position to oppress or exploit or *own* other people, but it is very likely that she or he has been inculcated with the values of possessive individualism so prevalent in the culture that she or he thinks a good life lies in owning property and making others toil for oneself. A man who has been exploited as a farmer by transnational agribusiness may have been so conditioned by the culture that he dreams of one day heading his own agribusiness and living off of the labor of other farmers. He may also have been conditioned to see his wife as a sex provider, a baby maker, a caregiver, and a house maintainer. Similarly, a woman who has been treated as an object for her whole life may have been treating her children as the only personal property she has, not entitled to any opinion of their own. By taking actions as such, one is not just an innocent victim of injustice, but is simultaneously a perpetuator of the ideology and behavioral pattern of treating others as mere means to one's self-centered interests and concerns. Being socio-psycho-physical compounds that co-arise and are interconnected, persons are hardly ever *mere* victims of the social injustice created by "the oppressors" without being complicit in some way in the values and conventions that make domination possible or even laudable. People co-write the cultural scripts and continue to re-write them together.

Therefore, Vietnamese *bhikṣu* Thích Nhât Hanh observes, the social system which we consider "imposes itself upon us, and we have become its slaves and victims" is the product of our own doing.[99] If we observe carefully and maintain mindfulness, he believes, we will see that social system and government policies reflect the values we hold in our daily life. With neither being aware of, nor working on, one's own thinking and emotions, no one is automatically above the three poisons of acquisitiveness (greed), aggression (hatred), and egocentric attachments (delusion). Historically, therefore, Buddhism has put much emphasis on doing the "inner" work of observing and confronting one's own thoughts and emotions that lead to the arising of *dukkha*-inducing social realities. "You may think that the way to change the world is to elect a new president," Venerable Nhât Hanh says, "but a government is only a reflection of society, which is a reflection of our own consciousness. To create fundamental change,

we, the members of society, have to transform ourselves."[100] In the
same vein, Sulak Sivaraksa comments, "We all have the power to cause
suffering in relationships and cannot attribute this only to the social
structure. The need for power stems from a desire to feel superior
in the vain quest to establish a unique self."[101] A society that values
aggression and worships consumption cannot but produce a government that enacts aggression for material gains.

Nonetheless, as shown in Chapter 1, the Buddhist masters' proximity to power and privilege has much to do with the internalization,
individualization, and masculinization of the Buddhist *Dhamma*. With
the significant exception of the early Buddhist texts, Buddhism has
not provided much direct critique of existing social structure or the
relation between social structure and the arising of *dukkha*. Cultivating
one's own mind has often been conceived to be the *only* task, instead
of the first task or one of the indispensable tasks. More often than not,
the existence of power and privilege in society is simply explained
away by saying that those powerful and privileged are reaping what
they have sown in previous lives, in the same way that the suffering
of women is often explained away by their bad *kamma* in past lives.
The operation of *dukkha*-inflicting social structure and *dukkha*-inducing
cultural norms is usually disregarded or neglected, and the here-and-
now *kamma* taught by the Buddha and the co-arising of "external"
socio-cultural phenomena and the "internal" mental processes of
individuals are yet to be sufficiently recognized.

Close to power or not, in accordance with the *Dharma*, a Buddhist
cannot find justification for violent means of restructuring society,
nor can a Buddhist easily translate the mission of saving all sentient
beings to the "preferential option for the poor," as one of the slogans
of Latin American liberation theology goes. It is in this aspect that
engaged Buddhists generally differ from Latin American liberation
theologians, to whom they are often compared. While understanding
that injustice and hatred "have their origin in human selfishness"[102]
and that people do not "automatically become less selfish,"[103] leading
Latin American liberation theologians nevertheless call for "an option
for one social class against another"[104] and differentiate the "unjust
violence of the oppressors" and *"just violence* of the oppressed."[105]
Gutiérrez equates the poor with the oppressed, who "are member
of one social class that is being subtly (or not so subtly) exploited
by another social class."[106] Even though Gutiérrez clarified elsewhere
that the oppressed should not assume any violence on their part is
"just," the dichotomy of, and the opposition between, the two social
groups, the oppressors and the oppressed, are much emphasized.[107]

Since the exploitative capital owners are the sinning oppressors who "refuse to love one's neighbor and, therefore, the Lord himself,"[108] redressing the situation entails siding with the righteous opposition, i.e., the poor, and combating the "class enemies"[109] to bring about immediate and radical change of the existing social structure. Along this line of thinking, Gutiérrez asserts, "Latin American misery and injustice go too deep to be responsive to palliatives. Hence we speak of social revolution, not reform; of liberation, not development; of socialism, not modernization of the prevailing system."[110]

Engaged Buddhists agree with Latin American liberation theologians in many regards, such as it is human beings (instead of a supernatural being of Evil) that should be responsible for the existence of suffering, and spirituality involves an ongoing effort in redressing the social wrongdoings and injustices. Gutiérrez, for example, believes that to be a Christian is to follow Jesus Christ whose work "is presented simultaneously as a liberation from sin and from all its consequences: despoliation, injustice, hatred," and so to be a Christian is "to preach the universal love of the Father is inevitably to go against all injustice, privilege, oppression, or narrow nationalism."[111] With the understanding of interdependent co-arising, however, engaged Buddhists cannot *dhammically* espouse oppositional thinking or violent change.[112] All are to some extent complicit in the perpetuation of *dukkha*-producing ideologies and behavioral patterns, and therefore the *dukkha* in the world will not cease simply by deposing the "class enemies" and placing the downtrodden on top. This, however, is not to say that Buddhists in history have never countenanced violence based on oppositional thinking, even though one of the founding figures of contemporary peace studies, Johan Galtung, believes that "by no stretch of imagination can Buddhism be used to justify direct and structural violence, war and exploitation."[113] On occasion, some Buddhist masters would support or even advocate military actions. In the twentieth century, in particular, the world has witnessed large-scale violence sanctioned or even initiated by Buddhists.[114] In all cases of which I am aware, the words of the Buddhist masters who endorsed or encouraged violent measures betray their strong attachments to their ethnic or national identity,[115] as if that identity had an intrinsic, permanent, and unchanging value that warranted its preservation at all cost. However, if one takes seriously the Buddhist deconstruction of self-identity, which is recognized as one of the core teachings across Buddhist traditions, one has to conclude that those violence-advocating Buddhists were twisting the *Dhamma*, behaving and thinking *undhammically*. This is to be discussed more fully in the final chapter.

To emphasize interdependent co-arising and to restrain from oppositional thinking and violent change, of course, is not to say that the current structure is to be preserved as it is. Fair social structures are the *necessary* condition for the alleviation of *dukkha*. They are not the *sufficient* condition, however. As noted above, the currently poor and powerless may not be as responsible for the arising of *dukkha* on the large scale as those who have been rich and powerful, but they have the same capability—and very likely the same underlying egocentric tendency, too—to inflict injustice. Seeing sufferings firsthand on a daily basis may prompt the deprived and oppressed to view things differently and develop different ways to relate to one another, but it does not guarantee they will. Once the conditions present themselves, they may soon manifest the same greed and aggression as their exploiters/ oppressors, and they may soon partake in the injustice and coercion that they once resented. At one point Gutiérrez makes the assertion that "[t]he poor countries are not interested in modeling themselves after the rich countries, among other reasons because they are increasingly more convinced that the status of the latter is the fruit of injustice and coercion."[116] Elsewhere, however, he remarks that the ruling élite of the poor countries "are generally in complicity with large interests at the international level" and do want to model themselves after the élite of the rich countries.[117] Very often the poor *are* interested in having the life of the élite. That is, they are not necessarily kinder or calmer or wiser than those who have been more responsible in inflicting *dukkha*, and they are not necessarily above seeing other people as property or instruments. Through repeated exposures and disciplines, all people alike may be conditioned by some socio-cultural norms to be acquisitive and aggressive. All may be driven by deeply-seated defilements, including disturbing emotions of greed and hatred, and the deluded thinking of an independent Self. Without conscious and conscientious dealing with one's own *dukkha*-producing tendencies, structural change simply changes the identity of the inflictors of *dukkha*, but not the socio-cultural patterns of *dukkha* production. Peace scholar Kenneth E. Boulding expresses a similar qualm: "a 'liberationism' which operates primarily in the dialectical mode and looks to the solution of human problems by getting rid of top dogs simply produces another set of top dogs, often worse than the last."[118]

Just as the currently poor and powerless are not inherently righteous, the currently privileged and powerful are not inherently evil, either. Though more responsible, the latter are not necessarily people who consciously and volitionally "refuse" to love their neighbors. While some of them may intend to keep the social structures unjust for their own benefits, others may simply be imperceptive of the co-arising of their own privileges and others' sufferings. Some of the people living in the "first world" may be ignorant of their role in creating *dukkha* in the same way that some of the people living in the "third world" may be ignorant of their agency. Once educated and conscientized, the privileged may strive diligently to utilize the resources at their hands to remedy the injustice they have encountered or possibly have caused. Branding all privileged people as the evildoers is not only unfair; it is as unbeneficial in changing the *dukkha*-producing socio-cultural norms as romanticizing about the righteousness of the poor as a whole, who may have been longing for the same privileges of their exploiters/oppressors. As pointed out in the section "The Liberative Is Ethical" in Chapter 2, the Buddha himself did not associate privileges with evil. The Dalai Lama does not think being rich itself is immoral, either. He comments that being rich is "a tremendous opportunity to benefit others."[119]

Oppositional thinking and hatred might on occasion effect changes faster for certain groups, but they will surely increase and intensify the ill will in others and deepen the roots of conflicts. Drawing from the *Dhammapada*, Cambodian engaged Buddhist Venerable Somdech Preah Maha Ghosananda says, "In those who harbor thoughts of blame and vengeance toward others, hatred will never cease. . . . For hatred is never appeased by hatred."[120] Thích Nhât Hanh provides a drastic instance of how oppositional thinking can result in violence or exacerbate conflicts: during the wars between the Northern Communist force based in Hanoi and the Southern anti-Communist government based in Saigon in Vietnam in the 1970s, Vietnamese Buddhist monks and nuns, in the spirit of nonviolence, promoted peace and protested against military dictatorships. "When others see that we oppose the Saigon government," Nhât Hanh relates, "they often think we support Hanoi" and assume that "we cooperate with the Communists in order to destroy anti-Communist elements in the country."[121] As a result, Vietnamese Buddhist monks and nuns were put in jails or even massacred, by both sides of the antagonism. Nhât Hanh himself went into exile and was not allowed to return to Vietnam until very recently. The "if you are not with us, you are against us" oppositional thinking on the part of the Hanoi supporters and Saigon supporters drove them to be violent toward people whose goal was to save lives and alleviate suffering.

Furthermore, in the analysis of the five aggregates, the pitfall with opposition and hatred goes deeper than the truism that "violence begets violence." Clinging to the mental construction (*saṇkhāra*) of opposition, one generates the volition (also part of *saṇkhāra*) of manifesting the opposition in one's actions, and the repeated exercise of volition in this way congeals to be one's disposition (*saṇkhāra*), which further affects one's mental construction and blocks one's perception of interconnectedness. That is, not only do hostilities get sedimented "externally" to be the socio-cultural norms of aggression and violence that will beget more aggression and violence, but they also get sedimented "internally" to be one's habitual way of mental construction and one's disposition. Harboring hatred and seeing others as the enemy, one is making oneself a hateful person; opting for violent change and enacting it, one is acculturating oneself to be violent while legitimizing violence. One cannot possibly all of a sudden revert to nonviolence if one has resorted to a series of violent actions to achieve one's end (surely age-long social structure cannot be changed with merely one action), nor can one possibly convince others not to use violence on one's self when they do not agree, given that one has already legitimized violence by repeatedly resorting to it. In the Buddhist perspective informed by the teachings of interdepedent co-arising and the five aggregates, opposition, hatred, and violence perpetuate the cycle of *dukkha* both "internally" and "externally." Along this line, the current Dalai Lama's response to those who comment that his commitment to nonviolence is impractical is, "Actually, it is far more naïve to suppose that the human-created problems which lead to violence can ever be solved through conflict."[122] Therefore, even if these means *might* bring forth a seemingly desirable "end," that "end" is at most one temporary stop in the cycle of *dukkha* production and is not really an end. It certainly is not an "end" that can justify the means.

In the interconnected web of existence, individual persons are conditioned by the *rūpa* to which they have been exposed, and yet what people do and how people act in turn become the *rūpa* with which new consciousnesses and new behavioral patterns co-arise. The actions people take, particularly the actions that powerful and privileged people take, inevitably reverberate through the web of interconditionality and become part of the culture as well as part of themselves. While acknowledging that all people alike, currently powerful or powerless, may be acquisitive, aggressive, and egocentric, Buddhism also affirms the possibility of change and teaches that people do have the ability to put an end to the cycles of *dukkha*-production, for others as well as for themselves. With the same reality of interconditionality, benevolence and *dukkha*-alleviating actions can travel on the *kammic* network just

as malice and *dukkha*-producing actions do. With repea
and disciplines, generosity and benevolence can becc
sediments on the top of deeply-seated acquisitiveness anc
Egalitarianism and cooperation can replace competition and
as the social norms. Seemingly minor effort, through repe
accumulation, may change the direction of society. Interconc ɔ̃iality
means that beings, through their repetitive actions, can perpetuate
samsāra, the endless cycle of *dukkha*-production, as much as they can
transform it into *nibbāna*, the cessation of *dukkha*.

In order to reach *nibbāna* and ceasing *dukkha* for all, Buddhists
take refuge in the Three Gems, the Buddha, the *Dhamma*, and the
Sangha. That is, besides learning from the Teacher and knowing that
it is possible to reach *nibbāna*, Buddhists are supposed to learn and
practice his Teaching of the Noble Eightfold Path, as well as building
spiritual communities that prompt and facilitate the behavioral, emotive, and conceptual transformations for the cessation of *dukkha*. As
pointed out in Chapter 2, the "forerunner and precursor" of the arising
of the Noble Eightfold Path is the association with "good friends,"
the "others" who inspire and/or support one to be "wholesome." The
Three Learnings contained in the Noble Eightfold Path allow one to
recondition oneself behaviorally, emotively, and conceptually, while
the process of building communities allows the results of this self-
reconditioning to travel farther and faster through the *kammic* network
in which all are implicated. The following chapter will deal with the
Buddhist program of self-reconditioning and community-building.

Buddhist Self-Reconditioning and Community-Building

In the Buddhist worldview of interdependent co-arising, society and individuals condition one another, and neither one is the uncreated creator of the other. Depending on each other to exist, both are impermanent and subject to change. In fact, both need to be changed, according to the Buddhist teaching of the Four Noble Truths. The First and Second Noble Truths state that existence is filled with *dukkha* and that *dukkha* arises due to craving. Besides being matter-of-fact statements about the unavoidable existential anguish in life and their causes, these two Noble Truths are simultaneously criticisms of the conventional *dukkha*-filled ways of life, particularly when they are viewed together with other teachings of the Buddha, such as *kamma*. The Third Noble Truth unequivocally upholds the cessation of *dukkha* as a goal and states that it is possible. The Fourth Noble Truth provides a program that enables individuals to go beyond their socio-cultural conditionings and transform the ways in which they live together and relate to each other. What the Buddha taught with the Four Noble Truths, then, was not a pessimistic or fatalistic view of life, but an indication of the Buddha's nonaggressive yet unyielding stance that the *dukkha*-inducing socio-cultural conventions and the *dukkha*-producing individuals, as they were, needed to be changed through the participation of all who are implicated.

Recognizing that individual persons were conditioned and constrained by their material and socio-cultural surroundings, the Buddha however manifested much confidence in individuals' potential in reconditioning their selves, being wholesome, and stopping the cycle of *dukkha*-production. In addition to tending the "outward" behavior and their ramifications, Buddhists are taught that it is equally important, if not more important, to turn "inward" and to know and work on their thoughts, emotions, and deeply-seated tendencies. In the Buddhist analysis of personhood through the five aggregates, the way one conducts oneself is not only conditioned by social conventions and norms, but is also a product of one's own mental formations and dispositions (saṇkhāra), which are more often than not gravitated toward the ego and tinted with egocentric emotional investments, such as attachment to the extent of greed, and aversion to the extent of hatred.[1] As the path to the cessation of dukkha, therefore, the Noble Eightfold Path consists of mental training and wisdom development in addition to ethical discipline. That is, in addition to reconditioning interpersonal relationships and behavioral patterns through ethical discipline, the Buddhist Dhamma teaches that individuals need to simultaneously work on their "inner" states through meditative practices and understand the co-arising nature of worldly phenomena through wisdom development.

The global understanding of interdependent co-arising related in the last chapter can be discouraging and downright paralyzing. Where does one even begin if all in the kammic network are interconnected and correlated? How does one face oneself when she or he realizes that, more often than not, she or he lapses into the mindless performances of conventions that are perpetuating dukkha? Even if one manages to be mindful and take wholesome actions for most of the time, what difference do a few wholesome actions make if unwholesome actions abound in the interconnected web of life? How does one know what to do and what not to do if one is yet to develop the kind of wisdom that sees all ramifications of one's own actions? Ideally, Buddhists are to develop the wisdom to see the reverberations of their actions through the web of interconditionality and take wholesome bodily, verbal, and mental actions for the well-being of all sentient beings, irrespective of their current connections, or their seeming lack of connections, with oneself. Realistically, however, it is impractical to expect someone to care for all sentient beings with equanimity when that someone is yet to acquire such wisdom to see the multiple, intricate, and dynamic interconnections among all. A pre-enlightened person can only be expected to develop and increase her or his social conscience and benevolence while inevitably continuing to engage in the world through bodily, verbal, and mental actions. To develop social concerns as such, one needs small enough social circles in which one can really see the consequences of one's own actions as well as feel the impact of others' actions. However, in the samsāric world, not everyone in one's immediate geographical community inspires or supports wholesome and socially responsible actions. One therefore needs spiritual communities that guide and reinforce *dukkha*-reducing thinking and behavioral patterns, so that one can be encouraged to try to continue her or his best in making positive differences, without being overwhelmed with the pervasiveness of *dukkha* in the world. The latter kind of communities is not necessarily congruent with the former kind, in the same way that the *ārya-sangha* of stream-enterers is not necessarily congruent with the *bhikkhu-sangha* in a certain geographical location, as discussed in Chapter 2.

In whichever way a community is defined, from a Buddhist perspective, it is a social construct and not something that one should cling to as one's permanent identity or as something inherently sacred. To reiterate the Buddha's analysis, clinging to a piece of mental or social construct as if it were the permanent "Self" is at the root of the generation of *dukkha*. Geographical or spiritual communities are indispensable in nurturing the sense of interconnections and socially conscionable actions. In the contemporary globalized world, they are also invaluable in that they can provide guidance and hope, preventing their members from feeling helpless in the global co-arising of *dukkha*. However, communities are subject to change and are conducive to *dukkha* when being "affected by clinging," just as individual persons are. Group identity-views can be as *dukkha*-inflicting as individual ones.

The Three Learnings:
Socially Conscionable Self-Reconditioning

As Rita Gross points out, one of the convergences between Buddhism and feminism is that both recognize habitual and conventional patterns of thinking and behaving can operate to block the basic well-being of people and cause great suffering.[2] The Buddha's discourses on the pervasiveness of *dukkha* indicated his criticism of the cultural scripts that people had written together and imposed on each other. His teaching of non-Self further instructed that identity views were *dukkha*-producing. In order to counteract the *dukkha*-producing conventional ways of life, including the identity views they supported and reinforced, and in order to volitionally recondition (and not just de-condition[3]) the conventionally constructed individual persons, the Buddha taught the Noble Eightfold Path. The Noble Eightfold Path is an eight-part program that seeks not only to stop persons from being further conditioned by *dukkha*-generating social conventions and egoistic desires, but also to recondition or reprogram persons so that they can reverse the vicious cycle of *dukkha*-production and work for the benefits of all sentient beings.

The Noble Eightfold Path can be grouped under three headings: ethical discipline, mental training, and wisdom development. The fact that the Buddhist path to the cessation of *dukkha* is comprised of these Three Learnings points to the three factors that set in motion the cycle of *dukkha*-production: lack of mutually beneficial behavioral patterns, lack of awareness and benevolent concern, and lack of wisdom. Lacking the wisdom to see the interconditionality of phenomena, people wrongly identify a social construct or a mental construct to be the "Self-Essence," and then seek to *real*-ize or aggrandize that Self, failing to consider the ramifications of their physical, verbal, and mental actions (*kamma*). The lack of wisdom is closely related to the lack of awareness, both in terms of the arising of one's mental formations and emotional states, and of how those "inner" functions are conditioned by social conventions on the one hand, and driven by egocentric desires on the other. The social behavioral norm of possessive individualism exacerbates the situation by implicitly legitimating self-centered *dukkha*-producing behaviors, which further condition more people to adopt an each-person-for-himself/herself attitude and behave selfishly. The conventional ways of life nurture and reinforce *dukkha*-inducing identities and social norms. The cessation of *dukkha*, therefore, hinges on counteracting, through the Three Learnings, all of the three factors that set the conventional ways of life in motion.

Wrongfully perceiving or conceiving a mental or social construct to be the Self, the Buddha taught, is at the root of the generation of *dukkha*. Delusion or ignorance in Buddhism refers to such misapprehension. Wisdom, by contrast, refers to the ability to "see as it really is," to apprehend truthfully the co-arising of phenomena and the concomitant impermanence, and to dwell in impermanent worldly phenomena without clinging or agitation:

> And, bhikkhus, from what are sorrow, lamentation, pain, displeasure, and despair born? How are they produced? Here, bhikkhus, the uninstructed worldling, who is not a seer of the noble ones and is unskilled and undisciplined in their Dhamma, who is not a seer of superior persons and is unskilled and undisciplined in their Dhamma, regards *rūpa* as self, or self as possessing *rūpa*, or *rūpa* as in self, or self as in *rūpa*. That *rūpa* of his changes and alters. With the change and alteration of *rūpa*, there arise in him sorrow, lamentation, pain, displeasure, and despair.

> He regards feeling . . . perception . . . volitional formations . . . consciousness as self, or self as possessing feeling/perception/volitional formations/consciousness, or feeling/perception/volitional formations/consciousness as in self, or self as in feeling/perception/volitional formations/consciousness. That feeling/perception/volitional formations/consciousness of his changes and alters. With the change and alteration of feeling/perception/volitional formations/consciousness, there arise in him sorrow, lamentation, pain, displeasure, and despair.
>
> But, bhikkhus, when one has understood the impermanence of *rūpa*/feeling/perception/volitional formations/consciousness, its change, fading away, and cessation, and when one sees as it really is with correct wisdom thus: "In the past and also now all *rūpa*/feeling/perception/volitional formations/consciousness is impermanent, suffering, and subject to change," then sorrow, lamentation, pain, displeasure, and despair are abandoned. With their abandonment, one does not become agitated. Being unagitated, one dwells happily. A bhikkhu who dwells happily is said to approximate Nibbāna in that respect.[4]

Dukkha arises when one clings to a piece of social construct or mental construct, such as the status of "nobleman" or the beauty of one's physical body, to be the true nature or the most important part of the individual self. Having held onto as the Self a piece that is constructed and thus bound to change, one experiences anguish when one detects change and tries in vain to substantialize such unsubstantial identity: "Agitated mental states born of preoccupation with the change of *rūpa*/feeling/perception/volitional formations/consciousness arise together and remain obsessing his mind. Because his mind is obsessed, he is anxious, distressed, and concerned, and due to clinging he becomes agitated."[5] Clinging to self-view or identity-view inevitably leads to anguish.

The delusion or ignorance in the above sense creates *dukkha* not only for the individual self but for others as well. Attempting to create substance out of something that is unsubstantial, and to ground permanence in something that is impermanent, one imposes on the world and others one's identity-view and all those postulations that would support that identity-view. One deploys all means to create the physical environment, social regulations, and ideological aura in which one's identity-view would seem more real and more grounded. With the self-perceived superiority, for instance, ancient male brāhmins and warrior-nobles devised regulations and justifications to ensure the stratification of society, and the more the society was stratified, the more natural or real the superiority claim seemed. With the social arrangement in which only the upper-class boys had the leisure for, and access to, education, it surely seemed real that upper classes were inherently smarter than lower classes, and men inherently smarter than women. With the upper classes defining etiquettes and civilizations, it surely seemed that lower classes were uncouth and uncivilized. With such a vicious cycle of unjust distribution of resources and social stratification, it would then seem natural for upper-class men to claim that, due to women's and lower-class people's unintelligent and/or uncivilized "nature," their appropriate place in society was to provide services for the upper-class men, affording the latter the time and energy to perform their "nature" of religious authority and/ or political dominance. Class identity and gender identity on the part of the upper-class men were thus *real*-ized in social conventions that prescribed rigid class roles and gender roles, dehumanizing and stunting the development of lower-class men and all women.

As such, mis-identification leads to mis-behavior; an epistemological mistake becomes a socio-ethical problem. The Buddha therefore instructed his monastic followers to abandon identity-view "as if smitten by a sword, as if his head were on fire."[6] The abandoning of identity-view, however, is not to be mistaken with the "fear and disgust with identity," the latter being an annihilationist view and a manifestation of the craving for nonexistence, which still centers around the self[7] because it is still motivated by the complete absorption with the self's, and only the self's, feelings and experiences. Craving for static nonexistence brings forth *dukkha* as much as craving for eternal existence; fear and disgust with identity is as *dukkha*-producing as clinging to an identity.[8] Both can lead to complete disregard of others' well-being and downright hatred toward existence as a whole, including one's own existence. In the *Abhidhamma* analysis, shamelessness of wrongdoing (*ahirika*) and fearlessness of wrongdoing (*anottappa*) are listed as unwholesome mental factors (*cetasika*) that lead to evil doing. U Rewata Dhamma and Bhikkhu Bodhi explain that the proximate cause of shamelessness of wrongdoing is the lack of respect for oneself, and the proximate cause of fearlessness of wronging is the lack of respect for others.[9] In other words, lacking respect for others' and one's current identities leads to fearlessness and shamelessness of wrongdoing, and inasmuch as it contributes to *dukkha*-inflicting wrongdoing, it is clearly not taught by the Buddha. In the Buddha's teachings, the five aggregates, including both the body and the mental and social constructs, are neither the self nor not the self. Even the Buddha himself was said to be neither the same with the five aggregates nor apart from them.[10] The five aggregates are not in and of themselves *dukkha*;[11] they become *dukkha* when they are "affected by clinging."[12] What the Buddha taught, in other words, is abandoning the clinging to a social or mental construct as one's abiding identity, not denying or disrespecting individual selves in their different identities. The respect for oneself is the root of shame of wrongdoing (*hiri*), and respect for others, the root of fear of wrongdoing (*ottappa*).[13] Together, shame and fear of wrongdoing protect the world from widespread immorality and thus are called the "guardians of the world" by the Buddha.[14]

In the same way that wisdom and wholesome actions are positively correlated in classical Buddhist discourse, as discussed in Chapter 2, delusion/ignorance and unwholesome actions are correlated. For example, the *Samyutta Nikāya* says that the unwholesome states of shamelessness and fearlessness of wrongdoing follow ignorance/delusion, while the wholesome states of shame and fear of wrongdoing follow wisdom/true knowledge.[15] Yet most people in the world, yet to be enlightened, are not aware of the connection between their identity-views and the ways in which they conduct themselves, much less to comprehend the multifarious and multilayered ramifications of their actions. All too often people simply perform that which they have been conditioned to perform and hold the views they have been conditioned to hold, without seeing those ways of behaving and thinking as *dukkha*-inducing. People may hold onto their gender identities, performing and expecting others to perform rigid binary gender roles, without realizing that they are upholding and perpetuating a social system that delimits prematurely the possibilities of individual men and women, reduces each to a half of a whole person, creates unnecessary sense of lack, generates hierarchical and oppressive relationships, and promotes certain kinds of behaviors that are unbeneficial to the well-being of human society as a whole.

For example, the conventional expectation of men being strong, powerful, and dominating creates *dukkha* not only for women, but for men themselves, too. Besides justifying the domination and mistreatment of women, the conventional expectation of macho men forces men to suppress their emotions, truncates their capacity to relate to others as equals and to be caring and nurturing, and sanctions aggression or even encourages the use of violence in the process of seeking domination of women or of other men. The emphasis on power and dominance leads to all forms of violence, from bullying peers to domestic abuse to armed conflicts among nations. The conventional expectation of women being subservient and subordinated to men not only renders women appendages that are incapable of sustaining themselves, but also pushes women to vanity. Under the rigid binary gender system, beautifying and commodifying themselves becomes the only means by which women can indirectly secure resources. The deprivation of independence and resources easily pushes women to be manipulative and jealous, and the overemphasis on physical beauty often results in low self-esteem for women, on the one hand, and overconsumption of cosmetics and adornments. on the other. These are but a few ways in which the existing binary gender norms produce and perpetuate *dukkha* in life. Individual men and women do not necessarily intend to harm, but their unreflective performances of conventional binary gender roles have produced harmful effects.

As discussed in Chapter 4, *kamma* in Buddhist discourses is identified as volitional actions, and as such, unintentional actions generally do not count as *kamma*. The lack of intention, however, does not always excuse conventional or unconventional actions that produce harmful effects, immediately or in the future.[16] The Buddhist goal is the cessation of *dukkha*, or at least the alleviation of it, and therefore the Buddhist path does not stop at deterring intentional harmful actions and promoting intentional beneficial ones. It also seeks to reduce the occurrences of unintentional harm. Thus, besides ethical discipline and wisdom development, the Noble Eightfold Path is also composed of mental training that deals with deeply-seated emotive states and undercurrent mental formations. The Buddhist mental training includes proper effort, proper mindfulness, and proper concentration. Proper concentration culminates in the four advanced meditative states called *jhāna*-s (Sanskrit: *dhyāna*-s), which are marked by happiness, tranquility, clarity, and peacefulness.[17] Deep concentration is conducive to the wisdom of seeing into the arising and cessation of phenomena in the world as well as in one's own mind. Proper mindfulness is complete awareness of one's bodily, verbal, and mental actions, including emotive states and thought formations.

> And what, bhikkhus, is proper effort? Here, bhikkhus, a bhikkhu generates desire for the nonarising (*samvara-padhānam*) of unarisen evil unwholesome states; he makes an effort, arouses energy, applies his mind, and strives. He generates desire for the abandoning (*pahāna-padhānam*) of arisen evil unwholesome states . . . He generates desire

for the arising (*bhāvanā-padhānam*) of unarisen whole-some states . . . He generates desire for the maintenance (*anurakkhaṇa-padhānam*) of arisen wholesome states, for their nondecay, increase, expansion, and fulfillment by develop-ment; he makes an effort, arouses energy, applies his mind, and strives. This is called proper effort.[18]

It is worth reiterating that, as pointed out in Chapter 2, wholesome-ness involves, *inter alia*, consideration for others. The desire for the development and preservation of wholesome states, and the desire for the restraint and abandonment of unwholesome states, are thus closely connected with the desire for the well-being of all sentient beings. The "proper effort" in the Noble Eightfold Path is the effort to generate care and respect for all, and to apply one's mind and energy to act on such care and respect, via one's "outer" bodily and verbal actions as well as one's "inner" mental actions.

Mental training, though far from the entirety of Buddhism, is a crucial and indispensable component of the Buddhist Three Learnings. People cannot live a day without performing actions, and actions can be performed to the effect of perpetuating *dukkha*-inducing norms and structures, or they can be performed unconventionally to the effect of unsettling or even subverting the existing conventions. However, one may not be aware of the ways in which she or he is performing.[19] Or one may happen to perform the norms unconventionally and subver-sively without meaning to do so. Or one may be aware of some of the negative consequences of her or his actions but remain indifferent, especially if she or he is currently benefiting from those conventional performances as well as from the existing social structures.[20] Or one may care enough to want to change the existing norms and structures but is not aware of the ways in which she or he is exacerbating the situation and inducing suffering in the process of trying to stop suf-fering.[21] That is, *dukkha*-producing performances result from either the lack of awareness, or the lack of benevolent social concerns, or the lack of both. For people to act, volitionally, in ways that would redirect the co-arising from *dukkha*-inflicting to *dukkha*-alleviating, both awareness and benevolent social concerns are needed. Mental train-ing allows practitioners to develop the mental states of full aware-ness (proper mindfulness) and clarity (proper concentration), as well as the emotive qualities of intending the wellbeing for all[22] (proper effort), while generating happiness and equanimity from within oneself (proper concentration).

One of the most basic kind of mental training along the line of the "proper effort" of cultivating benevolent social concerns is the development of the "Four Boundless States," otherwise termed the "Four Immeasurable Deliverances of Mind" and the "Four Divine Abidings" (*brahmavihāras*): loving-kindness (Pāli: *mettā*; Sanskrit: *maitrī*), compassion (Pāli/Sanskrit: *karuṇā*), altruistic joy (Pāli/Sanskrit: *muditā*), and equanimity (Pāli: *upekkhā*; Sanskrit: *upekṣā*). In this type of mental training, generally referred to as "metta meditation," a practitioner consciously reconditions oneself through repeated practice, gradually replacing the old habit of possessive individualism with the new habit of bearing best intentions for all in the interconnected web of life, including one's self:

> Here a bhikkhu abides pervading one quarter with a mind imbued with loving-kindness, likewise the second, likewise the third, likewise the fourth; so above, below, around and everywhere, and to all as to himself, he abides pervading the all-encompassing world with a mind imbued with loving-kindness, abundant, exalted, immeasurable, without hostility and without ill will. He abides . . . with a mind imbued with compassion . . . with altruistic joy . . . with equanimity, abundant, exalted, immeasurable, without hostility and without ill will.[23]

Cultivated and nurtured, the Four Immeasurable Deliverances of Mind supplant the "three poisons" of acquisitiveness, aggressiveness, and self-attachment, which have been deeply habituated in our psyche and can be removed and transformed only after repeated practice over a very long period of time. Loving-kindness is the wish for others to be happy, while compassion is the wish for others not to suffer. Stated negatively, loving-kindness is the absence of ill will, and compassion is non-cruelty. Both, as Sallie B. King states, are concerns for the welfare of others and ways of being benevolent.[24] Altruistic joy is to be joyful on account of others' achievements, particularly spiritual achievements. The cultivation of altruistic joy palliates both envy and resentment. Equanimity, quieting of both aversion and attachment, is predicated on seeing the transience of all phenomena and hence on seeing the relativity of truth claims and the seeing equality of all beings.[25] Equanimity is neither apathy, nor indifference, nor not distinguishing wholesome practices from unwholesome practices. Rather, it is being concerned with one person's welfare as much as the next person's, and therefore developing loving-kindness, compassion, and altruistic joy toward all beings equally.[26]

Charles Prebish and Damien Keown expound the progression from loving-kindness to equanimity thus,

> Love [loving-kindness] is a feeling of friendship and brotherhood with all beings. But this emotion many easily degenerate into lust, so it is followed by compassion, an awareness of the pitiful state into which these beings have fallen through ignorance. But again this may lead to spiritual pride and a feeling of superiority, so the meditator trains himself [sic] in sympathetic [altruistic] joy, that he [sic] may share the happiness of others and rejoice in the merits they have accumulated. And finally he [sic] achieves a state of equanimity wherein he makes no distinction between friend or enemy, but is even-minded toward all creatures.[27]

To put it simply, the mental training of the Four Boundless States reconditions a person to be benevolent, wishing the best for others and not wanting anyone to suffer, while not being self-righteously or arrogantly attached to a certain course of actions or a certain mode of being. A variety of volitional actions can be ethical, wholesome, and conducive to the cessation of *dukkha*; neither wholesomeness nor *dukkha*-alleviating behavior requires uniformity. What wholesomeness and *dukkha*-alleviating behavior does require is benevolent social concern, which has to be repeatedly cultivated to be developed. The meditative training of the Four Immeasurable Deliverances of Mind, through repetition, nurtures good will and enhances social concerns in the meditator.

The cultivation of the Four Boundless States remains indispensable to all branches of Buddhism, including various forms of Socially Engaged Buddhisms such as the Sarvodaya Shramadāna movement and the Tzu-Chi (Compassionate Relief) Foundation based off of Taiwan.[28] In Tibetan Buddhist practices, the cultivation of the Four Immeasurable Deliverances of Mind is incorporated into the liturgical routine. Before reciting any scripture, one would routinely recite the following for three times:

> May all mother sentient beings, infinite as the sky, have happiness and the causes of happiness.
> May they be liberated from suffering and the causes of suffering.
> May they never be separated from the happiness which is free from sorrow.
> May they rest in equanimity, free from attachment and aversion.

The first line aims at cultivating loving-kindness, and the second to fourth lines deal with compassion, altruistic joy, and equanimity, respectively.

Sometimes people do not intend to inflict sufferings or do want to stop sufferings, but are caught up in the compulsory performances of the various norms within the systems, and/or are driven by their emotional turbulences and habitual egocentric ways of thinking and (re-)acting, and/or are not aware of the reverberations of their actions. The Buddha taught his followers to be mindful and fully aware of every single bodily, verbal, and mental action and its consequences. Needless to say, this kind of complete awareness cannot be achieved overnight, just as a gender identity or a social norm is not constituted with one single act. Full awareness, like steady calmness and habitual benevolent concerns for all, requires repetitive practice.

In the early texts, the cultivation of mindfulness usually begins with being aware of one's bodily actions, such as breathing and postures. When one breathes in, she or he strives to be aware of it; when one breathes out, she or he strives to be aware of it; when one walks, stands, sits, and lies down, she or he strives to be aware of it.[29] Sarah Shaw notes, "The fact that the postures are so often mentioned as a group of four assumes that change of posture in the course of the day and frequent movement between different postures is to be encouraged."[30] Gradually one may come to be aware of every action performed by the body: flexing limbs, putting on clothes, consuming food, defecating, urinating, etc. Being aware of the sensuous experiences of the body may sound simple, but probably every beginner of meditation who tries to be aware of her or his own breath for fifteen minutes experiences something similar to this description given by Stephen Batchelor:

> Then suddenly we are no longer in touch with these experiences. A memory, a fantasy, a fear has snatched us away into the dim, seductive twilight of unawareness. We mentally blink, and the fascinating array of sensations vanishes. A single moment of forgetfulness lets the surge of impulses rush in again and sweep us away. Minutes pass before we even notice that we are distracted. We come back with a shock: our thoughts are racing (although we may have already forgotten why), our heart pumping, our forehead sweating. We return shakily to the breath.
>
> The practice of mindfulness entails patiently returning to the object of meditation again and again . . .[31]

One is unaware of the level of one's own unawareness until one finds out that she or he cannot even stay steadily aware of her or his own breath for a mere fifteen-minute session of sitting. Even with a relaxed posture and within a quiet environment, minutes will pass before one is even aware that one is not being aware. Likewise, most of the time one acts and reacts in the ways that she or he has been conditioned to act and react, without being aware of the action or reaction itself, let alone the process of being conditioned by multiple material and socio-cultural forces to act and react in certain ways.

To recondition, actively, the *dukkha*-inducing socio-cultural sediments that have been conditioning one's "self," first of all, one has to be aware of the subtle ways in which socio-cultural conditioning is taking place. To be aware of the conditioning, one has to be aware of one's feelings and mental formations that co-arise with the socio-cultural *rūpa*. Needless to say, awareness of mental activities, which are intangible and changing very fast, is much more difficult than awareness of bodily activities. Therefore the classical Buddhist mindfulness training begins with being mindful of one's own breath, a bodily activity that is crucial in sustaining one's life and is reflective of one's physical and emotive states. Concentrating on the process of breathing and patiently bringing one's attention back to it, one trains oneself to be calm and focused, as well as strengthens one's will power through repetition. One then gradually extends that focused awareness to other bodily experiences and activities, expanding the scope and raising the level of one's mindfulness. With sufficient awareness of bodily activities, one moves on to the subtler activities of the mind, striving to be aware of the arising and vanishing of every feeling and every thought, including the arising of acquisitiveness, aggressiveness, and egocentric attachment.[32]

It is significant that "volition" and "mental formations" are included in the same category of *saṅkhāra* in the Buddhist analysis of the five aggregates—the exercise of volition has everything to do with the awareness of mental formations. On the one hand, one has to have volition that is strong and benevolent enough to put oneself through the repetitive mental training, striving to be more mindful and aware. Any long-term meditator can testify that the repetitive mental training is time-consuming and mentally strenuous. On the other hand, one has to be aware of the ways in which one's actions, feelings, and thoughts co-arise with, and are conditioned by, the existing material environment and socio-cultural conventions, to be willing to recondition oneself as well as to reconstruct the socio-cultural *rūpa*. Mindfulness, Kalupahana points out, "is not merely an awareness of what is immediately given in experience, but understanding the present in relation to the past."[33] One has to be aware of the busy and turbulent "mental formations" that are shaping one's "dispositions," which further affect one's ways of thinking and acting, before one can see with clarity into the co-arising of worldly phenomena and one's own experiences, past and present. Such clear seeing into the multiple and dynamic interrelations between the socio-cultural *rūpa* and one's self, then, will further motivate one to exercise one's volition in ways that will benefit all sentient beings. Proper effort, proper mindfulness, and proper concentration support and enhance each other. The threefold Buddhist mental training calms the practitioner, allows wisdom to arise, generates or intensifies one's care for others, and strengthens one's volition to discipline one's self and work for the wellbeing of all.

Japanese scholar Kenneth K. Inada rightly maintains that mental training is a necessary ingredient in the Buddhist life, for it equips a person with the capacity to "sense the natural dynamic bond of the self-other relationship" that is "prevailing at all times" but not graspable with bare reason.[34] Daniel Goleman, based on a review of various neurological studies, finds that meditation enables people to be relaxed and yet highly attentive at the same time,[35] and it has the effect of reorienting one's consciousness.[36] This reoriented consciousness with intuitive understanding of interconnectedness and "reflective awareness (*anupassanā*) in the form of constant mindfulness (*sati*)," Kalupahana asserts, "is the means of discovering an appropriate method of behavior in a world of bewildering variety, richness, and creativity."[37] In other words, mental training is indispensable in Buddhist ethics because it reconditions people to be more aware of their bodily, verbal, and mental actions, while at the same time allowing them to see more directly into the interconnection among all beings, thereby nurturing their care for the well-being of others as well as enabling them to see more clearly the social ramifications of their actions so that they will take volitional actions that are more socially beneficial. In the *Mahācattārīsaka Sutta*, it is said that right view, right effort, and right mindfulness run and circle around right intention, which includes renunciation, non-ill will, non-cruelty, and noble and taintless thinking patterns.[38] John Ross Carter explains the requirement of awareness and benevolent concern for others in Buddhist ethics,

> Given a moral situation demanding a response, being aware
> of what has been done and is going on, both generally
> and particularly, responding in a way that is beneficial

for one and for others, and also understanding the causal sequences that have given rise to this or that particular situation, puts one in a position to reflect with insight on the proper course of action.[39]

Being more aware of the co-arising of one's "self" and others, one is more likely to care for others and less likely to be driven by egocentric concerns. Bearing stronger benevolent social concerns, one is less likely to take any *dukkha*-inducing action intentionally. Being more aware of arising and vanishing of one's own feelings and thoughts, one is less likely to take any action unintentionally. Mental training thus allows one to take wholesome actions volitionally and *consistently*, reducing the frequency of both intentional unwholesome actions and unintentional actions of all kinds.

It is worth reiterating that meditation is not all there is in Buddhism, despite the proliferation of modern literature that isolates meditation as the heart of Buddhism that is to be practiced for mystical experience, self-discovery, and stress reduction.[40] The Three Learnings of the Noble Eightfold Path require each other and fortify each other. Meditation is not the end of the Noble Eightfold Path and, according to the mainstream understanding of the interrelation between the Three Learnings, it is not the beginning, either. Ethical discipline is usually considered the logical first. Ethical discipline, in the form of precepts, enables one to attenuate the egoistic attachments to sensual enjoyments. It also functions to dilute the already-formed excessive concern for the self. The most basic five precepts (*pañca-śīla*) in Buddhism were formulated so that "immeasurable beings" could be free from fear, hostility, and oppression, which in turn would free oneself from fear, hostility, and oppression:

> By abstaining from the destruction of life . . . By abstaining from taking what is not given . . . By abstaining from sexual misconduct . . . By abstaining from false speech . . . By abstaining from wines, liquors and intoxicants, the noble disciple gives to immeasurable beings freedom from fear, freedom from hostility and freedom from oppression. By giving to immeasurable beings freedom from fear, hostility and oppression, he himself will enjoy immeasurable freedom from fear, hostility and oppression.[41]

Sallie B. King expounds, "in the end, responsibility to oneself and responsibility to others, my good and the good of others come to coincide. The former is fulfilled in the latter; that is, the two become, in a practical sense, coinherent."[42] A sociological study conducted by Thai scholar Somsuda Pupatana finds that laypeople who observe the five basic precepts are more careful with their own actions and speeches and hold a more positive attitude toward both others and themselves.[43] The Dalai Lama speaks in the same spirit of the Nikāya quote above when he comments that we should think of Buddhist precepts "less in terms of moral legislation than as reminders always to keep others' interests at heart and in the forefront of our minds."[44]

Distance from sensual enjoyments is a prerequisite for concentration, the needed component in any type of Buddhist meditation. David Kalupahana argues, "a strong moral life is a prerequisite for mental concentration. Excessive desire (kāma) and unwholesome mental tendencies (akusala dhamma) naturally obstruct concentration. Therefore, during the initial stage a person is expected to cultivate aloofness from such tendencies."[45] Conceivably, one's ability to concentrate is vitiated by unconstrained sensual desires. Therefore, when talking about advanced meditative states, the Buddha always posed as a precondition "being detached from all sense-desires" or "quite secluded from sensual pleasures."[46] Thai Buddhist philosopher Phra Prayudh Payutto explains the interrelation between ethical discipline and mental training in Buddhism thus: "Buddhism teaches that proper ethics have value because they nurture and improve the quality of the mind; ethics make the mind clean, clear, and pure; . . . they lead to liberation and freedom of the mind, which allows a person to go forth and act with wisdom in skillful and wholesome . . . ways."[47] Pupatana's study also indicates a positive correlation between taking basic Buddhist precepts and meditating on the one hand, and between taking basic Buddhist precepts and having "internal tranquility" and "a focused and still mind"[48] on the other hand.

Ethical discipline allows the mind to calm and concentrate. Concentrated meditation, then, enables one to attain wisdom and see the dynamic co-arising of phenomena in the world while at the same time fueling one with compassionate volition to engage in the world in the effort of alleviating suffering. It is significant that, when the Buddha decided to teach the Dhamma and considered "Who will understand this Dhamma quickly?," the first persons he thought of were his former teachers Ālāra Kālāma and Uddaka Rāmaputta, and the five ascetic friends with whom he had practiced, all of whom were very advanced in meditation.[49] The Dhamma of co-arising is "unattainable by mere reasoning"[50] but requires various kinds of meditative practices that help practitioners to recognize, examine, deal with, and eventually transform their conditioned behavioral habits and thinking patterns, emotional turbulences, and deeply-seated egocentric propensities. Saying that the *Dhamma* is unattainable by mere reasoning is very different from saying that it is entirely beyond human reasoning. Likewise, saying that one needs meditative discipline to see dependent origination does not mean that *nibbāna* is a mystical feeling. The rash rational-mystical dichotomy proposed by Max Weber should be avoided. In the Buddhist framework, just as greed and hatred are closely related to the delusion of egocentric attachment, the emotive transformation enabled by mental training is closely related to the conceptual trans-formation fostered by wisdom development.[51] Repeated meditative practices help a person work through her or his "inner" problems and acquire "inner peace." They also afford one the calmness and clarity to see deeper into the dynamic relationships between self and others, which furthers compassion and fortifies the volition for taking wholesome actions. "Inner calm and clear understanding produce a heightened moral sensibility which helps us distinguish more clearly between right and wrong," Prebish and Keown point out.[52] Advanced meditative states and wisdom, in the very practical, this-worldly clas-sical Buddhist discourses, are to be manifested in wholesome ethical behavior that is beneficial to all sentient beings.

The fact that traditional Buddhist teachers commonly teach that change *starts* with working on one's own mind does not indicate that the whole Buddhist *dukkha*-alleviating project also *stops* at creating peaceful mental states. In the Buddha's teachings, people are socio-psycho-physical compounds that are conditioning, and conditioned by, each other. Social realities and cultural norms find their ways into people's consciousness and are reflected in their bodily, verbal, and mental actions. Mental constructions and emotive states of people, in turn, may materialize through actions and become part of the social realities that condition people. Greedy, aggressive, egocentric individu-als and social injustices and conflicts beget each other, whereas "inner" peace and fair social structures nourish each other. Traditionally, Bud-dhist ethics places much emphasis on each individual's conscientious effort of working on her or his own mind and behaviors, but that does not negate the importance of reconstructing social structures so that they are humane and conducive to proper behaviors and peaceful and benevolent mental states.

If the cessation of *dukkha* can be compared to road safety, it can be understood that, besides infrastructures and traffic laws, road safety also requires each individual on the road to have adequate driving skills, to abide by the traffic laws, to be concerned with others' safety as much as with one's own, and to be fully aware of what is happening around her or him. One is less likely to be law-abiding or fully aware if one is self-absorbed and only concerned with getting to the destination as soon as possible. Self-concern, however, is not categorically negative, for a person may train herself or himself to be a very skillful driver and may be very cautious and law-abiding out of the concern for her or his own safety. However, a skillful, cautious, law-abiding driver may still be involved in accidents because there are drivers who do not care how their driving is going to affect others. Likewise, wide, smooth roads and sound traffic laws, albeit necessary, in and of themselves cannot guarantee road safety. Driving as recklessly as others rarely, if ever, achieves the goal of waking others up to reflect on the damages they have caused or may cause. Implementing more severe punishments has not effectively made all drivers more mindful. Giving up on others' potentials of changing themselves and giving up driving altogether will not ensure one's own safety, either, for one may still be hit as a pedestrian by someone who is driving under the influence of alcohol or narcotics, or by someone who is distracted by various electronic devices. Real road safety depends on finding ways to prompt all people, especially those whose driving has been causing the most harm, to improve their driving skills, to observe the laws more closely, to build safe roads and implement reasonable traffic laws, and to maintain lucidity and be more mindful, out of the concern for their own safety if not for others'.

The cessation of *dukkha*, likewise, depends on explicating the interconditionality of human existence to all and convincing each and every person to work on their own conduct and be aware of their mental states, while simultaneously striving for fair and humane social structures out of the concern for the well-being of all. "It is wrong," Sulak Sivaraksa avers, "to try to adjust the external world without training one's mind to be neutral and selfless. It is also wrong to be calm and detached without a proper concern to bring about better social conditions for all who share our planet."[53] The Buddhist path to the cessation of *dukkha* seeks to address both the "inner" mental states and tendencies, and the "outer" behaviors and practices.

Person-in-Community: Buddhist Community-Building Ideals

The view of interdependent co-arising, the view that the effects of any action travel in multiple directions simultaneously and will have layers of repercussions, can be very frightening. Considering that any harmful move on anyone's part may be broadcast through the entire web due to the unavoidable interrelationships, the day may never come when one can congratulate oneself that the job is done. One may not even find the world making enough progress, if in a greater scheme it is making progress at all. Even if one can be sure that she or he is heading toward the right direction with regard to a certain issue, the situation may still be dreadful considering that one may be surrounded by people who do not see the interconnectedness, keep operating in the same self-centered, *dukkha*-inflicting mode, and even demand others to do so. To make it worse, one may have familial and emotional ties with those who demand one's self to conform to the *dukkha*-inducing "norms" and so may fear the consequences of giving up the conventional ways. In Minnie Bruce Pratt's words, "This is a fear that can cause us to be hesitant in making fundamental changes or taking drastic actions that differ from how we were raised. We don't want to lose the love of the first people who knew us; we don't want to be standing outside the circle of home, with nowhere to go."[54] It is a fear of being alienated, isolated, and rejected by the people with whom one is most familiar and to whom one is most close.

Worse still, in the interconnected web, there is no center to be found, nor is there any clearly defined path that can guarantee one's rightness and/or righteousness. The interconnectedness indicates that moral codes do not have intrinsic value or ontological significance. Rather, in the "contextual pragmatism" of Buddhism discussed in Chapter 2, the right and wrong of an action are determined only when all dimensions of that action are put into consideration, including one's mentality at the time of taking the action, the concrete results produced by the action, and the impacts on the well-being of both self and others. The Dalai Lama expresses a similar view when he says,

> We have no means of discriminating between right and wrong if we do not take into account others' feelings, other' suffering. . . . ethical conduct is not something we engage in because it is somehow right in itself but because, like ourselves, all others desire to be happy and to avoid suffering. . . . if we cannot at least imagine the potential impact of our actions on others, then we have no means to discriminate between right and wrong, between what is appropriate and what is not, between harming and non-harming.[55]

Furthermore, with any bodily, verbal, or mental action taken, either by self or by others, one's "self" may be changed in the sense that one's ideological or social position may be shifted, one's interrelationships with others may be reconstituted, and one's familiar behavioral patterns may become inadequate (if they are ever adequate). As a result, it becomes exceedingly difficult to console oneself of doing the right thing, or to reckon oneself a good, righteous person without any doubt. It is overwhelming to have to face and respond to the new situations that ever present themselves, to engage in continuous self-reflection and self-criticism, and to readjust and re-discipline oneself constantly in accordance with the ever-changing-ness of the world.

That is, in light of interdependent co-arising, being ethical is not the same thing as following rules in a manner as if those rules represent any inalterable Truth. Instead, being ethical is a never-ending challenge. Sallie King explains this "developmental aspect" of Buddhist ethics: "[W]e will never reach the ideal or perfect level of development, but we orient ourselves by reaching toward it and we never stop trying to get closer."[56] Accordingly, nibbāna is better understood as a perfection of ethics rather than a state that transcends ethics; one can go beyond following rules, but one does not "transcend" being ethical. To be ethical, one has to be acutely aware of the intricate interconditionality and to strive for the most wholesome actions possible at every moment, in accordance with any shifting of position and any changing of interrelationships. Along this line, Payutto states, "Good deeds can be far reaching, endless, and changeable, depending on particular circumstances and contexts."[57] Likewise, the Dalai Lama maintains, "the moral value of a given act is to be judged in relation both to time, place, and circumstance and to the interests of the totality of all others in the future as well as now."[58] "Wisdom" in the Buddhist sense is the ability to see the interconditionality among people and among things so that one can, at every step, choose the most dukkha-alleviating course of actions possible. The farther and wider one sees on the intricate web of causes and conditions, the more likely one is to discipline one's self and train one's mind in order to perform the most socially responsible actions possible. And yet it is through self-discipline that one can begin to attenuate egocentric attachment and attune oneself to the kind of mental training that will lead to the wisdom that sees co-arising. As explicated in the section above, in the Three Learnings of the Noble Eightfold Path, wisdom development and ethical discipline inform and fortify each other.

However, the characteristic of samsāra is that most people, Buddhists and non-Buddhists alike, are not enlightened. Most people in samsāra are yet to develop the kind of complete awareness that sees all the causes and repercussions of one's action in the interconnected web of existence. Most people in samsāra are yet to forgo the self-centered patterns of thinking and behaving. Considering the phenomena in the world as either for or against themselves, most people in samsāra lack the volition/disposition to strive for the well-being of all and do not subject themselves to either ethical self-discipline or mental training. Without ethical discipline and mental training, it is unlikely that the wisdom that sees interconditionality will be developed. In the same way that ethical discipline, mental training, and wisdom development enhance and reinforce each other, the lack of any one of the three impedes the development and maturation of the other two. In terms of taking actions, the difficulty with the network causality conveyed by co-arising is not that it is an inaccurate description of the reality of social existence. Rather, the difficulty lies in the fact that too much needs to be reworked at the same time in order to transform *samsāra* into *nibbāna*. As Sulak Sivaraksa aptly puts it, "Merely tinkering with one link in the complex circle of causation does not stop the process that leads to violence and warfare. Rather, the practice of Buddhism strives to address each aspect of the process in a holistic way. This requires not just a counter-psychology, but also a counter-culture, a counter-economy, and counter-policies."[59] Ahangamage Tudor Ariyaratne, the leader of the Sarvodaya Shramadāna movement in Sri Lanka, similarly states, "In the Buddhist perspective, development is an awakening process. . . . It is a sustained effort to awaken in all aspects, spiritual and ethical as well as social and economic, the individual, the family, the community, rural as well as urban groups, nations, and the world community."[60]

Daunting as it may be, the Third Noble Truth in Buddhism teaches that cessation of *dukkha* is possible. It is possible to reach *nibbāna*. In the Buddhist program of reconstructing both of one's self and the world, one begins with tending one's bodily, verbal, and mental actions here and now, which is reflected in the fact that ethical discipline is generally considered the logical first among the Three Learnings, even though there is really no linear "first" in the *kammic* network and the reconstruction can theoretically begin anywhere. As a matter of fact, all continue to act in the world, and as such all continue to co-construct the world as well as the beings embedded and entangled in it, irrespective of the levels of mental calmness and wisdom attainment. It is therefore urgent that one be prompted, persuaded, and trained, to position oneself among others and consider the repercussions of one's actions. One may still be very far from seeing all directions and all layers of the repercussions of any single action, but one can begin with considering the ways in which one's actions affect others in one's immediate social circles.

This is why, I contend, the *Sangha* is one of the Three Jewels in Buddhism, in which Buddhists take refuge alongside the Buddha and the *Dhamma*. Recalling the political assembly of the Sākya tribe at the time of the Buddha, the *Sangha* was established to be a nonhierarchical community in which people who held the cessation of *dukkha* as their goal made decisions together and shared resources, keeping in mind their individual actions affected the well-being of all. Instead of a collective term denoting exclusively the monastic males who pursued *nibbāna* individually, the *Sangha* was an institutional device that brought the sociality of existence front and center, thereby allowing people to see the co-arising of self and others, motivating them to recondition themselves and to behave in more socially conscionable ways. In the turbulent ocean of *samsāra*, Buddhists are taught to take refuge in the Teacher, in his teachings, and in a community of "good friends" who, in their different personalities and perspectives, inspire and support the development of virtue, benevolence, and wisdom, which are essential in transforming *dukkha*-inducing behaviors to *dukkha*-alleviating ones.

With regard to the ways in which members of the *Sangha* should behave toward each other, the Buddha taught the "six principles of cordiality" (*sārāṇīyā dhammā*). They are: (1) to maintain "bodily acts of loving-kindness both in public and in private" toward one's companions in the holy life; (2) to maintain "verbal acts of loving-kindness both in public and in private" toward one's companions in the holy life; (3) to maintain "mental acts of loving-kindness both in public and in private" toward one's companions in the holy life; (4) to share without reservation "any gain of a kind that accords with the Dhamma and has been obtained in a way that accords with the Dhamma" with one's companions in the holy life; (5) to dwell both in public and in private possessing in common with one's companions in the holy life those liberating virtues that are conducive to concentration; and (6) to dwell both in public and in private possessing in common with one's companions in the holy life "that view that is noble and emancipating, and leads one who practices in accordance with it to the complete destruction of suffering."[61]

It is illuminating that all of the six principles revolve around sociality. A member is taught to evince loving-kindness toward one's companions in the *Sangha* through their bodily, verbal, and mental actions. She or he is to maintain that benevolence even in private, which means she or he is to keep the interconditionality with others constantly in mind and to conduct oneself accordingly in deeds, speeches, and thoughts. Always situating oneself among others as such, one shares resources instead of claiming them for oneself or acquiring them through unwholesome means. One nurtures in others as well as in oneself wholesome mental states. Moreover, one cultivates and helps others to cultivate the wisdom that sees co-arising while manifesting that wisdom in practices. As shown in Chapter 2, good friends, i.e., companions in the effort of ceasing *dukkha*, prompt one to engage in wholesome practices and help bring those practices to fruition. Through maintaining loving-kindness and sharing resources, members of the *Sangha* were to live "in concord, with mutual appreciation, without disputing, blending like milk and water, viewing each other with kindly eyes."[62]

Besides good companionship, ethical discipline is another precursor of the Noble Eightfold Path that is effective in bringing Buddhist practices to fruition. The teaching that consciousness depends on the socio-cultural environment to arise suggests the primacy of conduct and directs people's attention to the roles that their own actions play in molding one's own "self" as well as the socio-cultural norms. Recognizing people's responsibilities for their own individual characters as well as for the social realities, from its beginning Buddhism has emphasized ethics.[63] Buddhist ethics is often carried out in the form of moral self-conquest (*dharmavijaya*), which is to be taken up voluntarily by individual persons as a result of seeing the fundamental sociality of human life and realizing that any mental, verbal, and physical behavior has its impacts, on oneself as well as others. Therefore Buddhist ethical discipline takes the form of vows or precepts, rather than regulations or commandments. People cannot "blend like milk and water" if rules are imposed on them instead of being voluntarily taken up by them. In Buddhist thought, the need of discipline has to be recognized by the individual self, the practice of it has to be out of a sense of social responsibility and a desire for social well-being, and the methods of discipline have to be agreed upon by the self as well as holding the prospect of initiating positive chains of reactions throughout the network of social living. The practice of *self*-discipline is to usher in a more just and peaceful mode of coexistence by means of altering people's consciousness and behavioral patterns, starting with oneself.

It is significant that the collective term for the precepts that *Sangha* members voluntarily vow to take is *Vinaya*, which is *vi-naya*, literally meaning "leading in a different direction."[64] Though one is conditioned by the socio-cultural contexts, one can make a difference by leading the co-arising in a different direction, instead of repeating and reinforcing the currently existing *dukkha*-inducing conditions. Instead of expecting others to perform rigid binary gender norms that have caused *dukkha* of many kinds, for example, one can train oneself to be concerned with "wholesomeness" first and to be acceptant when seeing different performances of gender. Instead of justifying aggression or even glorifying war, one can train oneself to adhere to nonviolence in behavior and to dissolve from within the emotive and intellectual dregs that lead to aggression. Instead of mindlessly pursuing material gains at the expense of others, one can train oneself to be mindful with one's consumption and to uproot the seeds of acquisitiveness from one's mentality. Therefore, in explaining the reason for keeping the *Vinaya*, Indian Buddhist scholar G. S. P. Misra notes, "With the help of this [i.e., *Vinaya*], man can bring about a change in the circumstances he has been put in."[65] Ethical discipline is one of the means by which one changes the socio-cultural *rūpa* as well as oneself.

The *Vinaya* was formulated in the context of the *Sangha* and for the existence and cohesion of the *Sangha*. Therefore, even though the *Vinaya* is a set of monastic precepts that lay people generally do not take, the intentions of its formulation are worth considering in exploring the Buddhist ideals of community building. The Pāli *Vinaya* states that the precepts in the Buddhist monastic community were established with ten intentions:

1. Protecting the community
2. Insuring the community's comfort
3. Warding off ill-meaning people
4. Helping well-behaved monks and nuns
5. Destroying present defilements
6. Preventing future defilements
7. Benefiting non-followers
8. Increasing the number of followers
9. Establishing the discipline
10. Observing the rules of restraint.[66]

As an individual is a socio-psycho-physical compound that interdependently arises with others, she or he is conditioned by as well as conditioning the socio-cultural sediments: what is outside of the individual's skin goes in, and what is inside of the individual's skin comes out. Buddhist self-discipline is to stop flowing unconsciously with the dominant socio-cultural forces and to stop unreflectively reproducing and perpetuating the existing norms. Instead, through self-discipline one actively monitors the dialectical relation between what is outside of oneself and what is inside. Besides consciously screening what comes in ("observing the rules of restraint"—number 10 in the quote above), it is also necessary to eliminate some of that which has already gotten in ("destroying present defilements"—number 5). When the conditioning forces in the society are revealed and critiqued as such, it is then possible to have a psychological space in which a different perspective can be opened up, a different kind of consciousnesses can be developed, and the volition to resist the power structure, or the volition to change the reality, can be generated and sustained. When what goes out is carefully watched, one may be able to stop reinforcing the current way of life that may be mutually destructive, and one may proceed to unsettle those socio-cultural sediments that have been problematic. Then it is possible to bring about a more mutually beneficial way of coexistence, and thereby benefit non-followers (number 7) and prevent future defilements (number 6), both on the part of the self and on the part of others.

Some of the reasons for having precepts in the Buddhist communities (or any other communities for that matter) are very practical. For one thing, people in the same community often do not think and act the same, which may become problematic when some members disregard community interests altogether and take advantage of others' good behaviors. They deplete the resources shared by the whole community and erode the mutual trust that has been built over time by all community members. This type of behavior, unfortunately, has become all too familiar in modern times, with corporations depleting both moral capital and natural capital of the global community.[67] Therefore, some precepts are needed in order to protect those who behave themselves out of their care for the whole community (number 4) and to ensure the long-term comfort and harmony of the community (number 2).

For another, when individuals or communities need to network for a cause that is of mutual concern, keeping mutually agreed-upon precepts is an effective means of preventing individuals or communities from getting into conflicts. Roongraung Boonyoros puts it well when he expounds the reason that householders need the Five Precepts, "The reality is that, of necessity, we already have relationships with people everywhere. We are surrounded by people with different duties and needs, different habits and immediate goals, with whom we must associate simply to accomplish the diverse tasks of our daily lives."[68] Self-discipline denotes that each party, be it an individual or a community, should take responsibility for the well-being of all parties, given the existing and inevitable interconnections amongst them. The practice of self-discipline is thus mutually protective (number 1).

Moreover, it helps to establish the reputation of the community (or the network of communities; number 9) and enhance its ability in moving toward the greater goal that all parties involved desire to reach. In addition, the voluntary self-discipline on the part of individuals in the community (or individual communities in the network) may have the double effects of attracting those who envision a harmonious life with others (number 8), and of warding off those self-indulgent people who only want to take advantage of others (number 3). As such, "The monastic discipline (Vinaya) developed by the Buddha was designed to shape the Sangha as an ideal community, with the optimum conditions for spiritual growth."[69]

Providing "the optimal conditions for spiritual growth," the Sangha that the Buddha set up was to operate by consensus. Peter Harvey notes, "The Buddha advocated frequent meetings of each local Sangha, with the aim of reaching a unanimous consensus in matters of common concern (D.II.76–7). If necessary, there was also provision for voting and majority rule (Vin.II.84)."[70] This participatory decision-making process, Simon Zadek points out, was to help overcome egocentric attitudes and thus can be considered an aid to achieving nibbāna.[71] It is another way of putting the sociality of existence front and center, reminding people that any decision affects the well-being of all, themselves included. No one should be making decisions for others based on her or his own perspective and concerns alone.

To share resources and make decisions communally is not to eliminate individual differences and make everyone the same. To begin with, in the analysis of the five aggregates, due to the differences in individuals' life experiences and their unique ways of putting things together (saṅkhāra), no two persons are ever the same, nor is it practical to expect them to be the same. Additionally, according to the Nikāya texts, the Buddha never seemed to expect, much less demand, uniformity. Quite the contrary, he affirmed his disciples for what they had been, each in his own right. In the Mahāgosiṅga Sutta, six of the Buddha's disciples were asked the question, "What kind of bhikkhu could illuminate the delightful Gosiṅga Sāla-tree Wood?"[72] Judging from their answers, they all understood the question to be: What kind of bhikkhu was the ideal and could bring the most good to that local sangha where they were dwelling. Each of the six answered by describing the kind of bhikkhu he himself was, with the talent and achievement for which he himself was known. Each of these disciples naturally perceived and pursued the ideal in different ways because their dispositions and capacities had been conditioned by different co-arising and because of the working of their different *saṇkhāra*. Sāriputta finally brought the question to the Buddha and asked, "Which of us has spoken well?"[73] Essentially Sāriputta was asking the Buddha to identify one single ideal for the whole *sangha*. The Buddha said, "You have all spoken well, Sāriputta, each in his own way."[74] Anyone who was determined to dedicate oneself to the realization of the *Dhamma* could bring good to the *sangha*. This is further implied in the following words of the Buddha:

> Hear also from me what kind of bhikkhu could illuminate this Gosinga Sāla-tree Wood. Here, Sāriputta, when a bhik-khu has returned from his almsround, after his meal, he sits down, folds his legs crosswise, sets his body erect, and establishing mindfulness in front of him, resolves: "I shall not break this sitting position until through not clinging my mind is liberated from the taints." That kind of bhikkhu could illuminate this Gosinga Sāla-tree Wood.[75]

In this manner, "Buddhism does not recognize one single way,"[76] and uniformity is not expected, much less demanded. "Contrary to the sectarian assumptions of our various sub-traditions past and present," John Makransky maintains, "the history of Buddhist praxis and doctrine would indicate that there has never been only one narrowly delimited way to waken, and that any means to awaken is also a potential object of clinging."[77] Differences in terms of understanding of, and approach to, the cessation of *dukkha*, as long as they do not result in unwholesome consciousness and conduct, need to be appreciated and respected. What makes it possible for individuals with different ideals and temperaments to live in concord is mutual appreciation, but not uniformity.

Uniformity, some theorists point out, may negatively affect movements for justice and peace, and even reinforce domination and intensify conflict. Refusing the peace theories of the élite, which rest on order, Johan Galtung asserts that "peace has something to do with *entropy*, here taken in the sense of 'disorder,'" which does not denote "messiness in any pejorative sense."[78] Rather, it points to "high complexity of the system: many and diverse components, and many and diverse ties of interaction between them."[79] He explains,

> [T]he moment the system tends to crystallize, becomes more orderly, then the number of social types (such as nations,

blocs, alliances) becomes smaller; the concentration on one point more pronounced. And the links of interaction no longer fill the total space of possibilities, but tend to connect certain types only, and often mainly in a negative, hostile way. At that point the system may look very orderly, but is in fact poised for destructive battle. . . . With significant diversity and symbiosis deficits our world becomes a war-like system, with efforts to control violence through power balance of power monopoly policies. . . . We are building war structures, not peace structures, very low on diversity and symbiosis; very low on entropy.[80]

The expectation or even imposition of uniformity, in Galtung's view, is precisely what leads to power struggle and warlike behaviors. Long-term peace depends on the presence of different views and possibilities, and the appreciation for such differences. Judging from the criteria for "good friends" mentioned in Chapter 2, it seems that the Buddha would agree. After all, one of the criteria for "good friends" is being able to provide oneself with different perspectives. Diversity and the appreciation for diversity are in fact necessary in reducing egocentrism and egocentric conflicts.

Understandably, the greater the community grows, the less likely is it for consensus to be reached or for the decision-making process to be participatory, and more and more behavioral codes are needed to ensure the day-to-day operation of the community. Ethical discipline has always been a part of the Noble Eightfold Path, but as the early Buddhist *Sangha* gradually reached "the acme of worldly gain," "the acme of fame," "the acme of great learning," and "the acme of long-standing renown," more and more precepts were needed in order to "ward off those things that are the basis for taints" so that the *Sangha* members would not be affected negatively by the newly-gained fame and the gradually-accrued material goods.[81] Later in the Theravāda tradition the number of precepts for *bhikkhus* evolved to be 227, and that for *bhikkhunīs*, 311. Since these precepts were added in response to the situation at that particular time, and given the fact that situations would be constantly changing, the Buddha told Ānanda before his passing: "If they wish, the order may abolish the minor rules after my passing."[82] However, there has been disagreement as to which precepts could be considered "minor," and as a result no precept, not even the *garudhamma* (the eight revered conditions) that were probably interpolated at a later time, is officially abolished in any Buddhist tradition, even though the eight revered conditions have virtually been nonexistent in some modern-day Taiwanese *sanghas*.[83]

The enormous growth of the Buddhist *Sangha* also resulted in more hierarchical internal structure and eventually the split of the *Sangha*. It was recorded that, before his passing, the Buddha said, "whereas the *bhikkhus* are in the habit of addressing one another as 'friend,' this custom is to be abrogated after my passing. Senior *bhikkhus* shall address more junior *bhikkhus* by their name, their clan or as 'friend' (*āvuso*), whereas more junior *bhikkhus* are to address their senior either as 'Lord' (*bhante*) or as 'Venerable Sir' (*āyasmā*)."[84] Since then, the *Sangha* has been hierarchicalized according to seniority in all traditions of Buddhism. The hierarchicalization, however, could not effectively unify interpretations of the *Dhamma*. When differences in interpretations grew into disagreements in principles, the *Sangha* split. According to tradition, the first split happened at (or shortly after) the Second Council in Vaiśālī, which was held one hundred years after the Buddha's passing.

While it was uncertain whether or not the Buddha had foreseen the immense growth in size, the hierarchicalization, and the eventual split of the *Sangha*, it was clear that it did not take a large group of people to form a *sangha*, nor was hierarchy of seniority always present. The first *sangha* consisted of the Buddha and the five ascetics with whom the Buddha had practiced before his *nibbāna*. The presence of the mini-*sangha* of Anuruddha, Nandiya, and Kimbila, who had been living in concord and benefiting one another, was extolled as "a great gain for the Vajjians."[85] Considering the purposes of having communities, it may actually be more beneficial to have smaller egalitarian communities rather than big hierarchical ones. Sulak Sivaraksa maintains, "it is only through the establishment of a public sphere where one becomes engaged in the process of making decisions which will affect himself and other members of the community that one comes to recognize social responsibilities and the nature of human interdependence."[86] In a smaller social circle, it is easier for people to see the impacts of their actions on each other and to generate benevolent social concerns. It is also easier to include everyone in the decision-making process when the community is small. Genuine mutual appreciation and respect are more likely to be developed when the community is egalitarian and people in the community are not in any way coerced by people occupying the upper echelons in the hierarchy.

It remains that, in Buddhist thought, the wider that one sees the ways in which one's actions reverberate through the web of interconditionality, the wiser and the more *dukkha*-alleviating choices one will make. For this reason, small geographical or spiritual communities are not to be closed systems that reject exchanges with others. Communities are effective "skillful means" that help people generate benevolence and develop the wisdom of seeing co-arising, both of which are indispensable in actualizing the goal of *nibbāna*. They are not to become yet another object of ego-attachment. After all, communities change as individuals and the interconnections amongst them change; no community has an abiding, unchanging "Self." Therefore, no community or community identity is in and of itself so sacred that it should be preserved as it is, in all aspects, at all costs. Nor can a "sacred community" as such be built once and for all. New life situations, new people, and new interaction patterns among people will always emerge, and they demand new approaches and new codes of conduct. Previous decisions can serve as references, but no rule or custom will be "sacred" for all people at all times. With this understanding, Thích Nhât Hanh states in the Charter of the Order of Interbeing: "Every word and every sentence in this Charter is subject to change, so that the spirit of the Charter will be allowed to remain alive throughout the history of the practice. . . . This Charter . . . should be revised and amended . . . in order to keep it relevant to today's societies."[87]

Moreover, it is worth noting that, at the time of the Buddha, the *Sangha* was not geographically defined. The Buddha instructed his disciples to go forth for the welfare of many and maintain daily contact with people, which in effect meant that the *bhikkhus* and *bhikkhunīs* were to form a *sangha* with people of the localities to which they traveled. Thus one did not always have the same *sangha* members around; members of a *sangha* in any locality were not always one's old acquaintances and might not come from the same region. Being in a community helps one feel connected and see connections, so that one is prompted to dedicate oneself to wholesome and *dukkha*-alleviating practices out of benevolence and wisdom. Once sufficiently, though never fully, grounded in wholesomeness, one is encouraged to form connections with unfamiliar others, thereby influencing others to take up wholesome practices as well. Bhikkhu Puṇṇa, for example, was recognized by the Buddha as having enough self-control and peacefulness to go forth to the Sunāparanta country, where people were known for being "fierce and rough." Puṇṇa then went and "established five hundred men lay followers and five hundred women lay followers in the practice."[88]

A person needs a community, a small enough social circle, as the starting point of accustoming oneself to wholesome practices. Clinging to a certain geographical location or a certain community identity, however, is a form of ego-attachment and therefore is discouraged in Buddhism. Instead, one is encouraged to build more connections and form communities with multiple others, trying to maintain benevolence and wisdom at every moment, with every "other" that one encounters. Exactly as Dharmachari Lokamitra, Indian Buddhist scholar and the leader of the dalit group Trailokya Bauddha Mahasangha Sahayaka Gana, states: "Spiritual friendship is clearly more than just a context for practice, it is a practice in itself. It requires constant effort to be able to cultivate the friendship and trust necessary to be able to be fully open, confess, and rejoice in the merits of others."[89] It is *the process of community building*, rather than a particular community with its particular set of rules and customs, that matters. Additionally, with colonialism and capitalistic neo-colonialism broadening and deepening various forms of *dukkha* globally, it is increasingly difficult, and perhaps even socially irresponsible, for people to consider only the interests of their local communities.

Viewed from the perspective of interdependent co-arising, a socially constituted and constrained subject still can make a difference, and social institutions and cultural conventions can be changed in the same way that socialized individuals can be.[90] As a matter of fact, the very establishment of an alternative community that vows to "lead in a different direction" (*vi-naya*) indicates that, from the Buddha's point of view, many of the social institutions and cultural conventions *should* be changed, and socialized individuals are responsible for effecting those changes. The way in which a socialized individual can better society is through moral self-conquest on the one hand, and on the other hand building more connections with multiple others in manifold aspects. The Buddhist ideal of community-building is for people to train themselves to maintain benevolence for others in the community, to respect others as equals and decision-making partners, to share resources with them, and eventually to extend all these practices to all others via forming connections and building communities with them. On the Indra's Net, the change of the shade and color on some jewels will be reflected on others, and through enough connections can be reflected on all. Small enough communities allow people to see and feel the interconnections and thus motivate them to discipline themselves out of a sense of social responsibility. It is easier for people in small communities to feel the need to recondition their own attitudes, tendencies, and habitual behavioral patterns for the benefits of both self and others. By delimiting a tentative social circle in which one can more easily cultivate virtue, benevolence, and the wisdom of seeing co-arising, communities also provide temporary grounding and guidance in the overwhelming, seemingly impossible task of reaching *nibbāna*. Benevolence, sharing, and egalitarian practices, once sufficiently developed in some people through the help of small communities, can influence multiple others through interrelationships.

What the Buddhist path provides that does not exactly find a counterpart in contemporary justice discourses is its attention to, and techniques of dealing with, individuals' "inner" states.[91] Emotions, values, beliefs, dispositions, and thinking patterns affect not only the individuals who hold them, but manifest "outwardly" in their interactions with one another and thereby in social realities, which in turn condition the ways in which people think, feel, and act. From the perspective informed by the teaching of interdependent co-arising, it is insufficient to address only the societal or structural problems without at the same time addressing the ways in which people think and feel, and the ways in which people behave themselves and interact with one another. The Buddhist path therefore consists of three main parts that support and enhance each other. Ethical discipline is fundamental in generating social awareness and making concentrated meditation possible. Various meditative practices, through repetition, help generate compassion, sustain social engagement, heighten awareness, and remove the sources of emotional disturbance and epistemological prejudice, dissolving their residual effects. Together they are conducive to the rise of wisdom, which in Buddhism refers to both the cognitive aspect of seeing the interconditionality of each situation, and the volitional aspect of continuously striving to act in the most wholesome ways possible to break the cycle of *dukkha*-production.

While engaging in the *samsāric* world can be utterly enervating, which is exacerbated by the antagonistic reasoning in contemporary justice discourses, the Buddha's teachings provide a different way of thinking about and coping both "inner" troubles and "outer" obstacles. With the wisdom of seeing co-arising, one does not get engulfed in the animosity that arises with the "either with us or against us" oppositional thinking. Meditative practices, as Rita Gross finds, further tame aggression, bring forth clarity, and sustain continuous compassionate engagement in the world.[92] The Three Learnings contained in the Noble Eightfold Path, when practiced in the midst of spiritual communities that inspire and support such practices, allow practitioners to take a proactive role in reconditioning themselves and redirecting, together with other practitioners, the co-arising in the world from *dukkha*-inducing to *dukkha*-alleviating. They nurture in the practitioners the consideration for others, raise awareness of the co-arising both within and around themselves, direct them to see the myriad ways in which they are connected with others, strengthen their benevolent volition, and enable them to engage in the world with a clear mind and work on the myriad problems in the *samsāra* for the long haul.

6

Conclusion

This-Worldly *Nibbāna*
and Participatory Peacemaking

The Buddhist goal is *nibbāna*, the cessation of *dukkha*. In accordance with the Buddha's practical concerns and the socio-ethical implications of interdependent co-arising, *nibbāna* can be understood to have a very this-worldly and dynamic character. If all persons are socio-psycho-physical compounds whose actions are conditioning each other's behaviors, emotions, and consciousnesses, then for as long as they live as co-arisen beings, *nibbāna* is not a state of mind or a static existence in which co-arising stops. It is a never-ending process of alleviating *dukkha* and, more importantly, of discerning and removing the causes of *dukkha*, including egocentric attachments as well as the aspects of socio-cultural *rūpa* that justify or even encourage *dukkha*-producing actions. Given the interconnections among beings, it also involves building connections throughout the web of co-arising while continuously striving for "wholesome" actions and choosing the courses of actions that would be the most beneficial for both others and oneself.

Part of this dynamic, this-worldly sense of *nibbāna* finds a parallel in contemporary peace studies literature. In 1990, twenty-one years after theorizing about "structural violence," Johan Galtung introduced the concept of "cultural violence," which refers to "those aspects of culture, the symbolic sphere of our existence—exemplified by religion and ideology, language and art, empirical science and formal science (logic, mathematics)—that can be used to justify or legitimize direct or structural violence."[1] Galtung considers direct violence, structural

violence, and cultural violence to be forming a triangle and states
that the causal chain can begin with any one of the three. In terms
of time relation, however, he thinks cultural violence is the invariant,
the permanent condition underlying and justifying direct violence
and structural violence.[2] Cultural violence renders aggression (direct
violence) and domination (structural violence) normal and natural,
which on the one hand sanctions exploitation by the "topdogs" and
on the other hand pushes the "underdogs" to get even or get revenge.[3]
Peace, therefore, requires much more than simply removing direct violence. Galtung terms the absence of direct violence "negative peace."
"Positive peace"[4] requires the presence of social justice (the absence
of structural violence) and, more fundamentally, the restructuring of
cultural norms so that direct and structural violence become unacceptable (the absence of cultural violence). Similarly, the cessation of
dukkha entails far more than stopping suffering in its obvious forms
in the material and physical planes; it requires removing the causes
of dukkha embedded in the socio-cultural rūpa, including the unjust
social structures and the cultural values that encourage, sanction, and
glorify aggression, antagonism, domination, and so on.

At the same time, Buddhist Dhamma teaches that one cannot
attain nibbāna via dukkha-producing mental, verbal, and physical
actions. One who is bound by the disturbing emotions and delusional
thinking cannot bring about the cessation of dukkha. Acting out of the
"three poisons" of greed, aversion, and egocentrism, one is in effect
spreading and promoting greed, aversion, and egocentrism in the kammic network, even if one's purpose is to stop suffering. In Buddhist
thinking, to cease dukkha, one has to perform dukkha-ceasing actions
bodily, verbally, and mentally. The means and the end are not different things: "They coalesce, Nibbāna and the path, just as the waters of
the Ganges and the Yamunā coalesce and flow together."[5] "There is
no way to peace," Thích Nhât Hanh puts it well, "peace is the way."[6]
In other words, "Peace work means, first of all, being peace."[7] This
idea of "being peace" may seem simple. However, contained in it,
as Sallie King observes, are "the idea of approach conflict free of an
assumption of adversarial relations; a commitment to profound, prin-
cipled nonviolence; an understanding of the web of interdependence
as the fabric of our existence; and awareness of the great importance
of motivation and attitude in shaping the nature and outcome of an
action."[8] If samsāra is an ongoing cycle of the co-arising of dukkha, then
nibbāna is a dynamic process of striving for dukkha-free deeds, words,
and thoughts, instead of an endpoint that can be brought about by

dukkha-filled actions. "Being peace" is, in fact, a corollary of the Buddha's teachings, as shown so far in this book.

After listing twenty strong points of Buddhism in its possible contribution to world peace and six points in which Buddhism appears to be weak, Galtung concludes that "Buddhism has a tremendous potential as a source for active peace politics," albeit it remains largely untapped.[9] As a nontheistic tradition whose original Teacher discouraged egocentric attachment and emphasized the pragmatics of the well-being of all, Buddhism has much to contribute to contemporary peace and nonviolence movements. On the one hand, its non-dogmatic perspective allows accommodation of different views and, in fact, encourages its followers to develop all-encompassing "wisdom" by building connections with, and learning from, multiple "good friends." On the other hand, its nontheistic and pragmatic appeal makes it possible for people of a variety of religious affiliations to accept and adopt its teachings without giving up the religious or nonreligious identities with which they are familiar. More importantly, the dynamic constructiveness conveyed by the teaching of interdependent co-arising promotes a different way of considering ethics. With its central teaching refuting any static, eternal existence and any inherent, unchanging "nature," Buddhist ethics is an ongoing process of striving to be ethical in the ever-changing contexts rather than a prescribed, inalterable structure of behavioral codes. Upholding the cessation of *dukkha* as its unwavering goal, nonetheless, Buddhist ethics does not fall into extreme relativism but retains a universal character. Sallie King's description of Engaged Buddhist ethical theory may very well be a description of Buddhist social ethics in general:

> Engaged Buddhist ethical theory avoids both ethical relativism and rigid rule following. It maintains ethical objectivity with clear minimum standards that make clear what behaviors are unacceptable; however, it also maintains open-ended moral ideals or virtues that make flexibility possible as one responds to the particularity of each unique situation. The open-ended moral ideals also constitute a standing invitation to each individual to achieve ever higher moral standards.[10]

With its pragmatic, nontheistic teachings of dynamic, interrelational existence expounded through contemporary theories and studies, Buddhism has great potential in motivating people of different identities to engage in the world and participate, each in their own way, in the ongoing reconstruction of a peaceful, *nibbānic* culture for the welfare of all beings implicated in the interconnected web of life.

Boundary-Crossing Interconnections

In the Buddhist understanding of the interdependently co-arisen phenomena in the world, absolute demarcations between groups or schools of thought, like the absolute separation between self and others or between Pure Consciousness and Materiality, is a "mental formation" (*saṅkhāra*). That mental formation results from, and further results in, the ego's wish to reify itself, to isolate itself from non-self elements and beings, and to elevate itself above others. It has been found in some conflict studies that identity attachments play a central role in the inception and escalation of intergroup conflicts.[11] It has also been found that, if in the process of trying to solve conflicts between ethnic or political parties, a mediator reinforces the idea that the relation between them is necessarily adversarial, the parties involved will have difficulty in ever beginning a dialogue, let alone cooperating with each other.[12] Oppositional thinking, being rooted in the attachment to a certain identity-view and in the delusion of the separation of self and others, in Buddhist teachings, is an unenlightened, *dukkha*-producing way of thinking. Emphasizing the ever-changing-ness of an individual's identity as well as the interconnections between self and others, non-Self teaches that an individual person is being constituted and reconstituted in an intricate web of causal and conditional relationships. Understanding non-Self and interdependent co-arising, one will have the wisdom to recognize the expediency of categories and the continuous mutual influences between phenomena, entities, and beings. One who truly understands the Buddhist teaching of non-Self will not hold onto dichotomies or boundaries in an antagonistic manner.

It is worth noting that not to engage in oppositional thinking is not the same as not to be socially engaged. Not to act out of anger, likewise, is not the same as not to act at all. Quite the contrary, the cessation of *dukkha* hinges on ongoing effort of transforming both oneself and others and requires all to be actively involved in the never-ending process of removing *dukkha* as well as the social, cultural, and mental causes of *dukkha*. *Dhammic* actions do not at all exclude challenging the *status quo*, if the *status quo* has been causing suffering. They do, however, exclude the kind of actions taken out of attachment to a certain identity, such as ethnic or sectarian ones, or out of greed or hatred.

Identity attachments begin with naming and reifying the differences conveyed by names. The linguistic utility of naming the "self" easily morphs into the delusion of an ontological existence of a "self" that is separate and separable from all other animate and inanimate worldly phenomena. The reification of the name "self" provides the ground for excluding the non-self others and disregarding their well-being, in whatever way the others are defined. "If the self had intrinsic identity," the Dalai Lama points out, "it would be possible to speak in terms of self-interest in isolation from that of others'."[13] When differences are considered substantial and raised to the ontological level, interconnections amongst differences are nonexistent and unnatural by default, and benevolence is reserved only for one's own "kind," i.e., those whose connections with oneself are obvious and undeniable, such as blood relations. The needs and interests of others are therefore dismissed, and adversity and hostility easily ensue when conflict of interests arises. The attachment to a self-identity can thus obstruct the formation of relationships with others, diminish the benevolence one might have for them, debase them to various degrees, and disregard their needs and interests.

However, as pointed out in the section "The Three Learnings," the Buddhist injunction of abandoning identity-view is not to be mistaken with "fear and disgust with identity." Fear and disgust with identity and craving for static nonexistence, in the Buddha's teachings, are as *dukkha*-producing as clinging to a piece of social construct or mental construct to be one's eternal, unchanging "Self." As the Dalai Lama puts it,

> When we say that things and events can only be established in terms of their dependently originating nature, that they are without intrinsic reality, existence, or identity, we are not denying the existence of phenomena altogether. The "identitylessness" of phenomena points rather to the way in which things exist: not independently but in a sense interdependently. . . . It is, therefore, quite wrong to infer from the idea any sort of nihilistic approach to reality. . . . even the [concept of the] absence of intrinsic existence exists only conventionally.[14]

To say that individual or group differences are not everlasting, nonchanging essences, is not to say that all people are the same or different identities should not exist. Instead of focusing on either commonality or difference, or endorsing the validity of this dichotomy in any way, the Buddha taught interdependent co-arising. Non-Self, in its refusal of accepting any reified identity that is isolated from all others and is supposedly inherently superior (or inferior), is not the negation of any individual self or the denial of any existing difference in personalities and traits. Rather, with its understanding of the constructedness of both "self" and others, non-Self is an affirmation of all different selves embedded in the *kammic* web of existence, including one's own. Given the perspective of the interconnectedness and interconditionality of all, in Buddhism the welfare of oneself is inseparable from the welfare of all others, and the affirmation of oneself is realized through the affirmation of all others.

Like Buddhist teachings, Johan Galtung observes that the exaltation of the Self, and the concomitant debasement of the Other, is one of the major forms of cultural violence.[15] With the exaltation of Self, "Egotism and familism are considered normal. So is nationalism, and—within limits—sexism and racism," while "Altruism across boundaries . . . is easily seen as abnormal."[16] The perspective of network causality conveyed by interdependent co-arising dissuades clinging to a socially or mentally constructed idea of the self, and to the extensions of the self, including self-groups that are defined by blood relations and physical traits. Paradoxically, while buttressing the concept of non-Self, co-arising affirms diversity and emphasizes symbiosis. Diversity and symbiosis are two necessary conditions for the "positive peace" in Galtung's thinking. Galtung explains,

> In nature diversity and symbiosis would lead to ecological balance. In human beings diversity and symbiosis would lead to rich, mature human beings, to persons capable of developing several dispositions within themselves and letting them play together. At the social level diversity and symbiosis would lead to pluralistic, even fascinating societies, not only fragmented into diverse parts but with the parts interacting with each other, constantly evolving. And at the world level diversity and symbiosis would lead to active peace coexistence between several systems . . . Both social and world spaces can evolve so much better through symbiosis between diverse parts.[17]

Inasmuch as diverse beings and groups co-arise with one another, it is futile to pursue individual peace, if the beings in direct or indirect interconnections with the self or self-group do not approach the same kind of peace and liberation. Recognizing the co-constructedness of "self" and "others" and the tentativeness of the boundary between "self" and "others," one may be able to dedicate oneself to the welfare of all that are interconnected through their *kamma*. Maintaining benevolence toward diverse others and building connections and networking with them, therefore, is an indispensable part in attaining the cessation of *dukkha* in Buddhism or "positive peace" in Galtung's thinking. For this reason, I proposed in Chapter 5 that "taking refuge in the *Sangha*" involves dedicating oneself to the process of community-building and networking with myriad others, rather than identifying with, and getting attached to, any particular geographical location or drawing boundaries between "one's own kind" and other-groups.

The fact that the majority of the transmitters and exegetes of the Buddhist *Dhamma* were privileged males may have resulted in the under-emphasis of companionship and social relationship, as well as the elevation of seclusion and individualistic pursuit. With regard to the class bias that transmitters and exegetes of the Buddhist *Dhamma* might carry, Sulak Sivaraksa comments that "when the Sangha and/or members of the leading lay Buddhist communities were close to the rulers, they compromised the teachings of Buddha or lost their moral integrity for non-violent social change."[18] With regard to the transmitters and exegetes' gender bias, Rita Gross comments that "romanticization of aloneness is . . . a common, though unconscious strategy in our hypermasculine and highly alienated culture."[19] In a society highly stratified with class differences *and* gender differences, men of high social status are likely to have grown up perceiving others merely as service-providing instruments without recognizing that they are in fact dependent on those service-providing people. Worse, their life experiences often bring them to "opt for a social adjudication based on power."[20] In their privileged and dominant lifestyle, there is not much need to adjust, or to reconsider, the courses of their actions for the sake of others. When, on occasion, they do recognize their dependence on others' services and kindness, they may find it burdensome, for consideration for others involves thinking beyond their egocentric concerns and reining in their wayward behaviors. Not surprisingly, in the Buddhist *Dhamma* transmitted by such privileged men, isolated individual endeavor is often extolled while the importance of relationships is downplayed. The privileged male masters' class and gender biases not only affect the future generations of *Dharma* followers in their perception and assessment of relationships, but also diminish the privileged males' own experience of the profound joy that can be brought about by walking the Buddhist path with appreciation of interconnections with others. To say the least, the loving-kindness and altruistic joy that they cultivate and experience would be rather "thin" when, deep down, social relationships are considered burdens.

Nevertheless, based on interdependent co-arising, one is not completely liberated from *dukkha* unless all are. The "inner peace" brought about through seclusion is temporal, and it is futile to seek *nibbāna* without continually tending social structures and cultural norms that have been, and will be, conditioning one's emotions and consciousnesses. *Nibbāna* cannot be achieved with one or a few persons' effort, and it certainly cannot be completed with one action. Due to the interdependent nature of social existence, the task of transforming *samsāra* to *nibbāna* requires continuous and patient effort from those who are already aware of the interconditionality. It also depends on spreading through interrelationships wholesome, mutually beneficial practices, and the will to take on such practices. Socio-cultural sedimentation only happens when most people have been engaging in certain types of practices for a long enough time. That means, for one thing, that anyone who wants to alleviate *dukkha* needs to find a way to stay in the cause for the long haul, without feeling enervated or recoursing to *dukkha*-perpetuating measures out of prolonged frustration. In this regard, the "being peace" approach of Engaged Buddhists, Sallie King points out, "can help prevent burnout, a chronic problem among Western social activists."[21] For another, one would need to build connections with multiple and diverse others, engaging them in *dukkha*-alleviating *kamma*.

One may not be able to connect with and influence all kinds of others, especially if the "others" are indifferent to the *dukkha* they have caused or even intentionally uphold *dukkha*-inflicting social structures. Through building as many interconnections as one can, however, eventually someone in one's social circle may be able to reach out and "conscientize" someone in her or his social circle who has the ability and means to influence those who have been inflicting *dukkha*. Or, eventually the network of interconnections will be influential enough that new cultural norms can be reset through change of practices and social institutions, through change of *kamma* and socio-cultural *rūpa*. Anyway, besides continuous effort, one also needs tremendous patience in the ongoing process of reducing and alleviating *dukkha*. It is no accident that patience (Pāli: *khanti*; Sanskrit: *kṣānti*) has been extolled as a virtue together with effort (Pāli: *viriya*; Sanskrit: *vīrya*) throughout Buddhist history. Patience and effort are two of the ten virtuous qualities or "Perfections" (Pāli: *pāramī*; Sanskrit: *pāramitā*) in all Buddhist traditions.[22] It is also no accident that most Buddhist schools teach that it takes many lifetimes to reach *nibbāna*.

The network causality conveyed by interdependent co-arising may shed light on some of the deficiencies of some contemporary social theories and activisms, such as the "single issue" thinking that blames only one person or fixates on one social institution, and the oppositional thinking that fuels self-righteous anger, exhausts the activists, and exacerbates oppositions between individuals or groups. One person or one institution does not create all problems, and removing one person or restructuring one institution cannot solve all problems. For instance, without addressing the alienation that many non-Westerners feel under Westernization in general and U.S. dominance in particular, taking out Osama bin Laden alone cannot eliminate terrorism. Even in the "The Terrorist Threat to the US Homeland" released by the White House on July 17, 2007 that considers primarily the Al-Qa'ida and the threat it posts, the National Intelligence Estimate acknowledges that "violent Islamic extremists" and "non-Muslim terrorist groups" consisting of "small numbers of alienated people" are forming "self-generating cells" and becoming more connected globally, without a centralized "terrorist organization, training camp, or leader."[23] Clearly more people bear anti-U.S. sentiments than just Osama bin Laden, which is partially why many people warn of surge of anti-American violence immediately after bin Laden's death. According to the Pew Global Attitudes Project report released on July, 24, 2007, while 19 of the 47 publics surveyed worldwide consider the United States their most dependable ally, 17 deem it their greatest threat, including countries in South America, Asia, and Africa.[24]

In the same way that eliminating Osama bin Laden would not dissolve anti-American sentiments in many parts of the world, without examining and challenging the naturalized capitalist values and the imperialistic agenda, changing the president will not change U.S. foreign policies. Zillah Eisenstein characterizes U.S. foreign policies as being about "maintaining an imperial kind of globalization" that is composed of "unilateral nationalism and transnational capitalism."[25] David Loy relates that, in a personal communication, the social critic Micah Sifry writes, "Does anybody think that we can send the USS New Jersey to lob Volkswagen-sized shells into Lebanese villages—Reagan, 1983—or loose 'smart bombs' on civilians seeking shelter in a Baghdad bunker—Bush, 1991—or fire cruise missiles on a Sudanese pharmaceutical factory—Clinton, 1999—and not receive, someday, our share in kind?"[26] Loy then suggests some of the more hidden capitalistic and imperialistic concerns behind U.S. foreign policies by asking the question: "how much of U.S. foreign policy in the Middle East has been motivated by our love of freedom and democracy, and

how much by our need—our greed—for its oil?"[27] U.S. foreign policies have been based on corporate interests and backed with military
coercion, particularly since the Second World War, regardless which
political party holds the presidency.[28]

By the same token, advocating women's rights to paid jobs alone
cannot bring forth gender equality. In effect, it has further devalued
the work that most women have traditionally done at home, such as
nurturing, cooking, and cleaning. Domestic work, usually performed by
women, is crucial in both sustaining life and supporting the economy.
The fixation on women's rights to getting paid jobs outside of the home
the same as men, though not without its benefits, is indirectly endorsing
the value system that judges the worthiness of work by the monetary
return it produces, which then is underscoring the unworthiness of
domestic work since it is either unpaid or paid very little.[29] Rachel
Bowlby points out that the devaluation of the feminine-domestic (as
opposed to the masculine-worldly) is even reflected in the various
kinds of negative connotations of the word "domestication."[30] Anne
McClintock and Cynthia Enloe argue that the devaluation of domestic work is not only linked to the devaluation of women but is also
deeply connected to classism, racism, and imperialism.[31] All too often
fixating on one issue only leads to the exacerbation of problems in
other aspects of life, and targeting one individual or one group only
further widens the gap between "us" and "them," creating intense
ideological opposition and real-life hostility.

It is one thing that, out of compassion, one takes actions to rectify
the oppressive situation and redress the *dukkha* produced by those
who are most responsible. It is quite another that one begins with
identifying the enemy, *one* enemy, and then acts out of resentment
and hatred toward them. Being a product of mental formation, absolute demarcation between self and others needs to be perceived and
then disregarded, in the same manner that any beginner of Buddhist
meditation will be taught to deal with their ever-arising thoughts.
Clinging to oppositional demarcation one will act upon it, and acting
upon it one is simply deepening the hostility and planting the seed
of future antagonism, all the while enervating oneself. If one's goal
is the cessation of *dukkha* for all, one cannot afford excluding any
"other" on account of their differences. At the very least, it needs
to be recognized that any difference or opposition at the moment is
difference or opposition *at the moment*. Differences and oppositional
situations can be viewed as a "skillful means" for motivating and
inspiring one to expand the scope of one's benevolent concerns and
strive for a more universal liberation from *dukkha*.

It is also worth remembering that, in Buddhism, discerning those who have been more responsible in *dukkha*-production should not lead to aversion or animosity. The fact that some of the practices of the "others" are *dukkha*-inflicting does not mean that all of their practices are necessarily unwholesome, much less that all those "others" are inherently, inalterably "evil." The fact that certain unfamiliar and different others have inflicted *dukkha* also does not imply unfamiliarity or difference is in and of itself bad. As discussed in Chapter 2, different perspectives provided by "good friends" who are also dedicated to alleviate *dukkha* help one go beyond one's egocentric views and concerns. It is through knowing and interacting with multiple and different others and considering them "good friends" that one gradually grasps the manifold and multifarious ramifications of one's own actions, thereby developing more wisdom and being able to discern and adopt the courses of actions that can benefit many. "The assumption that similarity makes commonality makes alliance makes effective movement is mistaken," feminist activist and theorist Janet R. Jakobsen writes.[32] This view is shared by feminist Zillah Eisenstein, who advocates what she calls "polyversal humanism," which is enacted through "seeking out cultural differences in order to deepen understanding by sharing and decentering the self with a newly fulfilling complexity."[33] "Good friends" of different temperaments and perspectives who are also dedicated to alleviating *dukkha* help one along in the process of training oneself to be more all-encompassing in view and more wholesome in practice. They are therefore considered one of the forerunners of the Noble Eightfold Path.

Just as an individual moral agent needs to practice continuously within a community of different "good friends" so that they can continuously learn from each other and alleviate *dukkha* for each other, an intimate local community that can contribute to the culture of peace and the cessation of *dukkha* will have to be open enough to allow variety amongst its own members, as well as to build connections with various communities outside of itself, so that it can receive inputs from, and render assistance to, those other communities if the situation so requires. For the currently disadvantaged individuals and groups, in particular, it is crucial to cultivate the capacity to connect and work with multiple different other individuals and groups. As feminist Bernice Johnson Reagon puts it, coalition is necessary because the "barred rooms" where minority or minoritized people get together with one's own kind and feel at home "will not be allowed to exist. They will all be wiped out."[34] Disadvantaged people stand a chance to alleviate their own suffering when they are able to cross boundaries, coalesce strengths with people of different identities, and borrow from sources other than the tradition in which one is confined.

Furthermore, liberation from *dukkha* requires everyone's participation in *dukkha*-free actions, just as the cycle of *dukkha* has been set forth due to people's complicity in it. Joanna Macy points out that liberation or emancipation in the early Buddhist texts was not presented as an escape from causation, but was linked to co-arising. Hence Macy maintains that liberation is reached "by employing causation, by using the leverage of conditionality."[35] Living with "multiplicities of contacts and currents," Macy observes, is not only a source of constraint or reinforcement, but also a source of power as well.[36] On the Indra's Net where all jewels are reflecting, and reflected in, each other, a change with the color of a jewel could travel over on the Net and be reflected on other jewels. The more interconnections there are, the sooner and wider the change travels. It is through multiple interrelationships that any *dukkha*-reducing movement can take place, gain momentum, and eventually change the socio-cultural sediments.

Peace at Every Step

Recalling the Buddha's very practical concerns with being ethical in this world at every moment and his teachings against the pervasive social inequity and violence at his time, it is not too far-fetched to conclude that *nibbāna* has a very this-worldly meaning and encompasses enacting peace in everyday life, even though some Buddhist scholars may argue that peace in this world does not constitute the entirety of *nibbāna*. In the interconditioned web of worldly existence, problems or improvements in one aspect of life always reverberate through the web, generating problems or improvements in other aspects. Seeing the ways in which phenomena interdependently co-arise, it is delusional to assume that the rectification of social structures alone will bring forth justice and peace once and for all. It is equally delusional to assume all will be well once a person's "inner peace" is attained. In the same way that no individual can exist independently above the influences of social realities, no social structures can exist without individuals' continuous participation in them. Peace in the world therefore does not mean passivity, nonactivity, or purely "inner" peace in the form of training oneself to be content under whatever kind of *dukkha*-inflicting social structures. Quite the contrary, it involves being tirelessly yet mindfully active at all times, dedicating oneself to the never-ending task of alleviating and reducing *dukkha* for all who are embedded in the *kammic* network.

It is significant that the Buddha taught *kamma* as volitional action *here and now*. "Nonviolence as the Buddha taught it was directed at each interaction in each moment," Paul R. Fleischman observes.[37] Being peaceful or practicing nonviolence as such is by no means the same as being passive. The ethics based on interdependence is neither one-size-fits-all control nor let-it-be nonactivity. Renowned Buddhist leader on nonviolent social engagement Thích Nhât Hanh, for example, urges that people "work vigorously against the political and economic ambitions of any country" on national and international levels, in order to prevent societal violence.[38] While the Dalai Lama and Thích Nhât Hanh, two of the most famous Buddhist teachers on nonviolence in the contemporary world, do not mistake nonantagonism with social retreatism, nonviolence with no action, many do. Historically, Buddhist leaders have been more likely to fall short of actively removing the socio-political causes of *dukkha* than to engage in antagonistic belligerent activities driven by attachment to their ethnic or sectarian identities. "There are still those Buddhist leaders," Brian Daizen Victoria observes, "predominantly in Asia, who believe that Buddhists, especially clerics, should not take part in any form of social activism, most especially that which challenges either the political or social status quo."[39] Johan Galtung comments, "When Buddhism turns its less beautiful side up, it spells retreatism, ritualism."[40]

Based on the Buddha's teachings recorded in the early texts, however, "nonviolence does not mean turning way from violence or being passive. It means responding to violence with *upaya*, or skillful means, action appropriate to the time and circumstance."[41] Sulak Sivaraksa comments, "Peace is a proactive, comprehensive process of finding ground through open communication and putting into practice a philosophy of nonharming and the sharing of resources."[42] Aung San Suu Kyi, the Buddhist leader of Burma's National League for Democracy and Nobel Peace Prize laureate in 1991, expresses the same sentiment, "Non-violence means positive action. . . . It just means that the methods you use are not violent ones. Some people think that non-violence is passiveness. It's not so."[43] Scholars of peace and nonviolence studies agree. Gene Sharp, for instance, maintains that nonviolent action is neither passive nor an attempt to avoid or ignore conflict. "It is *not* inaction. It is *action* that is nonviolent."[44] Through actions such as giving public speeches, signing petitions, and organizing protests, one nonviolently sends a message[45] and deposits something nonviolent to the socio-cultural contexts. Through actions such as boycotting, going on strikes, or withdrawing one's cooperation, one nonviolently suspends social and economic relations.[46] Peace and nonviolence are different from pacifism and nonactivity.[47]

From the viewpoints of both Buddhism and peace studies, peace "can never come about through nonpeaceful means."[48] To be peaceful and nonviolent, one needs to refrain from enacting direct, structural, and cultural violence. With every direct or symbolic appeal to violent action, one is making violence more "citable" in the culture while constructing a violent disposition for oneself. Rita Gross comments about the symbolic appeal to violent action,

> I have always been horrified by the peace movement symbol of a clenched fist inside a circle. I am equally horrified by the phrase "fighting for" peace, justice, the environment, or any other worthy cause. These symbols and phrases indicate a great deal about the collective psyche of the culture, about its assumptions that only confrontation and overcoming opposition will gain any results.[49]

In the same way that individuals' states of "inner peace" will prove to be transitory if the social structure remains unjust and keeps causing *dukkha*, change of social order does not guarantee peace if violence remains the prevalent mode of action whenever there is a conflict of interests. *In trying to remove structural violence by resorting to direct violence, one only reinforces the grip of cultural violence that will further justify future implementation of both direct and structural violence.* The "end" of removing structural violence, therefore, does not justify the "means" of direct violence or the perpetuation of cultural violence. Aung San Suu Kyi refuses to adopt violent means against the military regime of Burma because "I'm afraid that if we achieve democracy in this way we will never be able to get rid of the idea that you bring about necessary changes through violence."[50] This Buddhist stance again finds echoes in contemporary Western feminist literature. For example, The Combahee River Collective states,

> In the practice of our politics we do not believe that the end always justifies the means. Many reactionary and destructive acts have been done in the name of achieving "correct" political goals. As feminists we do not want to mess over people in the name of politics. We believe in collective process.[51]

As long as the society at large continues to naturalize domination and violence, and as long as the society at large continues to foster the mentality of seeing all others in opposition to one's "self," people will perpetually create *dukkha* for each other as well as for themselves.

Peace requires dissolving cultural violence and restructuring cultural values. Since the nature of social existence is that any social phenomenon is continually being constructed and reconstructed by all involved, cultural values cannot be restructured once and for all. Likewise, peace is not an end point that can be reached once and for all. Rather, because of co-*arising*, peace is peace-*making*. And because of *co*-arising, peace-making is *participatory*. It requires the participation of everyone, and it requires everyone trying to be peaceful with every action, at every moment.

Emotively, one cannot enact peaceful actions if one is angry, or greedy, or so attached to an identity that one no longer finds it wrong to sacrifice the well-being of people of different identities for one's own benefit. This is where the Buddhist emphasis and techniques of mental training can contribute the most to contemporary movements and activisms for justice and peace.[52] From the perspective of interdependent co-arising, what is "inner" eventually finds its manifestations in the "outer" world. Buddhism thus places great emphasis on monitoring one's own state of mind in taking any actions. David R. Loy draws on the current Dalai Lama's call for "internal disarmament" and maintains,

> For genuine peace—which is much more than the absence of overt violence—such internal disarmament is as important as external disarmament, and this involves taming the greed, ill will, and delusion in the minds of all those involved, starting with ourselves. It is not possible to work toward peace in a confrontational, antagonistic way.[53]

Having mental training as one of its main components, the Buddhist Noble Eightfold Path provides a program for people to consciously and proactively recondition both their mental states as well as their behavioral patterns, both of which build up the cultural contexts.

Conceptually, being peaceful with every action at every moment depends on understanding the co-*arising* of things, thereby realizing that complete peace or total nonviolence is not a static condition that can be attained and preserved without change. Peace-*making* is a continuous effort and a never-ending process. Thích Nhât Hanh therefore teaches, "We cannot be completely nonviolent, but . . . we are going in the direction of nonviolence. If we want to head north, we can use the North Star to guide us, but it is impossible to arrive at the North Star. Our effort is only to proceed in that direction."[54] Along the same line, Fleischman argues,

> [N]onviolence is continuous, a pervasive and quotidian effort. . . . The student of Dhamma seeks the least harm *at all times*. . . . He or she will be called upon also to recognize the complexity and ambiguity that rests on the shoulders of those who have positioned themselves to make decisions in a world of turmoil and suffering. But the sincere devotee of Dhamma understands that the goal of *every moment* is to generate empathy and compassion, to minimize anger and hate.[55] (Italics added.)

In the ever-changing world of interdependent co-arising, peacemaking is participatory and ongoing in character. It requires each individual to examine scrupulously the co-arising in each situation, monitoring closely her or his own motives and mental states at every moment, and choosing carefully the most peaceful courses of actions possible, so that the interaction patterns and social structures that ensue can help nurture further *dukkha*-alleviating mentalities and behaviors. Every volitional action here and now matters because it is through every volitional action here and now that an individual's disposition is constructed, and it is through every volitional action here and now that socio-cultural norms are sedimented. In this spirit, Nhât Hanh says, "The way to take care of the future is also to take good care of the present moment."[56] The path to the cessation of *dukkha* in a co-arising world is *striving* for the cessation of *dukkha* at every present moment. There is no point at which effort can cease; *nibbāna* in an ever-changing world is a never-ending process.

Being ethical is a continuous effort and never-ending process, too. It involves far more than vowing to take a number of precepts. In the interconnected web of existence, being ethical involves being socially benevolent and conscionable. Furthermore, in the contextual pragmatism of Buddhism, being socially ethical involves attending and responding to the particulars of each situation. Doing the right thing means doing what is wholesome and proper in the context. One is not ethical simply by abiding by precepts, and one is not ethical simply by being ethical in one situation at one time. In the ever-changing world of interdependent co-arising, ethics is not something that one keeps for a while and then transcends, though certain precepts may be. Rather, being ethical is striving to be ethical in all arising situations, just like being peaceful and nonviolent is to be peaceful and nonviolent at all times.

The worldview of interdependent co-arising warrants that each situation, being co-arisen with the particular existing phenomena (*dhamma*) in its particular context, be given due consideration and be not judged by a universal rule imposed from the "outside." While the teaching of co-arising does not sit well with rigid universalism, the teaching of *anātta*—which has its rationale in co-arising—does not allow for complete relativism, either. In the same way that no individual independently exists, no ethical situation is a completely closed system. An individual does not exist independently because she or he is always subject to being conditioned by the phenomena arising around her or him, including the ideologies and symbols prevalent in the culture, as well as the actions and interactions of relatives, friends, and acquaintances. Other people's actions (*kamma*) and interactions not only condition their own habits and dispositions, but also construct the social realities that influence the "self." Any individual's actions, likewise, not only construct her or his own personality and character, but have wider effects on both the people directly and immediately involved, and the people who later interact with them. Along the same line, an ethical situation is never completely self-contained because the people directly involved in any one situation are also involved in numerous other situations, and the legacy of people's actions in one situation will live on through people's constant interactions with each other. Every new situation compels new courses of actions, and every action at every moment contributes to the shaping of cultural values. Since consequences of actions always reverberate through the interconnected web of life as such, universal principles are still needed. Therefore, the *dukkha*-ceasing Noble Eightfold Path taught by the Buddha was still meant to be universal and did not shy away from claiming the "proper" (Pāli: *sammā*; Sanskrit: *samyak*) view or action. However, the Buddha also cautioned against dogmatism and instructed his followers to determine what was proper on their own after careful examination of each situation. Similarly, feminist theorist Janet Jakobsen warns, "any attempt at complete or comprehensive representation of the moral 'universe' will erase some aspects of the context it claims to comprehend."[57] What is "proper" is seeing from the perspectives of all parties involved, considering all possible effects near and far, and then taking the actions that will ultimately cause the least harm or alleviate the most *dukkha* in the interconnected web of existence.

Striving to be ethical and peaceful *here and now* may not constitute the entirety of *nibbāna*,[58] but it is an aspect of *nibbāna* that needs to be emphasized in the spirit of the Buddha's own this-worldly concern and his refusal of discussing metaphysical questions. Not emphasizing the this-worldly aspect of *nibbāna*, the Buddhist *Dhamma* can easily be turned inward and individualized, morphing into something about an ineffable, mystical state of mind that each individual approaches on her or his own. Being turned inward and individualized, the *Dhamma*'s social ethics is attenuated, and its critiques of the *dukkha*-producing conditions in the world, mostly brought forth by the privileged and powerful, are neglected. Non-Self then loses its profound socio-ethical implications and becomes a philosophical game of the educated élite. *Kamma* becomes an excuse for the privileges enjoyed by the powerful, and it is used to blame the victims, most commonly women. The community-building and society-transforming dimensions of the *Sangha* are lost. With the this-worldly aspect of *nibbāna* neglected, being a Buddhist can easily translate to diminishing the underprivileged self, being content with the situations in which one finds oneself, no matter how oppressive they are, and paying obeisance to the males in the monastic order in the hope of accumulating merits so that one gets a less miserable rebirth in the next life.

The Buddhist *Dhamma* has an unequivocal this-worldly agendum, which is the cessation of the pervasive *dukkha* in this world. The teaching of interdependent co-arising conveys the interconditionality of "self" and "others." As every jewel at the node of the Indra's Net is reflecting and reflected by all others, what a self thinks, feels, and acts can influence and be influenced by what others think, feel, and act. It is because of this web-like mutual conditioning that neither one's consciousness nor one's identity can be static. It is because of this web-like mutual conditioning that every "individual" action has its social, accumulative effects, and as such the contextually constructed and constrained individual subjects are not exempted from the social responsibility of *dukkha*-alleviation. It is because of this web-like mutual conditioning that any individual person has the power to either reinforce or reconfigure the currently *dukkha*-filled sediments of social conventions via the volitional actions she or he takes and the interconnections she or he builds with multiple others. It is because of this web-like mutual conditioning that there is no point beyond which one can stop being peaceful or ethical in this world.

The Buddha consistently conveyed his very practical concerns and taught that the ultimate criterion for a view or a teaching was its ethical value: it should be learned and practiced if it leads to welfare and happiness, and it should be disregarded and abandoned if it leads to harm and suffering. Other considerations are either irrelevant or not practical enough. To reiterate, the ultimate goal of learning or teaching about the co-arising and interconditionality of existence is so that people will have the wisdom of understanding co-arising, will put that wisdom into practice, and thereby will put a stop to *dukkha*. Whether or not people call that wisdom *"Dhamma"* or recognize a *dukkha*-alleviating practice as "Buddhist" is, based on the teachings of the Buddha himself, beside the point. Bhikkhu Chao Chu puts it this way: "the only real Buddhism, the fulfillment of Buddhism, is no Buddhism at all."[59]

At the same time, one does not have to be a Buddhist (or a post-structuralist feminist) to understand that we come into being and learn how to think and behave in a web of material and symbolic forces constructed by people's *kamma*. One does not have to be a Buddhist to see that the *kammic* network, which seems to hold tremendous power over individuals, does not have any abiding essence and is subject to change by way of people's actions. One does not have to be a Buddhist to perceive the various forms of suffering existing in the world. One does not have to be a Buddhist to understand that the current suffering-filled realities have been constructed and maintained because of people's repeated participation in them. And one does not have to be a Buddhist to comprehend that it will take all people's participation to reorient the society and reduce the existing suffering.

Being Buddhist or not, spiritual self-discipline is an indispensable part of global justice and peace, for any form of violence or conflict or injustice is a product of the co-construction of what would be called "inner" or "individual" factors, and what would be called "outer" or "social" forces. Oppressive social structures contribute not only to conflicts between groups and individuals, but also breed bigotries and resentments. Bigotries and resentments reify themselves in social hierarchies, hate speeches, and violent actions, thereby creating *dukkha*-inducing social realities. The "internal" defilements and the "external" injustice feed and bounce off each other. Spiritual self-discipline is therefore needed so that one has the capacity to examine closely one's own mental states and the ways in which one interacts with others, thereby putting a stop to this reciprocity between the "internal" and "external" inducers of *dukkha*.

Sufficiently understood, the reality of interconditionality can compel people to strive continuously for the most wholesome, proper, nonviolent, peaceful, and least *dukkha*-producing actions possible, together with every "other" with whom they can build connections:

> Let us pray for world peace, social justice, and environ-
> mental balance, which begin with our own breathing.
> I breathe in calmly and breathe out mindfully.
> Once I have seeds of peace and happiness within me, I
> try to reduce my selfish desire and reconstitute my
> consciousness.
> With less attachment to myself, I try to understand the
> structural violence in the world.
> Linking my heart with my head, I perceive the world
> holistically, a sphere full of living beings who are all
> related to me.
> I try to expand my understanding with love to help
> build a more nonviolent world.
> I vow to live simply and offer myself to the oppressed.
> By the grace of the Compassionate Ones and with the
> help of good friends, may I be a partner in lessening
> the suffering of the world so that it may be a proper
> habitat for all sentient beings to live in harmony
> during this millennium.[60]

In the interconnected and interconditioned world, theoretically the task of transforming *samsāra* to *nibbāna* can start anywhere, be it a thought that a person generates, a relationship between two groups, a governmental policy, or an international agreement. The Buddhist Noble Eightfold Path, however, makes ethics first and last. Ethics is the first for very practical reasons: in the form of voluntarily-taken precepts, it makes mental training possible, and it makes cooperation and networking possible. Ethics is also the ever-elusive last that is manifest in the effort of always responding to every "other" in every situation with the most wholesome actions one can take. As such, an all-inclusive, rigorously ongoing, nonviolent social ethic has been built into the Buddhist *Dhamma* from the beginning. Therefore, instead of externalizing or extrapolating the Buddhist inner peace as if social ethics was prior to now nonexistent in the Buddhist *Dhamma*, follow-ers of the Buddha need only to heed the most basic teachings of the Buddha and to reclaim, revitalize, and actualize them.

Notes

Chapter 1

1. *Anguttara Nikāya*, I.186–187; duplicated in III.65.

2. The formulaic description of *dukkha* in the Pāli Canon is: "birth is *dukkha*, aging is *dukkha*, illness is *dukkha*, death is *dukkha*, union with what is displeasing is *dukkha*, separation from what is pleasing is *dukkha*; not to get what one wants is *dukkha*; in brief, the five aggregates subject to clinging are *dukkha*." *Samyutta Nikāya* V.421 (*Saccasamyutta*). For explication of the meaning of the quote above, see *Majjhima Nikāya* iii.248–52 (*Saccavibhanga Sutta*). "Unsatisfactoriness" rather than "dissatisfaction" is used as a translation because the word *dukkha* denotes much more than just outright dissatisfaction with life. Charles Prebish and Damien Keown expound that *dukkha*, besides referring to physical pains, also refers to emotional distress and psychological afflictions, and as such can be translated as suffering, pain, ill, unsatisfactoriness, anguish, stress, unease, and so on. Buddhist sources classify *dukkha* into three categories: *dukkha-dukkha* (Sanskrit: *duhkha-duhkha*; suffering due to biological causes, such as illness, aging, and death), *sankhāra-dukkha* (Sanskrit: *samskāra-duhkha*; suffering due to formations and conditioned states of beings), and *viparināma-dukkha* (Sanskrit: *viparināma-duhkha*; suffering due to change). *Samyutta Nikāya* IV.259 (*Jambukhādakasamyutta*); Charles S. Prebish and Damien Keown, *Introducing Buddhism*, 2nd edition (London and New York: Routledge, 2010), 43–6; Damien Keown, comp., *A Dictionary of Buddhism* (Oxford and New York: Oxford University Press, 2003), 81.

3. Bhikkhu Bodhi, "A Look at the Kalama Sutta," *Buddhist Publication Society Newsletter* 9 (Spring 1988), accessed May 24, 2011, http://www.access-toinsight.org/lib/authors/bodhi/bps-essay_09.html. Discussed in David L. McMahan, *The Making of Buddhist Modernism* (Oxford and New York: Oxford University Press, 2008), 248.

4. For the dating of the historical Buddha, see Charles S. Prebish, "Cooking the Buddhist Books: The Implications of the New Dating of the Buddha for the History of Early Indian Buddhism," *Journal of Buddhist Ethics* 15 (2008): 1–21.

5. Keown, *A Dictionary of Buddhism*, 74; Jonathan Z. Smith and William Scott Green, with the American Academy of Religion, eds., *The HarperCollins Dictionary of Religion* (New York: HarperCollins, 1995), 315–6.

6. Roger R. Jackson, "Buddhist Theology: Its Historical Context," in *Buddhist Theology: Critical Reflections by Contemporary Buddhist Scholars*, edited by Roger R. Jackson and John J. Makransky (Richmond, UK: Curzon Press, 2000), 5.

7. *Ibid.*

8. For discussion on the androcentric record-keeping in the Buddhist history, see Rita M. Gross, *Buddhism After Patriarchy: A Feminist History, Analysis, and Reconstruction of Buddhism* (Albany, New York: State University of New York Press, 1993), 18–54.

9. Rita M. Gross, "Where Are the Women in the Refugee Tree?" in *Religious Feminism and the Future of the Planet: A Buddhist-Christian Conversation*, by Rita M. Gross and Rosemary Radford Ruether (New York: The Continuum Publishing Company, 2001), 74–5.

10. Edmund F. Perry, "Foreword to the English Edition," in *The Heritage of the Bhikkhu: A Short History of the Bhikkhu in Educational, Cultural, Social, and Political Life* (New York: Grove Press, 1974), xii.

11. George Doherty Bond, *Buddhism at Work: Community Development, Social Empowerment and the Sarvodaya Movement*, foreword by Joanna Macy (Bloomfield, Connecticut: Kumarian Press, 2004), 11; also 74–5 and 2.

12. Perry, "Foreword to the English Edition," xii.

13. McMahan, *The Making of Buddhist Modernism*, 43.

14. Ken Jones, *The New Social Face of Buddhism: A Call to Action* (Boston, Massachusetts: Wisdom Publications, 2003), 180.

15. See Walpola Rāhula, *The Heritage of the Bhikkhu: A Short History of the Bhikkhu in Educational, Cultural, Social, and Political Life* (New York: Grove Press, 1974). May Ebihara's study also shows that Buddhist monasteries in Cambodia provide social services such as health care and education. May Ebihara, "Interrelation between Buddhism and Social Systems in Cambodian Peasant Culture," *Anthropological Studies in Theravada Buddhism*, edited by Manning Nash (New Haven, Connecticut: Yale University Press, 1966), 175–96.

16. Jones, *The New Social Face of Buddhism*, 222.

17. Robert Magliola, "Afterword," in *Buddhisms and Deconstructions*, edited by Jin Y. Park (Lanham, Maryland: Rowman & Littlefield, 2006), 260.

18. Peter Harvey introduces "Engaged Buddhism" as Asian Buddhists' borrowing characteristics of Protestant Christianity in order to fight back against Western colonial rule, which has led some to call it "Protestant Buddhism." Peter Harvey, *An Introduction to Buddhist Ethics: Foundations, Values and Issues* (Cambridge, United Kingdom: Cambridge University Press, 2000), 112. Robinson et al. in *Buddhist Religions* also describe engaged Buddhism as a Western reform that seems to be inspired by Christian social activists of the nineteenth century even though many of the pioneers of engaged Buddhism are Asian. Richard H. Robinson, Willard L. Johnson, and Thanissaro Bhikkhu, *Buddhist Religions: A Historical Introduction*, 5th edition (Belmont, California: Wadsworth/Thomson Learning, 2005), 304. They explain that the movement in Sri Lanka in the nineteenth century is called Protestant Buddhism both in the sense that it was a *protest* against

Portuguese Catholic rule, and in the sense that it was primarily led by educated laypeople (the Portuguese rule significantly reduced the number of Buddhist renunciates) who sought to strip away the elements that had no basis in the early texts. *Ibid.*, 154. As Harvey notes in *An Introduction to Buddhist Ethics*, "Social activist Buddhists in Asia often claim that they are simply reviving the best features of Buddhism from the pre-colonial era, before the colonial era cut back the social outreach of monks." Harvey, *An Introduction to Buddhist Ethics*, 112.

19. Christopher Ives, "Deploying the Dharma: Reflections on the Methodology of Constructive Buddhist Ethics," *Journal of Buddhist Ethics* 15 (2008): 24–5. See also McMahan, *The Making of Buddhist Modernism*, 152.

20. In addition to the opening quote, in the *Vīmamsaka Sutta* the Buddha invited his followers to investigate himself and taught that one should place confidence in him and his teaching only *after* investigating and gaining direct knowledge in this manner. *Majjhima Nikāya*, i.318–320 (*Vīmamsaka Sutta*). Ken Jones puts it this way: "Buddhism is essentially a tool of inquiry and an ideological solvent, open to untidy complexity and suspicious of fixed conclusions." Jones, *The New Social Face of Buddhism*, 57.

21. In this spirit, Vietnamese Chan Master Thích Nhât Hanh states, "If a teaching is not in accord with the needs of the people and the realities of society, it is not really Buddhist." Thích Nhât Hanh, *Interbeing: Commentaries on the Tiep Hien Precepts* (Berkeley, California: Parallax Press, 1987), 17.

22. John J. Makransky, "Contemporary Academic Buddhist Theology: Its Emergence and Rationale," in *Buddhist Theology: Critical Reflections by Contemporary Buddhist Scholars*, edited by Roger R. Jackson and John J. Makransky (Richmond, UK: Curzon Press, 2000), 18–9.

23. McMahan, *The Making of Buddhist Modernism*, 6, and also 20.

24. For examples, see Ouyporn Khuankaew, "Buddhism and Domestic Violence: Using the Four Noble Truths to Deconstruct and Liberate Women's Karma," in *Rethinking Karma: The Dharma of Social Justice*, edited by Jonathan S. Watts (Chiang Mai, Thailand: Silkworm Books, 2009), 202–4 and 207–8; Karen Derris, "When the Buddha Was a Woman: Reimagining Tradition in the Theravāda," *Journal of Feminist Studies in Religion* 24.2 (Fall 2008): 41–2; Ouyporn Khuankaew, "Buddhism and Violence against Women," in *Violence Against Women in Contemporary World Religion: Roots and Cures*, edited by Daniel C. Maguire and Sa'diyya Shaikh (Cleveland, Ohio: Pilgrim Press, 2007), 174–91; Chatsumarn Kabilsingh, *Thai Women in Buddhism* (Berkeley, California: Parallax Press, 1991), 31; Isaline Blew Horner, *Women Under Primitive Buddhism: Laywomen and Almswomen*, reprinted (Delhi, India: Motilal Banansidass, 1975), 28 and 48; Kajiyama Yuichi, "Women in Buddhism," *Eastern Buddhist*, New Series, 15, no. 2 (1982): 61–62; Gross, *Buddhism After Patriarchy*, 43.

25. Rita Gross comments that gender identity "is more basic for most people than identification in terms of color, shape, or even culture, and is far more addictive." Rita M. Gross, "The Dharma of Gender," *Contemporary Buddhism* 5, no. 1 (May 2004): 4.

26. Gross, *Buddhism After Patriarchy*, 128 and 158; also in Gross, "Buddhism and Feminism: Toward Their Mutual Transformation, Part I," *Eastern Buddhist* 19, no. 1 (Spring 1986): 49–50; Gross, "The Dharma of Gender," 6.

27. Damien Keown, *The Nature of Buddhist Ethics* (New York: Palgrave, 2001), 64–8.

28. *Samyutta Nikāya*, IV.251 (*Jambukhādakasamyutta*).

29. The same word is also translated as virtue, morality, or precepts. Ethical discipline includes proper speech (Pāli: *sammā vācā*; Sanskrit: *samyag-vāc*), proper action (Pāli: *sammā kammanta*; Sanskrit: *samyak-karmānta*), and proper livelihood (Pāli: *sammā ājīva*; Sanskrit: *samyak-ājīva*). The Pāli prefix *sammā* or the Sanskrit prefix *samyak* is often translated as "right" or "proper." The term itself, however, denotes comprehensiveness or completeness. The rightness or properness is predicated on being comprehensive and covering all grounds, not on being in accordance with any absolute truth. See David J. Kalupahana, *A History of Buddhist Philosophy: Continuities and Discontinuities* (Honolulu, Hawai'i: University of Hawai'i Press, 1992), 103.

30. This includes proper effort (Pāli: *sammā vāyāma*; Sanskrit: *samyag-vyāyāma*), proper mindfulness (Pāli: *sammā sati*; Sanskrit: *samyak-smrti*), and proper concentration (Pāli: *sammā samādhi*; Sanskrit: *samyak-samādhi*). Some consider "proper effort" part of ethical discipline.

31. This includes proper view (Pāli: *sammā ditthi*; Sanskrit: *samyag-drsti*) and proper intention (Pāli: *sammā sankappa*; Sanskrit: *samyak-samkalpa*).

32. In the Pāli Canon, the term *upāya-kosalla* (Sanskrit: *upāya kauśalya*), commonly translated as "skillful means" or "expedient means," occurs infrequently and simply denotes the Buddha's marvelous skills in expounding the *Dhamma*. In Mahāyāna texts, by contrast, the term has mainly been used to claim Mahāyāna's superiority to all older non-Mahāyānist schools. The followers of those schools might believe they had received and practiced the authentic, ultimate *Dhamma* directly from the Buddha. The early Mahāyānists, however, contend that the historical Buddha lied about the ultimacy, and the older teachings were in fact limited and restricted, for they were tailored for the early followers who were of more selfish inclinations and/or lesser spiritual potentials. At a glance, this Mahāyānist claim might seem to be disparaging of the Buddha (not to say disparaging of all older schools and all early followers), for it seems to accuse the Buddha of breaking the precept of no lying. In the Mahāyānist rendition, nonetheless, the seemingly morally wrong act of lying is in fact the Buddha's *upāya* for the purpose of convincing selfish people of lesser capacities to follow his teachings. By dismissing all older schools as the results of the Buddha's *upāya*, the early Mahāyānists branded them "Hīnayāna," the Small Raft, and considered itself providing "Mahāyāna," the Great Raft, an vehicle that is big enough to transport all sentient beings from the shore of endless suffering to the far-shore of *nibbāna*. Modern-day Mahāyānists who have been educated in Buddhist history do not hold this assumption any more, and yet less educated ones still commonly assume that Theravādins are the same as "Hīnayānists" and that "Hīnayānists" lack compassionate consideration for others. For the meaning of *upāya*, see Keown, comp, *A Dictionary of Buddhism*, 318.

33. Gross, *Buddhism After Patriarchy*, 30.

34. See Donald S. Lopez, Jr., *Modern Buddhism: Readings for the Unenlightened* (London: Penguin Books, 2002); Scott Pacey, "A Buddhism for the Human World: Interpretations of *Renjian Fojiao* in Contemporary Taiwan," *Asian Studies Review* 29 (March 2005): 61–77.

35. See Ian J. Coghlan, "A Survey of the Sources of Buddhist Ethics," *Journal of Buddhist Ethics* 11 (2004): 146.

36. In the Theravāda tradition, there are 227 vows or precepts for *bhikkhus* and, theoretically, 311 vows for *bhikkhunīs*, although the *bhikkhunī sangha* has died out in the Theravāda tradition in India and Sri Lanka since the eleventh century and was possibly never established in Cambodhia, Laos, or Thailand. See Nancy Auer Falk, "The Case of the Vanishing Nuns: The Fruits of Ambivalence in Ancient Indian Buddhism," in *Unspoken Worlds: Women's Religious Lives in Non-Western Cultures*, edited by Nancy Auer Falk and Rita M. Gross (San Francisco: Harper & Row, 1980), 207–24; Kabilsingh, *Thai Women in Buddhism*, 30; Karma Lekshe Tsomo, "Mahāprajāpatī's Legacy: The Buddhist Women's Movement: An Introduction," in *Buddhist Women Across Cultures: Realizations*, edited by Karma Lekshe Tsomo (Albany, New York: State University of New York Press, 1999), 9; Derris, "When the Buddha Was a Woman," 30. In the Mahāyāna Dharmagupta tradition there are 250 vows for *bhikṣus* and 348 for *bhikṣunīs*, and in the Tibetan Mūlāsarvāstivāda tradition there are 253 vows for *bhikṣus* and 364 for *bhikṣunīs*. See Karma Lekshe Tsomo, "Is the Bhiksunī Vinaya Sexist?" in *Buddhist Women and Social Justice: Ideals, Challenges, and Achievements*, edited by Karma Lekshe Tsomo (Albany, New York: State University of New York Press, 2004), 58. For the variances of the Vinaya texts, see Étienne Lamotte, *History of Indian Buddhism: From the Origins to the Śaka Era*, translated from French by Sara Webb-Boin under the supervision of Jean Dantinne (Paris: Institut Orientaliste de l'Université Catholique de Louvain, 1988), 165 and 171–6.

37. Greg Bailey and Ian Mabbett, *The Sociology of Early Buddhism* (Cambridge and New York: Cambridge University Press, 2006), 8; Charles S. Prebish, *Buddhist Monastic Discipline* (University Park and London: Pennsylvania State Press, 1975), 4.

38. For instances, see *Majjhima Nikāya* i.102 (*Cetokhila Sutta*), i.163 (*Ariyapariyesanā Sutta*), ii.181 (*Esukārī Sutta*), and iii.48 (*Sevitabbāsevitabba Sutta*). See also Lamotte, *History of Indian Buddhism*, 142–3.

39. Coghlan, "A Survey of the Sources of Buddhist Ethics," 147–8.

40. Phra Prayudh Payutto (Phra Rājavaramuni), "Foundations of Buddhist Social Ethics," in *Ethics, Wealth, and Salvation: A Study in Buddhist Social Ethics*, eds. Russell F. Sizemore and Donald K. Swearer (Columbia, South Carolina: University of South Carolina Press, 1990), 30.

41. Lamotte, *History of Indian Buddhism*, 163.

42. *Ibid.*, 156.

43. This collection consists of 34 suttas, divided into three sections. Its Sanskrit counterpart is the *Dīrghāgama*, which consists of 30 sūtras.

44. Nyanaponika Thera and Bhikkhu Bodhi, "Introduction I," in *Numerical Discourses of the Buddha: An Anthology of Suttas from the Anguttara Nikāya*,

selected and translated from the Pāli by Nyanaponika Thera and Bhikkhu Bodhi (Walnut Creek, California: AltaMira Press, 1999), 9.

45. This collection consists of 152 suttas. Its Sanskrit counterpart *Madhyamāgama* has 222 sūtras.

46. Nyanaponika Thera and Bhikkhu Bodhi, "Introduction I," 9.

47. This collection has 7,762 suttas, which are divided into six sections (*vagga*) and further subdivided into 56 assemblages (*samyutta*). It is referred to as Complete *Samyuktāgama* and Partial *Samyuktāgama* in Sanskrit sources and consisting of 1,362 and 364 sūtras, respectively.

48. Nyanaponika Thera and Bhikkhu Bodhi, "Introduction I," 9.

49. This collection consists of 9,557 suttas distributed into eleven groups (*nipāta*). Its Sanskrit counterpart *Ekottarāgama* has 364 sūtras.

50. Nyanaponika Thera and Bhikkhu Bodhi, "Introduction I," 10.

51. Lamotte, *History of Indian Buddhism*, 150–2 and 157–63; Steven Collins, "Introduction," in *Buddhist Monastic Life: According to the Texts of the Theravāda Tradition*, by Mohan Wijayaratna, translated by Claude Grangier and Steven Collins (Cambridge and New York: Cambridge University Press, 1990).

52. Elizabeth J. Harris, "The Female in Buddhism," in *Buddhist Women Across Cultures: Realizations*, edited by Karma Lekshe Tsomo (Albany, New York: State University of New York Press, 1999), 50–1, and endnotes 1–6.

53. For example, see Tavivat Puntarigvivat, *Budkkhu Buddhadasa's Dhammic Socialism in Dialogue with Latin American Liberation Theology* (PhD diss., Temple University, 1994), 104.

54. The Three Marks of Reality are impermanence (Pāli: *anicca*; Sanskrit: *anitya*), unsatisfactoriness (Pāli: *dukkha*; Sanskrit: *duhkha*), and lack of self-essence (Pāli: *anattā*; Sanskrit: *anātman*; more commonly translated as "no-Self" or "non-Self").

55. See Robinson et al., *Buddhist Religions*, 143; Paul Williams, *Buddhist Thought: A Complete Introduction to the Indian Tradition*, with Anthony Tribe (London and New York: Routledge, 2000), 32–3; David Seyfort Ruegg and Lambert Schmithausen, eds, *Earliest Buddhism and Madhyamaka* (Leiden, Netherlands: E. J. Brill, 1990), 1–2.

56. Robinson et al., *Buddhist Religions*, 146, 148, 150–3. See also Derris, "When the Buddha Was a Woman," 42–3.

57. Puntarigvivat, *Budkkhu Buddhadasa's Dhammic Socialism*, 104 and 108.

58. Mohan Wijayaratna, *Buddhist Monastic Life: According to the Texts of the Theravāda Tradition*, translated by Claude Grangier and Steven Collins, with an introduction by Steven Collins (Cambridge and New York: Cambridge University Press, 1990), 155, endnote 8; Tsomo, "Mahāprajāpatī's Legacy," 27.

59. *Samyutta Nikāya*, V.153 (*Satipaṭṭhānasamyutta*); duplicated in *Dīgha Nikāya* ii.100 (*Mahāparinibbāna Sutta*).

60. *Samyutta Nikāya*, III.42 (*Khandhasamyutta*) and V.154, 163–165 (*Satipaṭṭhānasamyutta*).

61. *Dīgha Nikāya*, ii.154 (*Mahāparinibbāna Sutta*).

62. *Majjhima Nikāya*, iii.9–10 (*Gopakamoggallāna Sutta*). See also *Dīgha Nikāya*, ii.100 (*Mahāparinibbāna Sutta*), and Lamotte, *History of Indian Buddhism*, 62–5.

63. Tsomo, "Mahāprajāpatī's Legacy," 2, 10, 12–13, 28, and 48, endnote 68; Senarat Wijayasundara, "Restoring the Order of Nuns to the Theravādin Tradition," in *Buddhist Women Across Cultures: Realizations*, edited by Karma Lekshe Tsomo (Albany, New York: State University of New York Press, 1999), 81, 85–6; David R. Loy, "The Karma of Women," in *Violence Against Women in Contemporary World Religion: Roots and Cures*, edited by Daniel C. Maguire and Sa'diyya Shaikh (Cleveland, Ohio: Pilgrim Press, 2007), 55; Khuankaew, "Buddhism and Domestic Violence," 210–1.

64. Gross, *Buddhism After Patriarchy*, 29.

65. Gregory Schopen, "Two Problems in the History of Indian Buddhism, The Layman/Monk Distinction and the Doctrines of the Transference of Merit," in *Bones, Stones, and Buddhist Monks, Collected Papers on the Archaeology, Epigraphy, and Texts of Monastic Buddhism in India* (Honolulu, Hawai'i: University of Hawai'i Press, 1997), 24–5; Nancy J. Barnes, "The Nuns at the Stūpa: Inscriptional Evidence for the Lives and Activities of Early Buddhist Nuns in India," in *Women's Buddhism, Buddhism's Women: Tradition, Revision, Renewal*, edited by Ellison Banks Findly (Boston, Massachusetts: Wisdom Publications, 2000), 18–9 and 29; Collins, "Introduction," xi; Williams, *Buddhist Thought*, 33.

66. Peter N. Gregory, "Is Critical Buddhism Really Critical?" in *Pruning the Bodhi Tree: The Storm Over Critical Buddhism*, edited by Jamie Hubbard and Paul Swanson (Honolulu, Hawai'i: University of Hawai'i Press, 1997), 286–297.

67. Nyanaponika Thera and Bhikkhu Bodhi, "Introduction I," 2–3.

68. *Ibid.*

69. Loy, "The Karma of Women," 50.

70. Bailey and Mabbett, *The Sociology of Early Buddhism*, 4.

71. Lamotte, *History of Indian Buddhism*, 163–4.

72. Bhikkhu Bodhi, "General Introduction," in *The Connected Discourses of the Buddha: A Translation of the Samyutta Nikāya*, translated from the Pāli by Bhikkhu Bodhi (Boston, Massachusetts: Wisdom Publications, 2000), 30.

73. See Uma Chakravarti, "The Social Background of the Early Buddhists," in *The Social Dimensions of Early Buddhism*, 2nd edition (Oxford, UK, and New York: Oxford University Press, 1987), 124–31 and 146–7. The predominantly upper-class backgrounds of the early followers of the Buddha can also be seen in the *Theragāthā* ("songs of the male elders") and the *Therīgāthā* ("songs of the female elders"). Among the 328 *bhikkhu*-s and *bhikkhunī*-s depicted in these two collections of songs and poems, 41 percent was of the *brāhmin* class and 23 percent was of the warrior-noble class (Pāli: *khattiya*; Sanskrit: *kṣatriya*). See Peter Harvey, *An Introduction to Buddhism: Teachings, History, and Practices* (Cambridge, UK: Cambridge University Press, 1990), 24. Greg Bailey and Ian Mabbett counted 1,359 members of the four social classes mentioned in the suttas and the *Vinaya*. Even though clearly not all of them were Buddhist renunciates or even Buddhist lay followers, it is still significant that 398 of these names mentioned in the texts were *brāhmin*s and 700 were *khattiya*s. Bailey and Mabbett, *The Sociology of Early Buddhism*, 87–8.

74. David Loy suggests that the Buddha's teachings reveal a struggle against the sexist social conditioning he received. Loy, "The Karma of Women," 50.

75. Tsomo, "Is The Bhiksuni Vinaya Sexist?" 48.

76. *Dīgha Nikāya*, ii.74.

77. Wijayaratna, *Buddhist Monastic Life*, 90.

78. Gross, *Buddhism After Patriarchy*, 46; also 52.

79. Horner, *Women Under Primitive Buddhism*, 155–7; Wijayaratna, *Buddhist Monastic Life*, 100.

80. Tsomo "Is the Bhiksunī Vinaya Sexist?" 50–3 and 61–7; Inyoung Chung, "A Buddhist View of Women: A Comparative Study of the Rules for Bhiksus and Bhiksunīs based on the Chinese Prātimoksa" (MA Thesis, Graduate Theological Union, Berkeley, 1995), 14; Gross, *Buddhism After Patriarchy*, 35–6 and 212; Kabilsingh, *Thai Women in Buddhism*, 28–9; Chakravarti, "The Political, Economic, Social, and Religious Environment at the Time of the Buddha," in *The Social Dimensions of Early Buddhism*, 62; Horner, *Women Under Primitive Buddhism*, 105-6, 109–10, 124, 130, 155.

81. Wijayaratna, *Buddhist Monastic Life*, 159.

82. Gregory Schopen, "The Suppression of Nuns and the Ritual Murder of Their Special Dead in Two Buddhist Monastic Texts," *Journal of Indian Philosophy* 24, no. 6 (December 1996): 563.

83. Wijayasundara, "Restoring the Order of Nuns to the Theravādin Tradition," 79; Edward J. Thomas, *The Life of the Buddha as Legend and History* (London: Routledge & Kegan Paul, 1969), 66; Horner, *Women under Primitive Buddhism*, 300; Tavivat Puntarigvivat, "A Thai Buddhist Perspective," in *What Men Owe to Women: Men's Voices from World Religions*, edited by John C. Raines and Daniel C. Maguire (Albany, New York: State University of New York Press, 2001), 230–1; Gross, *Buddhism After Patriarchy*, 42.

84. *Aṭṭhagarudhammā* is more popularly translated as the "eight special rules," "eight heavy rules," or "eight chief rules." Nirmala S. Salgado argues compellingly that it is better rendered the "eight revered conditions" given the nuances conveyed by the original Pāli/Sanskrit term. Nirmala S. Salgado, "Eight Revered Conditions: Ideological Complicity, Contemporary Reflections, and Practical Realities," *Journal of Buddhist Ethics* 15 (2008): 181ff. See also Bhikkhunī Kusuma, "Inaccuracies in Buddhist Women's History," in *Innovative Buddhist Women: Swimming Against the Stream*, edited by Karma Lekshe Tsomo (Richmond, Surrey: Curzon Press, 2000), 5–12; Tsomo "Is the Bhiksunī Vinaya Sexist?" 48–9; Puntarigvivat, "A Thai Buddhist Perspective," 217; Barnes, "The Nuns at the Stūpa," 19; Gross, *Buddhism After Patriarchy*, 33–8; Kajiyama, "Women in Buddhism," 53–70; Akira Hirakawa, *Monastic Discipline for the Buddhist Nuns: An English Translation of the Chinese Text of the Mahāsāmghika-Bhiksunī-Vinaya* (Patna: Kashi Prasad Jayaswal Research Institute, 1982), 47–98; Loy, "The Karma of Women," 51, footnote 3.

85. Tsomo, "Mahāprajāpatī's Legacy," 5; Nancy Auer Falk, "An Image of Woman in Old Buddhist Literature: the Daughters of Mara," in *Women and Religion*, edited by Judith Plaskow and Joan Arnold Romero, revised edition (Missoula, Montana: Scholars' Press, 1974), 105; Kajiyama, "Women in Buddhism," 53–70; Gross, *Buddhism After Patriarchy*, 33.

86. James William Coleman, *The New Buddhism: The Western Transformation of an Ancient Tradition* (Oxford and New York: Oxford University Press, 2001), 199.

87. Collins, "Introduction," xvii.

88. Alan Sponberg, "Attitudes toward Women and the Feminine in Early Buddhism," in *Buddhism, Sexuality, and Gender*, edited by José Ignacio Cabezón (Albany, New York: State University of New York Press, 1992), 3–4.

89. Loy, "The Karma of Women," 52; Gross, *Buddhism After Patriarchy*, 30–3.

90. Sallie B. King, *Being Benevolence: The Social Ethics of Engaged Buddhism* (Honolulu, Hawai'i: University of Hawai'i Press), 80–2; Santikaro Bhikkhu, "Buddhadasa Bhikkhu: Life and Society throught he Natural Eyes of Voidness," in *Engaged Buddhism: Buddhist Liberation Movements in Asia*, edited by Christopher S. Queen and Sallie B. King (Albany, New York: State University of New York Press, 1996), 156–7; Bhimrao Ramji Ambedkar, *The Buddha and His Dhamma*, 3rd edition (Bombay, India: Siddharth Publications, 1984), 254–5; Phra Prayudh Payutto, *Buddhadhamma: Natural Laws and Values for Life*, translated by Grant A. Olson (Albany, New York: State University of New York Press, 1995), 85–6 and 165.

91. *Anguttara Nikāya*, II.iv.6.

92. *Majjhima Nikāya*, i.66–67 (*Cūlasīhanāda Sutta*).

93. *Majjhima Nikāya*, i.140 (*Alagaddūpama Sutta*); see also *Samyuttaa Nikāya*, III.119 (*Khandhasamyutta*).

94. *Majjhima Nikāya*, i.134–135 (*Alagaddūpama Sutta*). See also Williams, *Buddhist Thought*, 38-40; Harvey, *An Introduction to Buddhism*, 31.

95. *Dīgha Nikāya*, ii.55 (*Mahānidāna Sutta*).

96. *Majjhima Nikāya*, i.190–191 (*Mahāhatthipadopama Sutta*).

97. *Samyutta Nikāya*, II.36 (*Nidānasamyutta*).

98. Kalupahana, *A History of Buddhist Philosophy*, 53.

99. Sulak Sivaraksa, *Conflict, Culture, Change: Engaged Buddhism in a Globalized World* (Boston, Massachusetts: Wisdom Publications, 2005), 71.

100. The traditional account relates that the Buddha-to-be, after experimenting with asceticism for six years and finally realized the value of the middle way between self-indulgence and self-mortification, sat down under a shady species of tree (the *pīpala* or *assattha*) at Bodhgayā (in the Ganges River plain of Northeastern India) and resolved not to rise until he had an awakening and attained liberative knowledge. The tree was retrospectively called the *bodhi* tree (or the *bo* tree), with the Pāli/Sanskrit word "bodhi" meaning "awakening" or "enlightenment." Robinson et al., *Buddhist Religions*, 1 and 8; Keown, comp., *A Dictionary of Buddhism*, 36; Harvey, *An Introduction to Buddhism*, 21–2.

101. Joanna Macy, *Mutual Causality in Buddhism and General Systems Theory: The Dharma of Natural Systems* (Albany, New York: State University of New York Press, 1991), 26–7 and 40.

102. *Anguttara Nikāya*, IV.94; also V.2, VIII.30, VIII.49, VIII.54, and IX.3.

103. *Samyutta Nikāya*, II.27 (*Nidānasamyutta*).

104. *Majjhima Nikāya*, i.55–63 (*Satipatthāna Sutta*).

105. Nicholas F. Gier and Paul Kjellberg, "Buddhism and the Freedom of the Will: Pali and Mahayanist Responses," in *Freedom and Determinism*, edited by Joseph Keim Campbell, Michael O'Rourke, and David Shier (Cambridge, Massachusetts: Massachusetts Institute of Technology Press, 2004), 284.

106. In the Pāli tradition, *hetu* (cause), *samudaya* (origin), and *paccaya* (condition) have been understood as synonyms. *Dīgha Nikāya* ii.57 (*Mahānidāna Sutta*). See also Bhikkhu Bodhi, "Introduction" to the Book of Causation (*Nidānavagga*), in *The Connected Discourses of the Buddha: A Translation of the Samyutta Nikāya*, translated by Bhikkhu Bodhi (Boston, Massachusetts: Wisdom Publications, 2002), 516.

107. *Samyutta Nikāya*, II.25; *Anguttara Nikāya*, III.134. See also Harvey, *An Introduction to Buddhism*, 29; Payutto, *Buddhadhamma*, 77.

108. David R. Loy, *The Great Awakening: A Buddhist Social Theory* (Boston, Massachusetts: Wisdom Publications, 2003), 7. See also Loy, "The Karma of Women," 59–60. The idea of performativity renders scriptural literalism invalid, and on this ground Loy suggests that Buddhists should not accept as literal truth everything said in the Pāli Canon.

109. Bailey and Mabbett, *The Sociology of Early Buddhism*, 241.

110. John J. Makransky, "Buddhist Perspectives on Truth in Other Religions: Past and Present." *Theological Studies* 64 (2003): 344 and 346; Loy, *The Great Awakening*, 7; Harvey, *An Introduction to Buddhism*, 29.

111. *Dīgha Nikāya*, i.246-251 (*Tevijja Sutta*). "Purity" and "impurity" in Buddhist discourses are redefined in ethical terms, and in this sutta the Buddha was exhorting Vāsettha to give up impurity *qua* moral transgression, rather than ritual imprecision. See Jayarava Michael Attwood, "Did King Ajātasattu Confess to the Buddha, and Did the Buddha Forgive Him?" *Journal of Buddhist Ethics* 15 (2008): 293–4.

112. Nyanaponika Thera and Bhikkhu Bodhi, "Introduction II," in *Numerical Discourses of the Buddha*, 13.

113. Donald S. Lopez, Jr., "Introduction," in *Buddhist Hermeneutics*, edited by Donald S. Lopez, Jr. (Honolulu, Hawai'i: University of Hawai'i Press, 1988), 3.

114. Bhikkhu Ānanda, "The Buddhist Approach to the Scriptures," *Journal of Dharma* 21, no. 4 (October–December 1996): 370–1.

115. *Majjhima Nikāya*, i.39 (*Vatthūpama Sutta*).

116. *Dīgha Nikāya*, iii.180–192 (*Sigālaka Sutta*).

117. *Dīgha Nikāya*, i.143–148 (*Kūtadanta Sutta*).

118. *Anguttara Nikāya*, V.12. See also Bhikkhu Chao Chu in "Buddhism and Dialogue Among the World Religions: Meeting the Challenge of Materialistic Skepticism," in *Ethics, Religion, and the Good Society: New Directions in a Pluralistic World*, edited by Joseph Runzo (Louisville, Kentucky: Westminster/ John Knox Press, 1992), 170–1.

119. *Majjhima Nikāya*, i.133 (*Alagaddūpama Sutta*).

120. Paul R. Fleischman, *The Buddha Taught Nonviolence, Not Pacifism* (Onalaska, Washington: Pariyatti Press, 2002), 33.

121. *Dīgha Nikāya*, ii.72–76 (*Mahāparinibbāna Sutta*).
122. King, *Being Benevolence*, 230–1, and also 72–80.
123. After Nāgārjuna of the Madhyamaka school, the most influential thinker in the Mahāyāna tradition, the principle of "Middle Way" has become the touchstone for the authentication of Buddhist doctrines. In the Mahāyāna setting, the middle also denotes a "combination of elements that, taken in isolation, would be considered extreme," and as such it also denotes the ultimate transcendence of isolated extremes. In Buddhism, it is in the avoidance of extremes that the ethical and soteriological path is to be found, although the exact locale of the middle remains elusive and is constantly being redefined. By contrast, Roger R. Jackson observes, the middle has multiple negative connotations in Western traditions. Roger R. Jackson, "In Search of a Postmodern Middle," in *Buddhist Theology: Critical Reflections by Contemporary Buddhist Scholars*, edited by Roger R. Jackson and John J. Makransky (Richmond, UK: Curzon Press, 2000), 227–37. See also Keown, *A Dictionary of Buddhism*, 162–3.
124. Rita M. Gross, "What Keeps Me in Buddhist Orbit?" in *Religious Feminism and the Future of the Planet: A Christian-Buddhist Conversation*, by Rita M. Gross and Rosemary Radford Ruether (New York: The Continuum Publishing Company, 2001), 114.
125. Harris, "The Female in Buddhism," 65, endnote 32.
126. James R. Egge, *Religious Giving and the Invention of Karma in Theravāda Buddhism* (Richmond, UK: Curzon Press, 2002), 41–67.

Chapter 2

1. *Samyutta Nikāya*, V.45-46 (*Maggasamyutta*).
2. Thomas Kochumuttom, "Ethics-Based Society of Buddhism," *Journal of Dharma* 16, no. 4 (October–December 1991): 410–20.
3. *Samyutta Nikāya*, IV.251 (*Jambukhādakasamyutta*).
4. Prebish and Keown, *Introducing Buddhism*, 49.
5. Keown, *The Nature of Buddhist Ethics*, 22.
6. *Majjhima Nikāya*, i.358 (*Sekha Sutta*).
7. *Anguttara Nikāya*, X.208.
8. *Anguttara Nikāya*, III.2.
9. *Dīgha Nikāya*, i.124 (*Soṇadaṇḍa Sutta*).
10. Keown, *The Nature of Buddhist Ethics*, 8-18 and 83–105.
11. *Ibid.*, 107–8. He further points out that "the view of ethics as preliminary or instrumental usually involves an understanding of karma as a mechanism for personal reward or retribution, which tends to corrode the framework of morality which is by nature interpersonal." *Ibid.*, 13. In the Buddha's own teachings recorded in the *Nikāya* texts, as will be shown in Chapter 4, the term *kamma* was not used in the passive sense, nor was it a strict mechanism that required calculation.
12. Prebish and Keown, *Introducing Buddhism*, 53.
13. *Anguttara Nikāya*, III.55.

14. *Anguttara Nikāya*, IX.7. Also see *Dīgha Nikāya*, iii.133 (*Pāsādika Sutta*) and iii.235 (*Saṅgīti Sutta*).

15. *Samyutta Nikāya*, I.139 (*Brahmasamyutta*); *Anguttara Nikāya*, III.126; *Dīgha Nikāya*, i.171–174 (*Mahāsīhanāda Sutta*), iii.217 (*Saṅgīti Sutta*).

16. Thomas William Rhys Davids, "Nibbāna," in *The Pāli Text Society's Pāli-English Dictionary*, edited by Thomas William Rhys Davids and William Stede (Oxford, England: The Pāli Text Society, 1995).

17. *Ibid.*

18. Payutto, *Buddhadhamma*, 37.

19. *Majjhima Nikāya*, iii.291–2 (*Nagaravindeyya Sutta*).

20. Caroline Augusta Foley Rhys Davids, "Introductory Essay," in *A Buddhist Manual of Psychological Ethics*, 3rd edition (London: The Pali Text Society, 1974), xxii.

21. King, *Being Benevolence*, 66.

22. *Majjhima Nikāya*, i.402–409 (*Apaṇṇaka Sutta*).

23. *Majjhima Nikāya*, i.428–430 (*Cūlamālunkya Sutta*).

24. *Majjhima Nikāya*, iii.187 (*Bhaddekaratta Sutta*).

25. *Majjhima Nikāya*, i.431 (*Cūlamālunkya Sutta*) and i.485–486 (*Aggivacchagotta Sutta*).

26. *Majjhima Nikāya*, i.8 (*Sabbāsava Sutta*).

27. David J. Kalupahana, *Ethics in Early Buddhism* (Honolulu, Hawai'i: University of Hawai'i Press, 1995), 35.

28. *Majjhima Nikāya*, ii.148 (*Assalāyana Sutta*).

29. *Majjhima Nikāya*, ii.148–153 (*Assalāyana Sutta*). See also *Majjhima Nikāya*, i.284 (*Cūla-Assapura Sutta*), ii.85-6 (*Madhurā Sutta*), and ii.128-30 (*Kaṇṇakatthala Sutta*).

30. *Majjhima Nikāya*, ii.178 (*Esukāri Sutta*).

31. *Majjhima Nikāya*, ii.86 (*Madhurā Sutta*).

32. *Majjhima Nikāya*, ii.179 (*Esukāri Sutta*).

33. *Ibid.* See also Bailey and Mabbett, *The Sociology of Early Buddhism*, 247–8.

34. *Sutta Nipāta*, 119–122 (*Vāseṭṭha Sutta*). This sutta is the ninety-eighth sutta in the *Majjhima Nikāya* but is not included in the edition published by the Pāli Text Society because it is identical with the sutta of the same name in the *Sutta Nipāta* that has been published in two versions by the Pāli Text Society. It is included in *Majjhima Nikāya* published by the Wisdom Publications.

35. *Dīgha Nikāya*, iii.271 (*Saṅgīti Sutta*).

36. *Dīgha Nikāya*, iii.81–3 (*Aggañña Sutta*).

37. Bailey and Mabbett, *The Sociology of Early Buddhism*, 196.

38. *Majjhima Nikāya*, i.279 (*Mahā-Assapura Sutta*).

39. *Anguttara Nikāya*, V.2. For passages of the same effect, see also *Majjhima Nikāya*, i.125 (*Kakacūpama Sutta*), ii.11 (*Mahāsakuludāyi Sutta*); *Dīgha Nikāya*, ii.312 (*Mahāsatipaṭṭhāna Sutta*); *Anguttara Nikāya*, I.58, I.204, V.96, and X.51.

40. *Majjhima Nikāya*, ii.25 (*Samaṇamaṇḍikā Sutta*).

41. *Majjhima Nikāya* ii.115-116 (*Bāhitika Sutta*).

42. *Majjhima Nikāya*, i.489–490 (*Mahāvacchagotta Sutta*). See also *Majjhima Nikāya*, iii.46–50 (*Sevitabbāsevitabba Sutta*).

43. *Majjhima Nikāya*, i.489 (*Mahāvacchagotta Sutta*).

44. *Anguttara Nikāya*, X.51.

45. For examples see *Majjhima Nikāya*, i.114 (*Bāhitika Sutta*) and *Samyutta Nikāya*, V.188 (*Satipaṭṭhānasamyutta*).

46. *Majjhima Nikāya*, i.415–419 (*Ambalaṭṭhikārāhulovāda Sutta*). See also *Majjhima Nikāya*, i.115 (*Dvedhāvitakka Sutta*).

47. Abraham Velez de Cea, "The Criteria of Goodness in the Pāli Nikāyas and the Nature of Buddhist Ethics," *Journal of Buddhist Ethics* 11 (2004): 134–5.

48. Loy, "The Karma of Women," 60–1.

49. Harvey, *An Introduction to Buddhist Ethics*, 51. Fitting Buddhist ethics into existing Western categories, however, is what many Buddhist scholars have been trying to do. Both Damien Keown and John Ross Carter, for example, align Buddhist ethics with Aristotelian virtue ethics, while Charles Hallisey considers it a system of moral realism. Keown, *The Nature of Buddhist Ethics*, 21; John Ross Carter, "Buddhist Ethics?" in *The Blackwell Companion to Religious Ethics*, edited by William Schweiker (Malden, Massachusetts: Blackwell Publishing, 2005), 279–80 and 283–4; Charles Hallisey, "Buddhist Ethics: Trajectories," in *The Blackwell Companion to Religious Ethics*, 320–1; also see Maria Heim, "Toward a 'Wider and Juster Initiative': Recent Comparative Work in Buddhist Ethics," *Religion Compass* 1, no. 1 (2007): 109–10.

50. King, *Being Benevolence*, 42-3, and also 60–61.

51. Ives, "Deploying the Dharma," 37–8.

52. Kalupahana, *A History of Buddhist Philosophy*, 102.

53. Gier and Kjellberg, "Buddhism and the Freedom of the Will," 284.

54. Kalupahana, *A History of Buddhist Philosophy*, 103.

55. *Majjhima Nikāya*, ii.25-28 (*Samaṇamaṇḍikā Sutta*).

56. Kulatissa Nanda Jayatilleke, "The Ethical Theory of Buddhism," *The Mahābodhi* 78 (July 1970): 192–7.

57. *Majjhima Nikāya*, i.77–9 (*Mahāsīhanāda Sutta*).

58. *Majjhima Nikāya*, i.440–1 (*Bhaddāli Sutta*). For the significance of the Buddha's admonition of Bhikkhu Bhaddāli in this sutta, see Attwood, "Did King Ajātasattu Confess," 289–90.

59. *Majjhima Nikāya*, i.64 (*Cūlaīhanāda Sutta*).

60. *Majjhima Nikāya*, i.512 (*Māgandiya Sutta*).

61. *Samyutta Nikāya*, V.29, 31, 32 (*Maggasamyutta*), and V.78, 101 (*Bojjhangasamyutta*).

62. *Samyutta Nikāya*, V.35 and 37 (*Maggasamyutta*).

63. *Samyutta Nikāya* I.87 (*Kosalasamyutta*) and V.2 (*Maggasamyutta*).

64. Sulak Sivaraksa, "The Virtuous Friends of Christianity and Buddhism," in *Conflict, Culture, Change: Engaged Buddhism in a Globalized World* (Boston, Massachusetts: Wisdom Publications, 2005), 52.

65. *Majjhima Nikāya*, i.11 (*Sabbāsava Sutta*).

66. Sulak Sivaraksa, "Blessings and Courage," in *Conflict, Culture, Change: Engaged Buddhism in a Globalized World* (Boston, Massachusetts: Wisdom Publications, 2005), 68.

67. *Anguttara Nikāya*, IX.3.

68. *Anguttara Nikāya*, VIII.54. Also see Carter, "Buddhist Ethics?" note 1.

69. For examples, see *Samyutta Nikāya*, V. 2, 30–32, 35–36, 38 (*Maggasamyutta*).

70. *Samyutta Nikāya*, III.15 (*Khandhasamyutta*), IV.80, 144 (*Salāyatanasa-myutta*), and V.414 (*Saccasamyutta*).

71. *Samyutta Nikāya*, II.210-1 (*Kassapasamyutta*), IV.225, 236 (*Vedanāsa-myutta*), V.198, 213 (*Indriyasamyutta*), and V.307 (*Jhānasamyutta*); *Majjhima Nikāya*, i.40 (*Sallekha Sutta*), i.89 (*Mahādukkhakkhandha Sutta*), i.117 (*Dvedhāvitakka Sutta*), i.174 (*Ariyapariyesanā Sutta*), i.246-7 (*Mahāsaccaka Sutta*), i.441 (*Bhaddāli Sutta*), iii.4 (*Gaṇakamoggallāna Sutta*); *Dīgha Nikāya*, iii.131 (*Pāsādika Sutta*); *Anguttara Nikāya*, IX.36.

72. Bailey and Mabbett, *The Sociology of Early Buddhism*, 161–2; Richard F. Gombrich, "Karma and Social Control," *Comparative Studies in Society and History 17* (1975): 212–20; McMahan, *The Making of Buddhist Modernism*, 154.

73. *Majjhima Nikāya*, ii.8–9 (*Mahāsakuludāyi Sutta*).

74. *Majjhima Nikāya*, ii.9–22 (*Mahāsakuludāyi Sutta*).

75. *Samyutta Nikāya*, II.210–1 (*Kassapasamyutta*), IV.225, 236 (*Vedanāsa-myutta*), V.198, 213 (*Indriyasamyutta*), and V.307 (*Jhānasamyutta*); *Majjhima Nikāya*, i.40 (*Sallekha Sutta*), i.89 (*Mahādukkhakkhandha Sutta*), i.117 (*Dvedhāvitakka Sutta*), i.174 (*Ariyapariyesanā Sutta*), i.246–7 (*Mahāsaccaka Sutta*), i.441 (*Bhaddāli Sutta*), iii.4 (*Gaṇakamoggallāna Sutta*); *Dīgha Nikāya*, iii.131 (*Pāsādika Sutta*); *Anguttara Nikāya*, IX.36.

76. *Majjhima Nikāya*, i.15–16 (*Dhammadāyāda Sutta*).

77. *Majjhima Nikāya*, i.90 (*Mahādukkhukkhandha Sutta*).

78. *Samyutta Nikāya*, I.197 (*Vanasamyutta*). See also Bailey and Mabbett, *The Sociology of Early Buddhism*, 166.

79. *Majjhima Nikāya*, iii.116–7 (*Mahāsuññata Sutta*).

80. Sangharakshita, *What Is the Sangha: The Nature of Spiritual Community* (Birmingham: Windhorse Publications, 2000), 244.

81. *Majjhima Nikāya*, i.17–21 (*Bhayabherava Sutta*).

82. *Majjhima Nikāya*, i.83 (*Mahāsīhanāda Sutta*) and *Anguttara Nikāya*, I.211.

83. Liz Wilson made this suggestion in "Celibacy and the Social World," in *Charming Cadavers: Horrific Figurations of the Feminine in Indian Buddhist Hagiographic Literature* (Chicago and London: The University of Chicago Press, 1996), 19–20.

84. Chai-Shin Yu, *Early Buddhism and Christianity: A Comparative Study of the Founders' Authority, the Community, and the Discipline* (Delhi, India: Motilal Banarsidass, 1981), 44–62.

85. Max Weber, *The Sociology of Religion*, translated by Ephraim Fischoff (Boston, Massachusetts: Beacon Press, 1993), 266.

86. Yu, *Early Buddhism and Christianity*, 47, 49, and 54.

87. *Ibid.*, 54.

88. For instances, see *Majjhima Nikāya*, ii.44 (*Vekhanassa Sutta*) and *Dīgha Nikāya*, iii.55 (*Udumbarika-Sīhanāda Sutta*).

89. Robinson et al., *Buddhist Religions*, 32. See also Wijayaratna, *Buddhist Monastic Life*, 173.

90. See *Samyutta Nikāya*, III.160–161 (*Khandhasamyutta*); III.203–216 (*Diṭṭhisamyutta*); III.225 (*Okkantisamyutta*); V.193–194, 205, 207 (*Indriyasamyutta*); V.357 (*Sotāpattisamyutta*); *Anguttara Nikāya*, I.235.

91. Keown, *A Dictionary of Buddhism*, 317. However, in the Mahāyana usage the word *Sangha* does not necessarily include lay followers, either. In the Chinese language, for example, the word used to translate *Sangha*, "*seng*," is also used to refer to *bhikkhu*s or, on occasion, the monastic order as a whole. That is to say, more often than not, the word "*seng*" only denotes male renunciates; neither female renunciates nor lay practitioners are included. Compounded by the traditional deference paid to teachers, for many Chinese Buddhists "taking refuge in the *Sangha*" translates to unconditional respect for monastic members of the *Sangha*, especially the *bhikkhus*.

92. Hammalawa Saddhatissa, *Buddhist Ethics* (Boston, Massachusetts: Wisdom Publications, 1997), 86. See also Ananda Kentish Coomaraswamy, *Buddha and the Gospel of Buddhism* (New Delhi: Munshiram Manoharlal, 1974), 212.

93. *Samyutta Nikāya*, II.107 (*Nidānasamyutta*). See also *Samyutta Nikāya*, V.357 (*Sotāpattisamyutta*); *Majjhima Nikāya*, i.491 (*Mahāvacchagotta Sutta*); and *Anguttara Nikāya*, III.211.

94. *Majjhima Nikāya*, ii.44 (*Vekhanassa Sutta*).

95. Edmund F. Perry and Shanta Ratnayaka, "The Sangha as Refuge: in the Theravāda Buddhist Tradition," in *The Threefold Refuge in the Theravāda Buddhist Tradition*, edited by John Ross Carter, George Doherty Bond, Edmund F. Perry, and Shanta Ratnayaka (Chambersburg, Pennsylvania: Anima Books, 1982), 51.

96. Robinson et al., *Buddhist Religions*, 58. The "first three degrees of Awakening" are stream-entry (*sotāpatti*), once-returning (*sakadāgāmitā*), and non-returning (*anāgāmitā*). The meaning of stream-entry was explained above. A once-returner is one who will come back to this world only one more time before reaching *nibbāna*, and a non-returner is one who is about to reach *nibbāna* but still has residues of clinging so that she or he cannot reach *nibbāna* in this lifetime as *arahant*-s do—after the end of this life, she or he will not come back to this world but will attain *nibbāna* at the time of death, or after death and before rebirth in one of the "Pure Abodes" (*suddhāvāsa*), or sometime after being reborn in one of the "Pure Abodes." The Buddhist cosmos is divided into three realms: the Sense-Sphere Realm, the Form Realm, and the Formless Realm. The Pure Abodes are the five highest planes in the Form Realm to which only non-returners are reborn. For a succinct account of the characteristics of the degrees of Awakening, see Harvey, *An Introduction to Buddhist Ethics*, 39–40.

97. Saddhatissa, *Buddhist Ethics*, 87.

98. *Anguttara Nikāya*, VIII.21.

99. Coghlan, "A Survey of the Sources of Buddhist Ethics," 152–153.

100. Tsomo, "Is The Bhiksuni Vinaya Sexist?" 63. Also see Chakravarti, *The Social Dimensions of Early Buddhism*, 62.

101. Wijayaratna, *Buddhist Monastic Life*, 128.

102. *Ibid.*, 20, 37, and 50–1.

103. Bailey and Mabbett, *The Sociology of Early Buddhism*, 181.

104. *Majjhima Nikāya*, ii.44 (*Vekhanassa Sutta*); Payutto (Phra Rājavara-muni), "Foundations of Buddhist Social Ethics," 29.

105. *Majjhima Nikāya*, i.210 (*Cūḷagosiṅga Sutta*).

106. Peter D. Hershock, "Family Matters: Dramatic Interdependence and the Intimate Realization of Buddhist Liberation," *Journal of Buddhist Ethics* 7 (2000): 103.

107. Perry and Ratnayaka, "The Sangha as Refuge," 49.

108. Chakravarti, "The Social Philosophy of Buddhism and the Problem of Inequality," 213.

109. Kalupahana, *A History of Buddhist Philosophy*, 28.

110. In the ancient patriarchal society at the time of the Buddha, a man was supposed to "own" his wife (or wives) and children, and an upper-class man was supposed to "own" some slaves in addition to his family.

111. Toward the end of the Buddha's life, the Sākyan republic was annexed by the monarchy of Kosala (Sanskrit: Kośala), which then was absorbed into the monarchial empire of Magadha. See Uma Chakravarti, "The Social Philosophy of Buddhism and the Problem of Inequality," *Social Compass* 33 (1986): 200–2 and 214–5; Bailey and Mabbett, *The Sociology of Early Buddhism*, 90–1; Robinson et al., *Buddhist Religions*, 5; Keown, *A Dictionary of Buddhism*, 244–5; Williams, *Buddhist Thought*, 25–6; Harvey, *An Introduction to Buddhism*, 11 and 14–5; William Theodore de Bary, ed., *The Buddhist Tradition in India, China, and Japan* (New York: Vintage Books, 1972), 4–5. For the pervasiveness of warfare at the time of the Buddha, see Bailey and Mabbett, *The Sociology of Early Buddhism*, 103–7 and 91. Evidence of preparation for wars can be seen in *Majjhima Nikāya*, iii.7ff (*Gopakamoggallāna Sutta*) and *Dīgha Nikāya*, ii.86 (*Mahāparinibbāna Sutta*).

112. Chakravarti, "The Social Philosophy of Buddhism and the Problem of Inequality," 202–6; also see Chakravarti, *The Social Dimensions of Early Buddhism*, 7–16; Robinson et al., *Buddhist Religions*, 1; George Erdosy, "City States of North India and Pakistan at the time of the Buddha," in *The Archaeology of Early Historic South Asia*, edited by F. Raymond Allchin (Cambridge and New York: Cambridge University Press, 1995), 99.

113. Uma Chakravarti, "The Social Philosophy of Buddhism and the Problem of Inequality," *Social Compass* 33 (1986): 204 and 206; also in *The Social Dimensions of Early Buddhism*, 16–29 and 67–71. See also Bailey and Mabbett, *The Sociology of Early Buddhism*, 49–51.

114. *Majjhima Nikāya*, i.452 (*Laṭukikopama Sutta*).

115. Chakravarti, "The Social Philosophy of Buddhism and the Problem of Inequality," 216.

116. Bailey and Mabbett, *The Sociology of Early Buddhism*, 50.

117. *Majjhima Nikāya*, i.345 (*Kandaraka Sutta*) and i.240 (*Mahāsaccaka Sutta*); *Dīgha Nikāya*, i.63 (*Sāmaññaphala Sutta*).

118. McMahan, *The Making of Buddhist Modernism*, 155.

119. Payutto (Phra Rājavaramuni), "Foundations of Buddhist Social Ethics," 31.

120. *Majjhima Nikāya*, i.472 (*Gulissāni Sutta*).

121. Bailey and Mabbett, *The Sociology of Early Buddhism*, 168 and 172.

122. See Chakravarti, "The Political, Economic, Social, and Religious Environment at the Time of Buddha," in *The Social Dimensions of Early Buddhism*, 7–64; Chakravarti, "The Social Philosophy of Buddhism and the Problem of Inequality," 200-8; Harvey, *An Introduction to Buddhist Ethics*, 354–5.

123. Harvey, *An Introduction to Buddhist Ethics*, 355.

124. *Anguttara Nikāya*, VIII.19 and IV.202.

125. Sukumar Dutt, *The Buddha and Five After-Centuries* (Calcutta: Sahitya Samsad, 1978), 62–5; Kalupahana, *Ethics in Early Buddhism*, 124–5; William Theodore de Bary, ed., *The Buddhist Tradition in India, China, and Japan* (New York: Vintage Books, 1972), 46 and 48–9; Harvey, *An Introduction to Buddhism*, 25.

126. For the specifics and ramifications of, and possible reasons for, these eight revered conditions, see Salgado, "Eight Revered Conditions," 182–3; Tsomo, "Is The Bhiksuni Vinaya Sexist?" 48–56; Tsomo, "Mahāprajāpatī's Legacy," 27–9; Lorna Dewaraja, "Buddhist Women in India and Precolonial Sri Lanka," in *Buddhist Women Across Cultures: Realizations*, edited by Karma Lekshe Tsomo (Albany, New York: State University of New York Press, 1999), 73; Ellison Banks Findly, "Women Teachers of Women: Early Nuns 'Worthy of My Confidence,' " in *Women's Buddhism, Buddhism's Women: Tradition, Revision, Renewal*, edited by Ellison Banks Findly (Boston, Massachusetts: Wisdom Publications, 2000), 135–40; Gross, *Buddhism After Patriarchy*, 36-8; Horner, "The Eight Chief Rules for Almswomen," in *Women Under Primitive Buddhism*, 118-61; and Khuankaew, "Buddhism and Domestic Violence," 206–7.

127. *Majjhima Nikāya*, i.490–491 (*Mahāvacchagotta Sutta*).

128. *Majjhima Nikāya*, iii.277 (*Nandakovāda Sutta*). Also see Harvey, *An Introduction to Buddhist Ethics*, 357–8.

129. *Samyutta Nikāya*, IV.374–380 (*Abyākatasamyutta*).

130. *Majjhima Nikāya*, i.299–305 (*Cūlavedalla Sutta*).

131. *Samyutta Nikāya*, V.396–397 (*Sotāpattisamyutta*).

132. For example, see *Majjhima Nikāya*, ii.209–213 (*Sangārava Sutta*); similar passage to be found in *Samyutta Nikāya*, I.160–161 (*Brāhmaṇasamyutta*). See also Findly, "Women Teachers of Women," 147.

133. Barnes, "The Nuns at the Stūpa," 28. See also Harvey, *An Introduction to Buddhist Ethics*, 380–1.

134. Barnes, "The Nuns at the Stūpa," 28, and endnote 15 on 32–33. See also Falk, "The Case of the Vanishing Nuns," 207–24.

135. Tsomo "Is the Bhiksunī Vinaya Sexist?" 48–9; Puntarigvivat, "A Thai Buddhist Perspective," 217; Bhikkhunī Kusuma, "Inaccuracies in Buddhist Women's History," 5–12; Barnes, "The Nuns at the Stūpa," 19; Gross, *Buddhism After Patriarchy*, 33-8; Kajiyama, "Women in Buddhism," 53–70; Hirakawa, *Monastic Discipline for the Buddhist Nuns*, 47–98.

136. Barnes, "The Nuns at the Stūpa," 29.

137. Chakravarti, *The Social Dimensions of Early Buddhism*, 50–1.

138. Gross, *Buddhism After Patriarchy*, 34.

139. *Anguttara Nikāya*, I.1–2.

140. *Anguttara Nikāya*, III.260–261. See also Harvey, *An Introduction to Buddhist Ethics*, 380.

141. Gross, *Buddhism After Patriarchy*, 44–5; Harvey, *An Introduction to Buddhist Ethics*, 379.

142. Payutto (Phra Rājavaramuni) speaks as a *bhikkhu* in the Theravāda tradition: "In principle, at least, a Buddhist monk cannot live even a single day without contact with lay people." See Payutto (Phra Rājavaramuni), "Foundations of Buddhist Social Ethics," 31.

143. In addition, it seems that the *bhikkhu*-s generally experience more difficulty with celibacy than the *bhikkhunī*-s and may have needed extra help in combating their desires, such as by conjuring negative images about women. This point is mentioned in Gross, *Buddhism After Patriarchy*, 46–7. *Bhikkhunī* Karma Lekshe Tsomo made the same observation in an oral presentation at the American Academy of Religion annual meetings in Philadelphia, 2005.

144. *Samyutta Nikāya*, I.86 (*Kosalasamyutta*).

145. *Samyutta Nikāya*, I.128–135 (*Bhikkhunīsamyutta*).

146. *Samyutta Nikāya*, I.129 (*Bhikkhunīsamyutta*).

147. *Samyutta Nikāya*, I.196 (*Vangīsasamyutta*).

148. *Dīgha Nikāya*, iii.123–124 (*Pāsādika Sutta*).

149. *Vinaya*, II.255; IV.52–53; Horner, "The Eight Chief Rules for Almswomen," 103–4.

150. For studies on the *Therīgāthā*, see Kathryn R. Blackstone, *Women in the Footsteps of the Buddha: Struggle for Liberation in the Therīgāthā* (Richmond, UK: Curzon Press, 1998); Susan Murcott, *The First Buddhist Women: Translations and Commentary on the Therigatha* (Berkeley, California: Parallax Press, 1991); Horner, *Women Under Primitive Buddhism*, 162–210.

Chapter 3

1. For examples, see Bernard Faure in *The Power of Denial: Buddhism, Purity, and Gender* (Princeton: Princeton University Press, 2003), 119–42; Lucinda Joy Peach, "Social Responsibility, Sex Change, and Salvation: Gender Justice in the *Lotus Sūtra*," *Philosophy East and West* 52, no. 1 (January 2002): 50–74; Miriam L. Levering, "The Dragon Girl and the Abbess of Mo-Shan: Gender and Status in the Ch'an Buddhist Tradition," *Journal of the International Association of Buddhist Studies* 5, no. 1 (1982): 19–35; and Nancy Schuster, "Changing the Female Body: Wise Women and the Bodhisattva Career in Some *Mahāratnakūtasūtras*," *Journal of the International Association of Buddhist Studies* 4, no. 1 (1981): 24–69. Also see Gross' discussion of the *Vimalakīrtinirdeśa Sūtra* in "The Dharma of Gender," 5–7.

2. Gross, "Buddhism and Feminism," 47–9; Gross, *Buddhism After Patriarchy*, 157.

3. Gross, *Buddhism After Patriarchy*, 130–2.

4. Gross, *Buddhism After Patriarchy*, 128 and 158; "Buddhism and Feminism," 49–50; "The Dharma of Gender," 6.

5. For examples, see *Samyutta Nikāya*, III.99, 109 (*Khandhasamyutta*) and III.206–207 (*Diṭṭhisamyutta*); *Dīgha Nikāya*, i.55–57 (*Sāmaññaphala Sutta*). See also *Majjhima Nikāya*, i.402 (*Apaṇṇaka Sutta*) and i.515–518 (*Sandaka Sutta*); *Samyutta Nikāya*, IV.400-1 (*Abyākatasamyutta*).

6. *Samyutta Nikāya*, III.99 and 182–183 (*Khandhasamyutta*), 204–205 (*Diṭṭhisamyutta*). See also *Majjhima Nikāya*, i.130–131 (*Alagaddūpama Sutta*) and i.256–257 (*Mahātaṇhāsankhaya Sutta*).

7. *Samyutta Nikāya*, III.204–205 (*Diṭṭhisamyutta*).

8. For examples, see *Samyutta Nikāya* III.22 and 45 (*Khandhasamyutta*).

9. See Peter Harvey, "The Mind-Body Relationship in Pali Buddhism: A Philosophical Investigation," *Asian Philosophy* 3, no. 1 (March 1993): 31. Also see Gier and Kjellberg, "Buddhism and the Freedom of the Will," 288–9. This view that an individual self, human or non-human, depends on non-self entities in the surrounding to exist supports an environmental ethic, and much has been written on the concept of interconnectedness and Buddhist ecology. It goes beyond the scope of this book.

10. Gier and Kjellberg, "Buddhism and the Freedom of the Will," 291.

11. *Ibid.*

12. *Samyutta Nikāya*, III.140–143 (*Khandhasamyutta*).

13. For examples, see *Samyutta Nikāya*, III.3–5, 16–18, 20–21, 46, 96–99, 102 (*Khandhasamyutta*); and III.196 (*Rādhasamyutta*).

14. *Samyutta Nikāya*, IV.7–15 (*Salāyatanasamyutta*), and V.426 (*Saccasamyutta*).

15. Gier and Kjellberg, "Buddhism and the Freedom of the Will," 282.

16. See *A Comprehensive Manual of Abhidhamma: Pāli Text, Translation and Explanatory Guide of the Abhidhammattha Sangaha of Ācariya Anuruddha*, 1st BPS Pariyatti edition, Pāli text originally edited and translated by Mahāthera Nārada, translation revised by Bhikkhu Bodhi, introduction and explanatory guide by U Rewata Dhamma and Bhikkhu Bodhi, Abhidhamma tables by U Sīlānanda (Onalaska, Washington: Pariyatti Press, 2000), 135–7.

17. Bhikkhu Bodhi, "General Introduction," in *The Connected Discourses of the Buddha: A Translation of the Samyutta Nikāya*, translated from the Pāli by Bhikkhu Bodhi (Boston, Massachusetts: Wisdom Publications, 2000), 45.

18. For examples, see *Samyutta Nikāya*, III.60–61, 63–64, 102–103 (*Khandhasamyutta*).

19. *Samyutta Nikāya*, III.104 (*Khandhasamyutta*).

20. For examples, see *Samyutta Nikāya*, II.28, 70, 78, and 95 (*Nidānasamyutta*). Bhikkhu Bodhi explains, "only when consciousness is present can a compound of material elements function as a sentient body and the mental concomitants participate in cognition." Bhikkhu Bodhi, "General Introduction," in *The Connected Discourses of the Buddha*, 48. Alternatively, *nāma* is understood by some to include consciousness as well. For example, Theravadin scholar Hammalawa Saddhatissa asserts, "*nāma-rūpa* should be understood as the

particularity or determinate character of individual things" and can be used as a synonym for individual beings. Saddhatissa, *Buddhist Ethics*, 5–6. In the early *Upaniṣads*, the term *nāma-rūpa* is used to refer to the things of common experiences, as opposed to the Absolute Reality of *Brāhman*.

21. *A Comprehensive Manual of Abhidhamma*, 26. For a list of the fifty-two mental factors, see *ibid.*, 79.

22. David J. Kalupahana, *The Principles of Buddhist Psychology* (Albany, New York: State University of New York Press, 1987), 20–1.

23. *Samyutta Nikāya*, II.95 (*Nidānasamyutta*).

24. Gross, "The Dharma of Gender," 4.

25. Karma Lekshe Tsomo, "Family, Monastery, and Gender Justice: Reenvisioning Buddhist Institutions," in *Buddhist Women and Social Justice: Ideals, Challenges, and Achievements*, edited by Karma Lekshe Tsomo (Albany, New York: State University of New York Press, 2004), 9–10.

26. Gross, "The Dharma of Gender," 3.

27. *Ibid.*, 7.

28. Sponberg, "Attitudes Toward Women and the Feminine in Early Buddhism," 3–36.

29. Susanne Mrozik, "Materialization of Virtue: Buddhist Discourses on Bodies," in *Bodily Citations: Religion and Judith Butler*, edited by Ellen T. Armour and Susan M. St. Ville (New York: Columbia University Press, 2006), 34–5.

30. Sheng-yen Shih, "Why Are There More Women Followers of Buddhism Than Men? (Weishenmo xuefo hui nu bi nan duo)," *Dharma Drum Monthly*, June 1, 2004.

31. Hsing Yun Shih, "Buddhist Perspective on Issues Concerning the Female Gender (Fojiao dui nuxing wenti de kanfa)," *Pu-Men Journal* (Pu-Men xuebao) *18* (November 2003), accessed May 24, 2011, http://www.fgs.org.tw/master/masterA/books/delectus/discussion/03.htm.

32. Chengyen Shih, *Master Chengyen's Still Thoughts*, Vol. 2, (Taipei: Tzu-Chi Cultural Publishing, 1994), 24 and 162.

33. Pacey, "A Buddhism for the Human World," 70–1.

34. Gross, *Buddhism After Patriarchy*, 117; Gross, "The Dharma of Gender," 11. Similar concerns are shown in Mrozik, "Materialization of Virtue," 35; Tsomo, "Family, Monastery, and Gender Justice," 2; Sara McClintock, "Gendered Bodies of Illusion: Finding a Somatic Method in the Ontic Madness of Emptiness," in *Buddhist Theology: Critical Reflections by Contemporary Buddhist Scholars*, edited by Roger R. Jackson and John J. Makransky (Richmond, UK: Curzon Press, 2000), 261; Faure, *The Power of Denial*, 119–42.

35. Judith Butler, *Gender Trouble: Feminism and the Subversion of Identity* (London and New York: Routledge, 1990), 43–4.

36. *Ibid.*, 173.

37. The idea "gender core" was discussed by Robert Stoller in *Presentations of Gender* (New Haven: Yale University Press, 1985), 11–4, and was referenced by Butler in *Gender Trouble*, 32.

38. Zillah Eisenstein, "Developing a Theory of Capitalist Patriarchy and Socialist Feminism," in *Capitalist Patriarchy: The Case for Socialist Feminism*,

edited by Zillah R. Eisenstein (New York and London: Monthly Review Press, 1979), 27.

39. Iris Marion Young, "Throwing Like a Girl: A Phenomenology of Feminine Body Comportment, Motility, and Spatiality," in *The Thinking Muse: Feminism and Modern French Philosophers*, edited by Jeffner Allen and Iris Marion Young (Bloomington, Indiana: Indiana University Press, 1989), 53–6.

40. Margaret Mead, *Sex and Temperament in Three Primitive Societies* (New York: Morrow, 1935).

41. See, for example, Gunnel Forsberg, "The Difference That Space Makes: A Way to Describe the Construction of Local and Regional Gender Contracts," *Norsk Geografisk Tidsskrift-Norwegian Journal of Geography* 55: 161–5; Simon Duncan and B. Pfau-Effinger, eds, *Gender, Economy and Culture in the European Union* (London and New York: Routledge, 2000).

42. Jean-Sébastien Marcoux, "Body Exchanges: Material Culture, Gender and Stereotypes in the Making," *Home Cultures* 1, issue 1 (2004): 51–60.

43. Michél Foucault, *Discipline and Punish: The Birth of the Prison*, translated from the French by Alan Sheridan, 2nd edition (New York: Vintage Books, 1995), 139.

44. Foucault, "The Means of Correct Training," in *Discipline and Punish*, 170–94.

45. Foucault, *Discipline and Punish*, 169.

46. Judith Butler, *Excitable Speech: A Politics of the Performative* (New York and London: Routledge, 1997), 28.

47. Coincidentally, when explaining the "grammar" of the market, Herman E. Daly and John B. Cobb, Jr. make a similar reference to language: "Individuals are free to try to communicate in whatever ways they wish. But to succeed they have to conform to certain community conventions. The result is not a Tower of Babel, but an amazingly well-ordered structure, as is evident in the grammar of any language. No one designed a language, not even the French Academy. Yet language has an order and logic that would appear to have been the product of rational planning." See Herman E. Daly and John B. Cobb, Jr., *For the Common Good: Redirecting the Economy Toward Community, the Environment, and a Sustainable Future* (Boston, Massachusetts: Beacon Press, 1989), 44.

48. King, *Being Benevolence*, 234.

49. Rajesh Kumar, "Communicative Conflict in Intercultural Negotiations: The Case of American and Japanese Business Negotiations," *International Negotiation* 4, no. 1 (1999): 63–78; Hazel Rose Markus and Shinobu Kitayama, "Culture and the Self: Implications for Cognition, Emotion and Motivation," *Psychological Review* 98, no. 2 (1991): 224–53; Edward Twitchell Hall, *Beyond Culture* (Garden City, New York: Anchor Press, 1976).

50. Kam-hon Lee, Guang Yang, and John L. Graham, "Tension and Trust in International Business Negotiations: American Executives Negotiating with Chinese Executives," *Journal of International Business Studies* 37 (2006): 626. See also Prue Holmes, "Problematising Intercultural Communication Competence in the Pluricultural Classroom: Chinese Students in a New

Zealand University," *Language and Intercultural Communication* 6, no. 1 (2006): 18–34; Wendi L. Adair, Tetsushi Okumura, and Jeanne M. Brett, "Negotiation Behavior When Cultures Collide: The United States and Japan," *Journal of Applied Psychology* 86, no. 3 (June 2001): 371–85; Vairam Arunachalam, James A. Wall, Jr., and Chris Chan, "Hong Kong Versus U.S. Negotiations: Effects of Culture, Alternatives, Outcome Scales, and Mediation," *Journal of Applied Social Psychology* 28, no. 14 (1998): 1219–44; Geert Hofstede and Michael Harris Bond, "The Confucius Connection: From Cultural Roots to Economic Growth," *Organizational Dynamics* 16, no. 4 (Spring 1988): 5–21.

51. Butler, *Excitable Speech*, 16.

52. Linda Martín Alcoff, "The Problem of Speaking for Others," in *Who Can Speak? Authority and Critical Identity*, edited by Judith Roof and Robyn Wiegman (Urbana, Illinois: University of Illinois Press, 1995), 101.

53. Judith Butler, *Undoing Gender* (New York and London: Routledge, 2004), 41.

54. *Ibid.*, 48.

55. Loy, *The Great Awakening*, 182.

56. *Ibid.*, 135.

57. Macy, *Mutual Causality in Buddhism and General Systems Theory*, 58.

58. Loy, *The Great Awakening*, 87.

Chapter 4

1. The term "person-in-kammic-network" is inspired by Daly and Cobb's term "person-in-community" in *For the Commond Good*, in which the term first appeared on page 7. Stating from a theocentric Protestant Christian perspective, Daly and Cobb addressed the inadequacy of taking the abstract concept of *homo economicus* to be the social reality, and they reached a conclusion that is strikingly similar to non-Self and interdependent co-arising in Buddhism, a non-theistic tradition. Rather than a "pure individual" who is entirely independent and self-concerned, they point out, an human being is always a "person-in-community":

> People are constituted by their relationships. We come into being in and through relationships and have no identity apart from them. Our dependence on others is not simply for goods and services. How we think and feel, what we want and dislike, our aspirations and fears—in short, who we are—all come into being socially. . . . We are not only members of societies, but what more we are also depends on the character of these societies. The social character of human existence is primary. The classical *Homo economicus* is a radical abstraction from social reality.
>
> In the real world the self-contained individual does not exist.

Daly and Cobb, *For the Common Good*, 161.

2. Loy, *The Great Awakening*, 183.

3. Gananath Obeyesekere, *Imagining Karma: Ethical Transformation in Amerindian, Buddhist, and Greek Rebirth* (Berkeley, CA: University of California Press, 2002), 2–3; Harvey, *An Introduction to Buddhism*, 11.

4. Obeyesekere, *Imagining Karma*, 100.

5. *Bṛhadāraṇyaka Upaniṣad*, 3.2.12–13. See Obeyesekere, *Imagining Karma*, 4–5. The *Upaniṣads* date as early as 800 BCE and as late as 400 BCE, and *Bṛhadāraṇyaka Upaniṣad* and *Chāndogya Upaniṣad* are generally considered to be earlier than the time of the historical Buddha.

6. *Chāndogya Upaniṣad*, 5.10.8. See Obeyesekere, *Imagining Karma*, 11–2.

7. Kalupahana, *Ethics in Early Buddhism*, 22–4. Also see Harvey, *An Introduction to Buddhism*, 13.

8. Egge, *Religious Giving and the Invention of Karma in Theravāda Buddhism*, 41–67; see also Bailey and Mabbett, *The Sociology of Early Buddhism*, 122.

9. *Majjhima Nikāya*, i.93 (*Cūladukkhakkhandha Sutta*); also ii.214-5 (*Devadaha Sutta*).

10. *Ibid.*

11. For examples, see *Majjhima Nikāya*, i.22 (*Bhayabherava Sutta*), i.278 (*Mahā-Assapura Sutta*), i.347 (*Kandaraka Sutta*), i.357 (*Sekha Sutta*); *Samyutta Nikāya*, II.213 (*Kassapasamyutta*), V.265 (*Iddhipādasamyutta*), and V.305 (*Anuruddhasamyutta*).

12. *Anguttara Nikāya*, V.57.

13. *Samyutta Nikāya*, IV.230-1 (*Vedanāsamyutta*). See also *Majjhima Nikāya*, i.93 (*Cūladukkhakkhandha Sutta*) and ii.214ff (*Devadaha Sutta*).

14. *Samyutta Nikāya*, IV.230–1 (*Vedanāsamyutta*).

15. *Majjhima Nikāya*, ii.222 (*Devadaha Sutta*).

16. *Samyutta Nikāya*, IV.132–3 (*Salāyatanasamyutta*) and II.64–65 (*Nidānasamyutta*).

17. *Majjhima Nikāya*, iii.202–6 (*Cūlakammavibhanga Sutta*).

18. *Dīgha Nikāya*, iii.142–79 (*Lakkhaṇa Sutta*).

19. Kulatissa Nanda Jayatilleke, *The Message of the Buddha* (London: George Allen and Unwin, 1975; reprinted Kandy: Buddhist Publication Society, 2001), 149 and 223.

20. *Majjhima Nikāya*, iii.207–15 (*Mahākammavibhanga Sutta*).

21. McMahan, *The Making of Buddhist Modernism*, 175.

22. *Majjhima Nikāya*, i.44 (*Sallekha Sutta*) and ii.222 (*Devadaha Sutta*).

23. *Anguttara Nikāya*, VIII.12.

24. For examples, see *Majjhima Nikāya*, i.36 (*Ākankheyya Sutta*) and i.415 (*Ambalaṭṭhikārāhulovāda Sutta*); *Anguttara Nikāya*, V.7, V.114, VIII.2, IX.3, and X.20; and *Samyutta Nikāya* V.187 (*Satipaṭṭhānasamyutta*).

25. For examples, see Gier and Kjellberg, "Buddhism and the Freedom of the Will," 287; Luis O. Gómez, "Some Aspects of Free-Will Question in the Nikāyas," *Philosophy East and West* 25, no. 1 (January 1975): 82; Robinson et al., *Buddhist Religions*, 11–2; Williams, *Buddhist Thought*, 73–4; Harvey, *An Introduction to Buddhism*, 40; Harvey, *An Introduction to Buddhist Ethics*, 52–8.

26. *Samyutta Nikāya*, IV.132–3 (*Salāyatanasamyutta*) and II.64–65 (*Nidānasamyutta*).

27. *A Comprehensive Manual of Abhidhamma*, 80. Also see Bhikkhu Ñāṇamoli and Bhikkhu Bodhi, trans., *The Middle Length Discourses of the Buddha: A Translation of the Majjhima Nikāya*, 2nd edition (Boston, Massachusetts: Wisdom Publications, 2001), 1258, note 581.

28. Rita M. Gross, "What Buddhists Could Learn from Christians," in *Religious Feminism and the Future of the Planet: A Christian-Buddhist Conversation*, by Rita M. Gross and Rosemary Radford Ruether (New York: The Continuum Publishing Company, 2001), 176.

29. David J. Kalupahana, *Buddhist Philosophy: A Historical Analysis* (Honolulu, Hawai'i: University of Hawai'i Press, 1976), Chapter 3.

30. Gómez, "Some Aspects of Free-Will Question in the Nikāyas": 81–4.

31. Gier and Kjellberg, "Buddhism and the Freedom of the Will," 285–7.

32. Peter Harvey, "'Freedom of the Will' in the Light of Theravāda Buddhist Teachings," *Journal of Buddhist Ethics* 14 (2007): 37, and also 47–8.

33. Butler, *Gender Trouble*, 187.

34. *Ibid.*, 181.

35. Butler, *Excitable Speech*, 139. See also Janet R. Jakobsen, *Working Alliances and the Politics of Difference* (Bloomington, Indiana: Indiana University Press, 1998), 3.

36. Butler, *Gender Trouble*, 177–9, and 184–5.

37. Loy, *The Great Awakening*, 7.

38. *Ibid.*, 87.

39. Thích Nhất Hanh, *Being Peace* (Berkeley, California: Parallax Press, 1987), 47. See also King, *Being Benevolence*, 92–3.

40. Butler, *Excitable Speech*, 129.

41. Butler, *Undoing Gender*, 52.

42. H. H. the Dalai Lama, *Ethics for the New Millennium* (New York: Riverhead Books, 1999), 41.

43. Walpola Rāhula, *What the Buddha Taught*, revised and expanded edition with texts from Suttas and Dhammapada (New York: Grove Press, 1974), 54.

44. King, *Being Benevolence*, 96, and also 98.

45. See, for instance, Winston L. King, "A Buddhist Ethic without Karmic Rebirth?" *Journal of Buddhist Ethics* 1 (1994): 35.

46. *Samyutta Nikāya*, II.20 (*Nidānasamyutta*).

47. Gross, "What Buddhists Could Learn from Christians," 173.

48. Butler, *Excitable Speech*, 78–80.

49. Loy, *The Great Awakening*, 121.

50. Dalai Lama, *Ethics for the New Millennium*, 29.

51. Nhất Hanh, *Being Peace*, 62.

52. King, *Being Benevolence*, 224–8 and 237–9.

53. For instance, see Winston L. King, "A Buddhist Ethic without Karmic Rebirth?": 36.

54. For example, see McMahan, *The Making of Buddhist Modernism*, 176–7.

55. Gross differentiates "vertical karma," the individualistic, linear, and past-tense aspect of karma, from "horizontal karma," the karma that is being

produced socially, reticularly, and contemporarily. Gross, "What Buddhists Could Learn from Christians," 173–9.

56. *Samyutta Nikāya*, I.85 (*Kosalasamyutta*).

57. *Anguttara Nikāya*, V.292.

58. Attwood, "Did King Ajātasattu Confess," 294–7.

59. Roongraung Boonyoros, "Householders and the Five Precepts," in *Buddhist Behavioral Codes and the Modern World: An International Symposium*, edited by Charles Wei-hsün Fu and Sandra A. Wawrytko (Westport, Connecticut and London: Greenwood Press, 1994), 173.

60. This statement drawn from Buddhist view of dependent origination again coincides with Daly and Cobb's "basic conviction." See Daly and Cobb, *For the Common Good*, 169.

61. McMahan, "A Brief History of Interdependence," in *The Making of Buddhist Modernism*, 149–82, particularly 177–9, 172, and 154–6; Mark L. Blum, "Baptizing Nature: Environmentalism, Buddhism, and Transcendentalism," in *Bukkyo to Shizen* (Buddhism and nature) (Kyoto: Research Institute of Bukkyo University, 2005), 133–63.

62. Hershock, "Family Matters," 93–94.

63. Macy, *Mutual Causality in Buddhism and General Systems Theory*, 194.

64. Kathleen H. Dockett, "Buddhist Empowerment: Individual, Organizational, and Societal Transformation," in *Psychology and Buddhism: From Individual to Global Community*, edited by Kathleen H. Dockett, et al. (New York: Kluwer Academic/Plenum Publishers, 2003), 178–9.

65. Herbert Guenther, *Buddhist Philosophy in Theory and Practice* (Baltimore: Penguin Books, 1972), 75–6.

66. Regarding the Latin American liberation theologians' usage of the word "conscientization," see Paulo Freire, *Pedagogy for the Oppressed* (New York: Herder and Herder, 1970); 18–9; Phillip Berryman, *Liberation Theology: The Essential Facts About the Revolutionary Movement in Latin America and Beyond* (New York: Pantheon Books, 1987), 35–7; Gustavo Gutiérrez, *A Theology of Liberation: History, Politics, and Salvation*, trans. Sister Caridad Inda and John Eagleson, 15th anniversary edition (Maryknoll, New York: Orbis Books, 1988), xxiv, xxix, 57, 70; Ernani Fiori, "Education and Conscientization," in *Conscientization for Liberation*, edited by Louis M. Colonnese (Washington, D.C.: Division for Latin America-USCC, 1971), 123–44; Nigel W. Oakley, "Base Ecclesial Communities and Community Ministry: Some Freirean Points of Comparison and Difference," *Political Theology* 5, no. 4 (2004): 447–8 and 451.

67. *Dīgha Nikāya*, iii.65 (*Cakkavatti-Sīhanāda Sutta*).

68. Kalupahana, *Ethics in Early Buddhism*, 120–1.

69. *Dīgha Nikāya*, iii.86–94 (*Aggañña Sutta*).

70. Kalupahana, *Ethics in Early Buddhism*, 121.

71. *Ibid.*

72. Rebecca Todd Peters, *In Search of the Good Life: The Ethics of Globalization* (New York and London: Continuum, 2004), 43–5.

73. See also Michael D. Yates, *Naming the System: Inequality and Work in the Global Economy* (New York: Monthly Review Press, 2003), 34–5 and 155;

Berryman, *Liberation Theology*, 19–20, 88–91, 123, and 181–2; Gutiérrez, *A Theology of Liberation*, 17, 50–3, and 64; Gutiérrez, *The Density of the Present: Selected Writings* (Maryknoll, New York: Orbis Books, 1999), 73, 75–6, and 159–60.

74. Loy, *The Great Awakening*, 93.

75. Joseph M. Kitagawa, "Introduction," in *The Religious Traditions of Asia: Religion, History, and Culture*, edited by Joseph M. Kitagawa (London and New York: Routledge, 2002), viii.

76. Roksana Bahramitash, *Liberation from Liberalization: Gender and Globalization in Southeast Asia* (London and New York: Zed Books, 2005), 24–5. See also Y. Alvin So, *Social Change and Development: Modernization, Dependency, and World-Systems Theories* (Newbury Park, California: Sage Publications, 1990).

77. Berryman, *Liberation Theology*, 11–2.

78. See David C. Korten, *When Corporations Rule the World*, 2nd edition (Bloomfield, Connecticut: Kumarian Press, 2001), 165–6; also 59–92 and 107–20; Yates, *Naming the System*, 41, 47–8, 52, and 55–7; Bahramitash, *Liberation from Liberalization*, 19, 21, 24–5; Peters, *In Search of the Good Life*, 73–5 and 81–4; Thomas Pogge, "The First United Nations Millennium Development Goal: A Cause for Celebration?" *Journal of Human Development* 5, no. 3 (November 2004): 387–8; Gutiérrez, *The Density of the Present*, 131–2; Gutiérrez, *A Theology of Liberation*, 53; Berryman, *Liberation Theology*, 123 and 183; Bruce Cumings, "Still the American Century?" *Review of International Studies* 25, Special Issue (1999): 287; Ray Kiely and Phil Marfleet, *Globalisation and the Third World* (London: Routledge, 1998), 32–3; Catherine Caulfield, *Masters of Illusion: The World Bank and the Poverty of Nations* (New York: Henry Holt & Co., 1996); Bruce Rich, *Mortgaging the Earth: The World Bank, Environmental Impoverishment, and the Crisis of Overdevelopment* (Boston, Massachusetts: Beacon Press, 1994).

79. United Nations Development Programme, *Human Development Report 1999: Globalization with a Human Face*, 3, 22, 28, and 37, accessed May 24, 2011, http://hdr.undp.org/en/media/HDR_1999_EN.pdf.

80. United Nations Development Programme, *Human Development Report 2007/2008: Fighting Climate Change: Human Solidarity in a Divided World*, 25, accessed May 24, 2011, http://hdr.undp.org/en/media/HDR_20072008_EN_Complete.pdf.

81. Pogge, "The First United Nations Millennium Development Goal," 389.

82. Gutiérrez, *A Theology of Liberation*, 51 and 64; also in *The Density of the Present*, 76.

83. Yates, *Naming the System*, 44; see also 42, 48, and 155.

84. United Nations Development Programme, *Human Development Report 2003: Millennium Development Goals: A Compact Among Nations to End Human Poverty*, 9, accessed May 24, 2011, http://hdr.undp.org/en/media/hdr03_complete.pdf.

85. UNDP, *Human Development Report 2007/2008*, 25 and 45. See also Peters, *In Search of the Good Life*, 206–8.

86. Pogge, "The First United Nations Millennium Development Goal," 392.

87. UNDP, *Human Development Report 2003*, 310–30; Bahramitash, *Liberation from Liberalization*, 23–4; Pogge, "The First United Nations Millennium Development Goal," 386; Yates, *Naming the System*, 60–1; Korten, *When Corporations Rule the World*, 51.

88. Bahramitash, *Liberation from Liberalization*, 2.

89. For examples, see Sarah Kindon, "Of Mothers and Men: Questioning Gender and Community Myths in Bali," in *The Myth of Community: Gender Issues in Participatory Development*, edited by Irene Guijt and Meera Kaul Shah, with a foreword by Robert Chambers (London: Intermediate Technology Publications, 1998), 156–9; Morag Humble, "Assessing PRA for Implementing Gender and Development," in *The Myth of Community*, 35; Ranjani K. Murthy, "Learning About Participation from Gender Relations of Female Infanticide," in *The Myth of Community*, 80–2; Irene Guijt and Meera Kaul Shah, "Waking Up to Power, Conflict and Process," in *The Myth of Community*, 1–23.

90. See Patricia Maguire, "Proposing a More Feminist Participatory Research: Knowing and Being Embraced Openly," in *Participatory Research in Health: Issues and Experiences*, edited by Korrie de Koning and Marion Martin (London: Zed Books, 1996), 29–30; Bahramitash, *Liberation from Liberalization*, 24.

91. UNDP, *Human Development Report 2003*, 310–30; UNDP, *Human Development Report 2007/2008*, 326–9.

92. UNDP, *Human Development Report 2007/2008*, 43. See also Peters, *In Search of the Good Life*, 85–6.

93. UNDP, *Human Development Report 2007/2008*, 43–4. See also Peters, *In Search of the Good Life*, 114–5.

94. UNDP, *Human Development Report 2007/2008*, 25–31 and 73–89.

95. *Ibid.*, 81–2.

96. *Ibid.*, 81–2 and 76–7.

97. *Ibid.*, 86.

98. See Peters, *In Search of the Good Life*, 144–50.

99. Thích Nhât Hanh, "The Individual, Society, and Nature," in *The Path of Compassion: Writings on Socially Engaged Buddhism*, edited by Fred Eppsteiner, revised 2nd edition (Berkeley, California: Parallax Press, 1988), 42.

100. Thích Nhât Hanh, "Ahimsa: The Path of Harmlessness," in *Buddhist Peacework: Creating Cultures of Peace*, edited by David W. Chappell (Boston, Massachusetts: Wisdom Publications, 1999), 156.

101. Sulak Sivaraksa, "The Virtuous Friends of Christianity and Buddhism," in *Conflict, Culture, Change: Engaged Buddhism in a Globalized World* (Boston, Massachusetts: Wisdom Publications, 2005), 56.

102. Gutiérrez, *A Theology of Liberation*, 65.

103. Quoted by Gutiérrez in *A Theology of Liberation*, 66.

104. Gutiérrez, *The Power of the Poor in History*, trans. Robert R. Barr (Maryknoll, New York: Orbis Books, 1983), 45.

105. "Latin America: A Continent of Violence," a document signed by more than 900 Latin American priests, 1968, in *Between Honesty and Hope*, 84. Quoted by Gutiérrez in *A Theology of Liberation*, 64.

106. Gutiérrez, *The Power of the Poor in History*, 45. See also Gutiérrez, *The Density of the Present*, 32.

107. Gutiérrez, "The Meaning and Scope of Medellín," first published in 1989 and compiled in *The Density of the Present*, 59–101.

108. Gutiérrez, *A Theology of Liberation*, 24.

109. Gutiérrez, *The Power of the Poor in History*, 48

110. *Ibid.*, 45.

111. Gutiérrez, *A Theology of Liberation*, 90 and 135.

112. See King, *Being Benevolence*, 72–80 and 164–201.

113. Johan Galtung, *Buddhism: A Quest for Unity and Peace* (Ratmalana, Sri Lanka: Sarvodaya Book Publishing Services, 1993), 22.

114. David R. Loy, "Zen and the Art of War," in *The Great Awakening: A Buddhist Social Theory* (Boston, Massachusetts: Wisdom Publications, 2003), 143–56; Ananda Abeysekara, "The Saffron Army, Violence, Terror(ism): Buddhism, Identity, and Difference in Sri Lanka," *Numen* 48, no. 1 (2001): 1–46.

115. Brian Daizen Victoria, "Engaged Buddhism: A Skeleton in the Closet?" *Journal of Global Buddhism* 2 (2001): 72.

116. Gutiérrez, *A Theology of Liberation*, 14.

117. Gutiérrez, *The Density of the Present*, 76.

118. Kenneth E. Boulding, "Twelve Friendly Quarrels with Johan Galtung," *Journal of Peace Research* 14, no. 1 (1977): 81. He however does not address the "inner" factors of the *dukkha*-producing tendencies of people. Instead, he rests his hope of solving poverty and human misery on economic development and increased productivity.

119. Dalai Lama, *Ethics for the New Millennium*, 177.

120. Maha Ghosananda, *Step by Step: Meditations on Wisdom and Compassion* (Berkeley, California: Parallax Press, 1992), 27.

121. Thích Nhât Hanh and Daniel Berrigan, *The Raft Is Not the Shore: Conversations Toward a Buddhist-Christian Awareness*, foreword by bell hooks (Maryknoll, New York: Orbis, 2001), 75.

122. Dalai Lama, *Ethics for the New Millennium*, 202.

Chapter 5

1. Keown, *The Nature of Buddhist Ethics*, 64–8.

2. Gross, "Buddhism and Feminism," 47–9; Gross, *Buddhism After Patriarchy*, 157.

3. Regarding the popular modern Western (mis-)understanding of Buddhism as a way of de-conditioning through meditation, see McMahan, *The Making of Buddhist Modernism*, 195–9.

4. *Samyutta Nikāya*, III.42–4, 102 (*Khandhasamyutta*), IV.287 (*Cittasamyutta*); *Majjhima Nikāya*, iii.17–9 (*Mahāpuṇṇama Sutta*), iii.188–9 (*Bhaddekaratta Sutta*), iii.227-8 (*Uddesavibhanga Sutta*). Translation modified from Bhikkhu Bodhi, *The Connected Discourses of the Buddha*. See also *Samyutta Nikāya*, III.158–9 (*Khandhasamyutta*), IV.259 (*Jambukhādakasamyutta*); *Majjhima Nikāya*, i.299–300 (*Cūlavedalla Sutta*), iii.284–285 (*Chachakka Sutta*).

5. *Majjhima Nikāya*, iii.227–8 (*Uddesavibhanga Sutta*).
6. *Samyutta Nikāya*, I.13 (*Devatāsamyutta*).
7. *Majjhima Nikāya*, ii.232–3 (*Pañcattaya Sutta*) and iii.19–20 (*Mahāpuṇṇama Sutta*).
8. *Majjhima Nikāya*, iii.250 (*Saccavibhanga Sutta*).
9. *A Comprehensive Manual of Abhidhamma*, 83.
10. *Samyutta Nikāya*, III.111–2 (*Khandhasamyutta*).
11. *Dīgha Nikāya*, ii. 66–8 (*Mahānidāna Sutta*).
12. *Majjhima Nikāya*, iii.249 (*Saccavibhanga Sutta*).
13. *A Comprehensive Manual of Abhidhamma*, 86.
14. *Anguttara Nikāya*, I.51.
15. *Samyutta Nikāya*, V.1 (*Maggasamyutta*).
16. See Harvey, "Avoiding Unintended Harm to the Environment and the Buddhist Ethic of Intention," *Journal of Buddhist Ethics* 14 (2007): 2–4.
17. *Samyutta Nikāya*, II.211 (*Kassapasamyutta*), IV.236 (*Vedanāsamyutta*), V.198, 213–5 (*Indriyasamyutta*), and V.307 (*Jhānasamyutta*); *Majjhima Nikāya*, i.40-1 (*Sallekha Sutta*), i.89–90 (*Mahādukkhakkhandha Sutta*), i.117 (*Dvedhāvitakka Sutta*), iii.4 (*Gaṇakamoggallāna Sutta*); *Dīgha Nikāya*, iii.131 (*Pāsādika Sutta*); *Anguttara Nikāya*, IX.36.
18. *Samyutta Nikāya*, V.9 (*Maggasamyutta*); *Majjhima Nikāya*, iii.251–2 (*Saccavibhanga Sutta*); *Dīgha Nikāya*, ii.312-3 (*Mahāsatipaṭṭhāna Sutta*) and iii.226 (*Sangīti Sutta*).
19. In a rather personal example, when my father passed away, my mother insisted that my brother should get at least one half, preferably more, of everything that my father had owned (and she and I would divide up the rest), even though the current inheritance law in Taiwan stipulates that my father's property should be divided evenly among my mother, my brother, and I. She argued that "traditionally" the oldest son and the oldest grandson would both get a bigger cut, and that meant my brother should get a lot more since there was no grandson yet (that is, she thought my brother should take a bigger share for himself and receive an additional bigger share on behalf of his future oldest son). "*Traditionally*," I replied, "females do not count, and so everything should go to Brother." She knew it was true because she suddenly recalled that neither her mother nor any of the four sisters in her natal family inherited any of her father's property—it was divided into four portions, with her oldest brother claiming two portions and each of the other two brothers having one portion. As "traditional" as she would like to be, she thought that both she and I were still entitled to something. She did not appeal to the "tradition" again with regard to inheritance after that conversation. In this incident, she was not aware of her trying to carry out a gender-discriminative and age-discriminative cultural convention, even though she had resented that convention herself.
20. Lawrence Summers' memorandum to the World Bank regarding industrial pollution in 1991 is a glaring example. Knowing that industrial pollution causes cancerous diseases, deaths, and environmental damages, he however advocated the migration of dirty industries to the so-called "third-world" countries. People in poor countries, he argued, have less earning

potential and do not live that long anyway, so it is economically most efficient for rich countries to dump their toxic wastes in poor countries. Lawrence Summers, internal World Bank memorandum dated December 12, 1991, 5. See Yates, *Naming the System*, 151; Korten, *When Corporations Rule the World*, 91.

21. Oftentimes the well-intended Western feminists' criticisms against the patriarchal practices in non-Western societies have the effect of locking the latter in perpetual backwardness and giving the men in those societies more reasons to tighten up their control of women, in the name of resisting Western imperialism and protecting their traditions. See Rita M. Gross and Rosemary Radford Ruether, "Introduction: A Dialogue about Dialogue," in *Religious Feminism and the Future of the Planet* (New York: The Continuum Publishing Company, 2001), 19–21; Rey Chow, " 'It's you, and not me': Domination and 'Othering' in Theorizing the 'Third World'," in *American Feminist Thought at Century's End: A Reader*, edited by Linda S. Kauffman (Cambridge, Massachusetts: Blackwell, 1993), 95–106; Butler, *Undoing Gender*, 187.

22. See also King, *Being Benevolence*, 69–70.

23. *Majjhima Nikāya*, i.297 (*Mahāvedalla Sutta*) and iii.146 (*Anuruddha Sutta*).

24. King, *Being Benevolence*, 6 and 24.

25. Bhadantācariya Buddhaghosa, *The Path of Purification (Visuddhimagga)*, translated by Bhikkhu Ñānamoli (Boulder, Colorado: Shambhala, 1976), IX, 94–101.

26. Chris Frakes, "Do the Compassionate Flourish?: Overcoming Anguish and the Impulse towards Violence," *Journal of Buddhist Ethics* 14: 117–8 and 115.

27. Prebish and Keown, *Introducing Buddhism*, 122.

28. See King, *Being Benevolence*, 33–34 and 22–27.

29. *Majjhima Nikāya*, i.56–7 (*Satipatthāna Sutta*); *Dīgha Nikāya*, ii.291–2 (*Mahāsatipatthāna Sutta*).

30. Sarah Shaw, comp., *Buddhist Meditation: An Anthology of Texts from the Pāli Canon* (London and New York: Routledge, 2006), 18.

31. Stephen Batchelor, *Buddhism Without Beliefs: A Contemporary Guide to Wakening*, (New York: Riverhead Books, 1997), 64.

32. *Majjhima Nikāya*, i.59 (*Satipatthāna Sutta*); *Dīgha Nikāya*, ii.298–300 (*Mahāsatipatthāna Sutta*).

33. Kalupahana, *A History of Buddhist Philosophy*, 41.

34. Kenneth K. Inada, "The Nature of Emptiness and Buddhist Ethics," *Chung-Hwa Buddhist Journal* 13, no. 2 (May 2000): 256 and 272–3.

35. Daniel Goleman, *The Meditative Mind: The Varieties of Meditative Experience* (New York: Tarcher, 1996), 163–5 and 167.

36. *Ibid.*, 175.

37. Kalupahana, *A History of Buddhist Philosophy*, 117.

38. *Majjhima Nikāya*, iii.73 (*Mahācattārīsaka Sutta*).

39. Carter, "Buddhist Ethics?" 280–1.

40. McMahan, *The Making of Buddhist Modernism*, 184–6, 192–9.

41. *Anguttara Nikāya*, VIII.39.

42. King, *Being Benevolence*, 52.

43. Somsuda Pupatana, "The Development of Peace through the Process of Morality," *Chung-Hwa Buddhist Journal* 13, no. 2 (May 2000): 627–8 and 630.

44. Dalai Lama, *Ethics for the New Millennium*, 150.

45. Kalupahana, *A History of Buddhist Philosophy*, 35.

46. *Samyutta Nikāya*, II.210–1 (*Kassapasamyutta*), IV.225, 236 (*Vedanāsamyutta*), V.198, 213 (*Indriyasamyutta*), and V.307 (*Jhānasamyutta*); *Majjhima Nikāya*, i.40 (*Sallekha Sutta*), i.89 (*Mahādukkhakkhandha Sutta*), i.117 (*Dvedhāvitakka Sutta*), i.174 (*Ariyapariyesanā Sutta*), i.246–7 (*Mahāsaccaka Sutta*), i.441 (*Bhaddāli Sutta*), iii.4 (*Gaṇakamoggallāna Sutta*); *Dīgha Nikāya*, iii.131 (*Pāsādika Sutta*); *Anguttara Nikāya*, IX.36.

47. Payutto, *Buddhadhamma*, 248.

48. Pupatana, "The Development of Peace through the Process of Morality," 613–34.

49. *Majjhima Nikāya*, i.169–70 and i.164–5 (*Ariyapariyesanā Sutta*).

50. *Majjhima Nikāya*, i.487 (*Aggivacchagotta Sutta*) and i.167 (*Ariyapariyesanā Sutta*).

51. For the interrelation between reason and emotion in Buddhism, see King, *Being Benevolence*, 63–72.

52. Prebish and Keown, *Introducing Buddhism*, 53.

53. Sulak Sivaraksa, *A Socially Engaged Buddhism* (Bangkok: Thai Inter-Religious Commission for Development, 1988), 75–6.

54. Minnie Bruce Pratt, "Identity: Skin Blood Heart," in *Yours in Struggle: Three Feminist Perspectives on Anti-Semitism and Racism*, by Elly Bulkin, Minnie Bruce Pratt, and Barbara Smith (Brooklyn, New York: Long Haul Press, 1984), 47–8.

55. Dalai Lama, *Ethics for the New Millennium*, 28 and 73.

56. King, *Being Benevolence*, 54.

57. Payutto, *Buddhadhamma*, 246.

58. Dalai Lama, *Ethics for the New Millennium*, 152–3.

59. Sulak Sivaraksa, "Buddhism and Contermporary International Trends," in *Inner Peace, World Peace: Essays on Buddhism and Nonviolence*, edited by Kenneth Kraft (Albany, New York: State University of New York Press, 1992), 127.

60. Ahangamage Tudor Ariyaratne, "The Non-Violent Struggle for Economic and Social Justice." Address to the Sixth International Conference of the Society for Buddhist-Christian Studies, Tacoma, Washington, August 2000 (Ratmalana, Sri Lanka: Sarvodaya Vishva Lekha, 2000), 5.

61. *Majjhima Nikāya*, i.322 (*Kosambiya Sutta*) and ii.251 (*Sāmagāma Sutta*); *Dīgha Nikāya*, ii.80 (*Mahāparinibbāna Sutta*).

62. *Majjhima Nikāya*, i.206 (*Cūḷagosinga Sutta*) and iii.156 (*Upakkilesa Sutta*).

63. Loy, *The Great Awakening*, 180.

64. Kalupahana, *Ethics in Early Buddhism*, 131.

65. G. S. P. Misra, *The Age of Vinaya* (New Delhi: Munshiram Manoharlal, 1972), 90.

66. Wijayaratna, *Buddhist Monastic Life*, 122, quoting from the Pāli *Vinaya* III 21; IV 91, 120, 182, 299. See also Charles S. Prebish, "Varying the Vinaya: Creative Responses to Modernity," in *Buddhism in the Modern World: Adaptations of an Ancient Tradition*, edited by Steven Heine and Charles S. Prebish (New York: Oxford University Press, 2003), 61.

67. Relevant critiques can be found in Daly and Cobb, *For the Common Good*, 49–51.

68. Boonyoros, "Householders and the Five Precepts," 172.

69. Harvey, *An Introduction to Buddhism*, 73.

70. *Ibid.* See also Uma Chakravarti, "Buddhism As a Discourse of Dissent?: Class and Gender," *Pravada 1.5* (May 1992): 16.

71. Simon Zadek, "The Practice of Buddhist Economics: Another View," *American Journal of Economics and Sociology* 42, no. 4 (October, 1993): 435–6.

72. *Majjhima Nikāya*, i.212–9 (*Mahāgosinga Sutta*).

73. *Ibid.*, i.219.

74. *Ibid.*

75. *Ibid.*

76. Kalupahana, *A History of Buddhist Philosophy*, 117.

77. John J. Makransky, "Historical Consciousness as an Offering to the Trans-Historical Buddha," in *Buddhist Theology: Critical Reflections by Contemporary Buddhist Scholars*, edited by Roger Jackson and John Makransky (Surrey, UK: Curzon Press, 2000), 126.

78. Galtung, *Buddhism: A Quest for Unity and Peace*, 1.

79. *Ibid.*, 2.

80. *Ibid.*, 4.

81. *Majjhima Nikāya*, i.445 (*Bhaddāli Sutta*).

82. *Dīgha Nikāya*, ii.154 (*Mahāparinibbāna Sutta*).

83. See Elise Anne DeVido, *Taiwan's Buddhist Nuns* (Albany, New York: State University of New York Press, 2010), 105–10.

84. *Dīgha Nikāya*, ii.154 (*Mahāparinibbāna Sutta*).

85. *Majjhima Nikāya*, i.210 (*Cūḷagosinga Sutta*).

86. Sulak Sivaraksa, "An Alternative Agenda for a Global Economy," *Seeds of Peace 13*, no. 1 (January-April 1997): 15–6. Quoted in Sallie B. King, *Being Benevolence*, 114. For the development of such participatory small communities in Sri Lanka, see King, *Being Benevolence*, 114–7.

87. Thích Nhât Hanh, *Interbeing: Fourteen Guidelines for Engaged Buddhism*, 3rd edition (Berkeley, California: Parallax Press, 1998), 113.

88. *Majjhima Nikāya*, iii.267-270 (*Punnovāda Sutta*).

89. Dharmachari Lokamitra, "Buddhism and Society—the Dynamics of Right Livelihood" (paper presented at the Fourth Chung-Hwa International Conference on Buddhism: The Role of Buddhism in the 21st Century, Taipei, Taiwan, January 18–20, 2002), 11.

90. Macy, *Mutual Causality in Buddhism and General Systems Theory*, 191.

91. Regarding the difference between Buddhist approach and Western justice discourse, see King, *Being Benevolence*, 202–28.

92. Gross, "What Keeps Me in Buddhist Orbit?" 107–20.

Chapter 6

1. Johan Galtung, "Cultural Violence," *Journal of Peace Research* 27, no. 3 (August 1990): 291. See also Galtung, *Peace by Peaceful Means: Peace and Conflict, Development and Civilization* (Oslo, Norway: International Peace Research Institute; and London and Thousand Oaks, California: Sage Publications, 1996), 31.

2. Galtung, "Cultural Violence," 294–295.

3. *Ibid.*, 295.

4. Another renowned peace studies scholar Kenneth E. Boulding criticizes Galtung's careless definitions of the terms "negative peace" and "positive peace." While I do agree with Boulding's critique that Galtung seems to hold a very static view and seems to lack a grasp of the dynamics of social situations, unlike Boulding I find Galtung's distinction between "negative peace" and "positive peace" useful. At least by making the distinction he is pointing out that there is much more to be desired than just the absence of direct violence, thereby rejecting possible structural oppression done by the ruling class in the name of maintaining "peace" that is "negative" in nature. For Boulding's critiques on Galtung's static view and definitions of terms, see Boulding, "Twelve Friendly Quarrels with Johan Galtung," 78–9.

5. *Dīgha Nikāya*, ii.223 (*Mahāgovinda Sutta*).

6. Nhât Hanh, *Interbeing*, 6.

7. Nhât Hanh, *Being Peace*, 80. See also King, *Being Benevolence*, 230.

8. King, *Being Benevolence*, 175.

9. Galtung, *Buddhism: A Quest for Unity and Peace*, 4–22.

10. King, *Being Benevolence*, 230.

11. Jeffrey R. Seul, " 'Ours Is the Way of God': Religion, Identity, and Intergroup Conflict," *Journal of Peace Research* 36, no. 5 (September 1999): 553–69; Ronald J. Fisher, "Cyprus: The Failure of Mediation and Escalation of an Identity-Based Conflict to an Adversarial Impasse," *Journal of Peace Research* 38, no. 3 (May 2001; Special Issue on Conflict Resolution in Identity-Based Disputes): 307–26; Salman Elbedour, David T. Bastien, and Bruce A. Center, "Identity Formation in the Shadow of Conflict: Projective Drawings by Palestinian and Israeli Arab Children from the West Bank and Gaza" *Journal of Peace Research* 34, no. 2 (May 1997): 217–31.

12. Davin Bremner, "South African Experiences with Identity and Community Conflicts," *Journal of Peace Research* 38, no. 3 (May 2001; Special Issue on Conflict Resolution in Identity-Based Disputes): 393–405.

13. Dalai Lama, *Ethics for the New Millennium*, 47.

14. *Ibid.*, 45.

15. Galtung, "Cultural Violence," 298.

16. Galtung, *Buddhism: A Quest for Unity and Peace*, 65.

17. *Ibid.*, 3–4.

18. Sulak Sivaraksa, "Buddhism in Asia: Challenges & Prospects," *Just Commentary: International Movement for a Just World* 6, no. 9 (September 2006): 9.

19. Gross, *Buddhism After Patriarchy*, 263.

20. Ronald M. Green, "Buddhist Economic Ethics: A Theoretical Approach," in *Ethics, Wealth, and Salvation: A Study in Buddhist Social Ethics*, edited by Russell F. Sizemore and Donald K. Swearer (Columbia, South Carolina: University of South Carolina Press, 1990), 225.

21. King, *Being Benevolence*, 230.

22. For the complete lists of the ten *pāramī* or *pāramitā*, see Keown, *Dictionary of Buddhism*, 212.

23. The White House, "The Terrorist Threat to the US Homeland" (July 17, 2007), 6–7, accessed May 24, 2011, http://www.dni.gov/press_releases/20070717_release.pdf.

24. The Pew Global Attitudes Project, "Global Opinion Trends 2002-2007" (July 24, 2007), 45–54, accessed May 24, 2011, http://pewglobal.org/files/pdf/257.pdf.

25. Zillah R. Eisenstein, *Against Empire: Feminisms, Racism, and the West* (London and New York: Zed Books, 2004), 9.

26. Loy, *The Great Awakening*, 107.

27. *Ibid.*

28. For a short account of the imperialistic foreign policies of the U.S. based on corporate interests since the World War II, see Korten, *When Corporations Rule the World*, 136–42. For the component of military coercion in the U.S. global hegemony, see John Agnew, *Hegemony: The New Shape of Global Power* (Philadelphia, Pennsylvania: Temple University Press, 2005), 60–1, 71, 125, 133–4, 136–8, 148–9, and 187.

29. Relevant discussion on the capitalistic devaluation of women's domestic work can be found in Nancy Chodorow, "Mothering, Male Dominance, and Capitalism," in *Capitalist Patriarchy: The Case for Socialist Feminism*, edited by Zillah R. Eisenstein (New York and London: Monthly Review Press, 1979), 86–90.

30. Rachel Bowlby, "Domestication," in *Feminism Beside Itself*, edited by Diane Elam and Robyn Wiegman (London and New York: Routledge, 1995), 71–91.

31. Anne McClintock, "Soft-Soaping Empire: Commodity Racism and Imperial Advertising," in *Traveller's Tales: Narratives of Home and Displacement*, edited by George Robertson, Melinda Mash, Lisa Tickner, Jon Bird, Barry Curtis, and Tim Putnam (London and New York: Routledge, 1994), 131–54; Cynthia Enloe, " 'Just Like One of the Family': Domestic Servants in World Politics," in *Bananas Beaches Bases: Making Feminist Sense of International Politics* (Berkeley, California: University of California Press, 1989), 177–94.

32. Jakobsen, *Working Alliances and the Politics of Difference*, 59.

33. Eisenstein, *Against Empire*, 6.

34. Bernice Johnson Reagon, "Coalition Politics: Turning the Century," in *Feminism and Politics*, edited by Anne Phillips (New York: Oxford University Press, 1998), 247.

35. Macy, *Mutual Causality in Buddhism and General Systems Theory*, 60. See also *Samyutta Nikāya*, II.29–32 (*Nidānasamyutta*).

36. Macy, *Mutual Causality in Buddhism and General Systems Theory*, xv–xvi.

37. Fleischman, *The Buddha Taught Nonviolence, Not Pacifism*, 43.

38. Nhât Hanh, *Interbeing*, 48.

39. Victoria, "Engaged Buddhism: A Skeleton in the Closet?" 72.

40. Galtung, *Buddhism: A Quest for Unity and Peace*, 22.

41. Sulak Sivaraksa, "Buddhist Solutions to Global Conflict," in *Conflict, Culture, Change: Engaged Buddhism in a Globalizing World* (Boston, Wisdom Publications, 2005), 5.

42. *Ibid.*, 7.

43. Aung San Suu Kyi, *The Voice of Hope: Conversations with Alan Clements*, with contributions by U Kyi Maung and U Tin U (New York: Penguin, 1997), 7.

44. Gene Sharp, "Nonviolent Action: An Active Technique of Struggle," in *Nonviolence in Theory and Practice*, edited by Robert L. Holmes (Prospect Heights, Illinois: Waveland Press, 1990), 147.

45. Gene Sharp, "The Methods of Nonviolent Action," in *Waging Nonviolent Struggle: 20th Century Practice and 21st Century Potential* (Boston, Massachusetts: Extending Horizons Books), 51–4.

46. *Ibid.*, 55–9. See also King, *Being Benevolence*, 246–7.

47. King, *Being Benevolence*, 149. See also Mark Kurlansky, *Nonviolence: Twenty-Five Lessons from the History of a Dangerous Idea*, foreword by His Holiness the Dalai Lama (New York: Random House, 2006), 6.

48. Nhât Hanh, "Ahimsa," 156.

49. Gross, "What Keeps Me in Buddhist Orbit?" 119–20.

50. Suu Kyi, *The Voice of Hope*, 112.

51. The Combahee River Collective, "The Combahee River Collective Statement," in *Theorizing Feminism: Parallel Trends in the Humanities and Social Sciences*, edited by Anne C. Hermann and Abigail J. Stewart (Boulder, Colorado: Westview Press, 1994), 33.

52. King, *Being Benevolence*, 231.

53. Loy, *The Great Awakening*, 109. For the Dalai Lama's call to "internal disarmament," see H. H. the Dalai Lama, "Dialogue on Religion and Peace," in *Buddhist Peacework: Creating Cultures of Peace*, edited by David W. Chappell (Boston, Massachusetts: Wisdom Publications, 1999), 190.

54. Nhât Hanh, "Ahimsa," 155.

55. Fleischman, *The Buddha Taught Nonviolence, Not Pacifism*, 28.

56. Thích Nhât Hanh, "Community As a Resource," in *Engaged Buddhist Reader: Ten Years of Engaged Buddhist Publishing*, edited by Arnold Kotler (Berkeley, California: Parallax Press, 1996), 204.

57. Jakobsen, *Working Alliances and the Politics of Difference*, 33.

58. Some Buddhist scholars do consider it is, such as T. W. Rhys Davids and Caroline A. F. Rhys Davids. See the section "The Liberative Is Ethical" in Chapter 2.

59. Bhikkhu Chao Chu, "Buddhism and Dialogue Among the World Religions," 171.

60. Sulak Sivaraksa, "A Very Simple Magic," in *Conflict, Culture, Change: Engaged Buddhism in a Globalized World* (Boston, Massachusetts: Wisdom Publications, 2005), 59–60.

Bibliography

Primary Sources

Dialogues of the Buddha, Vols. 2 and 3, translated from the Pāli of the *Dīgha Nikāya* by Thomas William Rhys Davids and Caroline Augusta Foley Rhys Davids. London: Pāli Text Society, 1956–1966.

The Long Discourses of the Buddha: A Translation of the Dīgha Nikāya, translated from the Pāli by Maurice Walshe. Boston, Massachusetts: Wisdom Publications, 1995.

Further Dialogues of the Buddha, translated from the Pāli of the *Majjhima Nikāya* by Lord Chalmers. London: Pāli Text Society, 1956–1966.

The Middle Length Discourses of the Buddha: A Translation of the Majjhima Nikāya, 2nd edition, translated by Bhikkhu Ñāṇamoli and Bhikkhu Bodhi. Boston, Massachusetts: Wisdom Publications, 2001.

The Connected Discourses of the Buddha: A Translation of the Samyutta Nikāya, translated by Bhikkhu Bodhi. Boston, Massachusetts: Wisdom Publications, 2002.

The Anguttara Nikāya of the Sutta Pitaka, Eka Duka, and Tika Nipāta, translated from the Pāli by Edmund Rowland Jayetilleke Gooneratne. London: Pāli Text Society, 1885.

Numerical Discourses of the Buddha: An Anthology of Suttas from the Anguttara Nikāya, selected and translated from the Pāli by Nyanaponika Thera and Bhikkhu Bodhi. Walnut Creek, California: AltaMira Press, 1999.

A Comprehensive Manual of Abhidhamma: Pāli Text, Translation and Explanatory Guide of the Abhidhammattha Sangaha of Ācariya Anuruddha, 1st BPS Pariyatti edition, Pāli text originally edited and translated by Mahāthera Nārada, translation revised by Bhikkhu Bodhi, introduction and explanatory guide by U Rewata Dhamma and Bhikkhu Bodhi, Abhidhamma tables by U Sīlānanda. Onalaska, Washington: Pariyatti Press, 2000.

Secondary Sources

Abeysekara, Ananda. "The Saffron Army, Violence, Terror(ism): Buddhism, Identity, and Difference in Sri Lanka." *Numen* 48, no. 1 (2001): 1–46.

215

Adair, Wendi L., Tetsushi Okumura, and Jeanne M. Brett. "Negotiation Behavior When Cultures Collide: The United States and Japan." *Journal of Applied Psychology* 86, no. 3 (June 2001): 371–85.

Agnew, John. *Hegemony: The New Shape of Global Power*. Philadelphia, Pennsylvania: Temple University Press, 2005.

Alcoff, Linda Martín. "The Problem of Speaking for Others." In *Who Can Speak? Authority and Critical Identity*, edited by Judith Roof and Robyn Wiegman, 97–119. Urbana, Illinois: University of Illinois Press, 1995.

Allchin, F. Raymond, ed. *The Archaeology of Early Historic South Asia*. Cambridge and New York: Cambridge University Press, 1995.

Allen, Jeffner, and Iris Marion Young, eds. *The Thinking Muse: Feminism and Modern French Philosophers*. Bloomington, Indiana: Indiana University Press, 1989.

Ambedkar, Bhimrao Ramji. *The Buddha and His Dhamma*, 3rd edition. Bombay, India: Siddharth Publications, 1984.

Ariyaratne, Ahangamage Tudor. "The Non-Violent Struggle for Economic and Social Justice." Address to the Sixth International Conference of the Society for Buddhist-Christian Studies, Tacoma, Washington, August 2000. Ratmalana, Sri Lanka: Sarvodaya Vishva Lekha, 2000.

Armour, Ellen T., and Susan M. St. Ville, eds. *Bodily Citations: Religion and Judith Butler*. New York: Columbia University Press, 2006.

Arunachalam, Vairam, James A. Wall, Jr., and Chris Chan. "Hong Kong Versus U.S. Negotiations: Effects of Culture, Alternatives, Outcome Scales, and Mediation." *Journal of Applied Social Psychology* 28, no. 14 (1998): 1219–44.

Attwood, Jayarava Michael. "Did King Ajātasattu Confess to the Buddha, and Did the Buddha Forgive Him?" *Journal of Buddhist Ethics* 15 (2008): 279–307.

Bahramitash, Roksana. *Liberation from Liberalization: Gender and Globalization in Southeast Asia*. London and New York: Zed Books, 2005.

Bailey, Greg, and Ian Mabbett. *The Sociology of Early Buddhism*. Cambridge, UK: Cambridge University Press, 2006.

Barnes, Nancy J. "The Nuns at the Stūpa: Inscriptional Evidence for the Lives and Activities of Early Buddhist Nuns in India." In *Women's Buddhism, Buddhism's Women: Tradition, Revision, Renewal*, edited by Ellison Banks Findly, 17–36. Boston, Massachusetts: Wisdom Publications, 2000.

Batchelor, Stephen. *Buddhism Without Beliefs: A Contemporary Guide to Awakening*. New York: Riverhead Books, 1997.

Baumann, Martin, and Charles Prebish, eds. *Westward Dharma: Buddhism Beyond Asia*. Berkeley, California: University of California Press, 2002.

Berryman, Phillip. *Liberation Theology: The Essential Facts About the Revolutionary Movement in Latin America and Beyond*. New York: Pantheon Books, 1987.

Bhikkhu Ānanda. "The Buddhist Approach to the Scriptures." *Journal of Dharma* 21, no. 4 (October–December 1996): 364–77.

Bhikkhu Bodhi. "A Look at the Kalama Sutta." *Buddhist Publication Society Newsletter* 9 (Spring 1988). Accessed May 24, 2011. http://www.access-toinsight.org/lib/authors/bodhi/bps-essay_09.html

————. "General Introduction." In *The Connected Discourses of the Buddha: A Translation of the Samyutta Nikāya*, translated from the Pāli by Bhikkhu Bodhi, 21–55. Boston, Massachusetts: Wisdom Publications, 2000.

————. "Introduction" to the Book of Causation (*Nidānavagga*). In *The Connected Discourses of the Buddha: A Translation of the Samyutta Nikāya*, translated by Bhikkhu Bodhi, 515–32. Boston, Massachusetts: Wisdom Publications, 2002.

Bhikkhu Chao Chu. "Buddhism and Dialogue Among the World Religions: Meeting the Challenge of Materialistic Skepticism." In *Ethics, Religion, and the Good Society: New Directions in a Pluralistic World*, edited by Joseph Runzo, 167–71. Louisville, Kentucky: Westminster/John Knox Press, 1992.

Bhikkhu Santikaro. "Buddhadasa Bhikkhu: Life and Society through the Natural Eyes of Voidness." *Engaged Buddhism: Buddhist Liberation Movements in Asia*, edited by Christopher S. Queen and Sallie B. King, 147–94. Albany, New York: State University of New York Press, 1996.

Bhikkhunī Kusuma. "Inaccuracies in Buddhist Women's History." In *Innovative Buddhist Women: Swimming Against the Stream*, edited by Karma Lekshe Tsomo, 5–12. Richmond, UK: Curzon Press, 2000.

Blackstone, Kathryn R. *Women in the Footsteps of the Buddha: Struggle for Liberation in the Therīgāthā*. Richmond, UK: Curzon Press, 1998.

Blum, Mark L. "Baptizing Nature: Environmentalism, Buddhism, and Transcendentalism." In *Bukkyo to Shizen* (Buddhism and nature), 133–163. Kyoto: Research Institute of Bukkyo University, 2005.

Bond, George Doherty. *Buddhism at Work: Community Development, Social Empowerment and the Sarvodaya Movement*, foreword by Joanna Macy. Bloomfield, Connecticut: Kumarian Press, 2004.

Boonyoros, Roongraung. "Householders and the Five Precepts." In *Buddhist Behavioral Codes and the Modern World: An International Symposium*, edited by Charles Wei-hsün Fu and Sandra A. Wawrytko, 171–78. Westport, Connecticut and London: Greenwood Press, 1994.

Boulding, Kenneth E. "Twelve Friendly Quarrels with Johan Galtung." *Journal of Peace Research* 14, no. 1 (1977): 75–86.

Bowlby, Rachel. "Domestication." In *Feminism Beside Itself*, edited by Diane Elam and Robyn Wiegman, 71–91. London and New York: Routledge, 1995.

Bremner, Davin. "South African Experiences with Identity and Community Conflicts." *Journal of Peace Research* 38, no. 3 (May 2001; Special Issue on Conflict Resolution in Identity-Based Disputes): 393–405.

Buddhaghosa, Bhadantācariya. *The Path of Purification (Visuddhimagga)*, translated by Bhikkhu Ñāṇamoli. Boulder: Shambhala, 1976.

Bulkin, Elly, Minnie Bruce Pratt, and Barbara Smith. *Yours in Struggle: Three Feminist Perspectives on Anti-Semitism and Racism*. Brooklyn, New York: Long Haul Press, 1984.

Butler, Judith. *Gender Trouble: Feminism and the Subversion of Identity*. London and New York: Routledge, 1990.

———. *Excitable Speech: A Politics of the Performative*. London and New York: Routledge, 1997.

———. *Undoing Gender*. New York and London: Routledge, 2004.

Cabezón, José Ignacio, ed. *Buddhism, Sexuality, and Gender*. Albany, New York: State University of New York Press, 1992.

Campbell, Joseph Keim, Michael O'Rourke, and David Shier, eds. *Freedom and Determinism*. Cambridge, Massachusetts: Massachusetts Institute of Technology Press, 2004.

Carter, John Ross, George Doherty Bond, Edmund F. Perry, and Shanta Ratnayaka, eds. *The Threefold Refuge in the Theravāda Buddhist Tradition*. Chambersburg, Pennsylvania: Anima Books, 1982.

Carter, John Ross. "Buddhist Ethics?" In *The Blackwell Companion to Religious Ethics*, edited by William Schweiker, 278–85. Malden, Massachusetts: Blackwell Publishing, 2005.

Caulfield, Catherine. *Masters of Illusion: The World Bank and the Poverty of Nations*. New York: Henry Holt & Co., 1996.

Chakravarti, Uma. "The Social Philosophy of Buddhism and the Problem of Inequality." *Social Compass* 33 (1986): 199–221.

———. *The Social Dimensions of Early Buddhism*, 2nd edition. Oxford, UK, and New York: Oxford University Press, 1987.

———. "Buddhism As a Discourse of Dissent?: Class and Gender." *Pravada* 1.5 (May 1992).

Chappell, David W., ed. *Buddhist Peacework: Creating Cultures of Peace*. Boston, Massachusetts: Wisdom Publications, 1999.

Chodorow, Nancy. "Mothering, Male Dominance, and Capitalism." In *Capitalist Patriarchy: The Case for Socialist Feminism*, edited by Zillah R. Eisenstein, 83–106. New York and London: Monthly Review Press, 1979.

Chow, Rey. " 'It's you, and not me': Domination and 'Othering' in Theorizing the 'Third World,' " In *American Feminist Thought at Century's End: A Reader*, edited by Linda S. Kauffman, 95–106. Cambridge, Massachusetts: Blackwell, 1993.

Chung, Inyoung. "A Buddhist View of Women: A Comparative Study of the Rules for Bhiksus and Bhiksunīs based on the Chinese Prātimoksa." MA Thesis, Graduate Theological Union, Berkeley, 1995.

Coghlan, Ian J. "A Survey of the Sources of Buddhist Ethics." *Journal of Buddhist Ethics* 11 (2004): 143–66.

Coleman, James William. *The New Buddhism: The Western Transformation of an Ancient Tradition*. Oxford and New York: Oxford University Press, 2001.

Collins, Steven. "Introduction." In *Buddhist Monastic Life: According to the Texts of the Theravāda Tradition*, by Mohan Wijayaratna, translated by Claude Grangier and Steven Collins, ix–xxiv. Cambridge and New York: Cambridge University Press, 1990.

Colonnese, Louis M., ed. *Conscientization for Liberation*. Washington, D.C.: Division for Latin America-USCC, 1971.

Combahee River Collective. "The Combahee River Collective Statement." In *Theorizing Feminism: Parallel Trends in the Humanities and Social Sciences,* edited by Anne C. Hermann and Abigail J. Stewart, 26–33. Boulder, Colorado: Westview Press, 1994.

Coomaraswamy, Ananda Kentish. *Buddha and the Gospel of Buddhism*. New Delhi: Munshiram Manoharlal, 1974.

Cumings, Bruce. "Still the American Century?" *Review of International Studies* 25, Special Issue (1999): 271–99.

Dalai Lama. *Ethics for the New Millennium*. New York: Riverhead Books, 1999.

———. "Dialogue on Religion and Peace." In *Buddhist Peacework: Creating Cultures of Peace*, edited by David W. Chappell, 189–97. Boston, Massachusetts: Wisdom Publications, 1999.

Daly, Herman E., and John B. Cobb, Jr. *For the Common Good: Redirecting the Economy Toward Community, the Environment, and a Sustainable Future*. Boston, Massachusetts: Beacon Press, 1989.

de Bary, William Theodore, ed. *The Buddhist Tradition in India, China, and Japan*. New York: Vintage Books, 1972.

de Cea, Abraham Velez. "The Criteria of Goodness in the Pāli Nikāyas and the Nature of Buddhist Ethics." *Journal of Buddhist Ethics* 11 (2004): 123–42.

de Koning, Korrie, and Marion Martin, eds. *Participatory Research in Health: Issues and Experiences*. London: Zed Books, 1996.

Derris, Karen. "When the Buddha Was a Woman: Reimagining Tradition in the Theravāda." *Journal of Feminist Studies in Religion* 24.2 (Fall 2008): 29–44.

DeVido, Elise Anne. *Taiwan's Buddhist Nuns*. Albany New York: State University of New York Press, 2010.

Dewaraja, Lorna. "Buddhist Women in India and Precolonial Sri Lanka." In *Buddhist Women Across Cultures: Realizations*, edited by Karma Lekshe Tsomo, 67–77. Albany, New York: State University of New York Press, 1999.

Dockett, Kathleen H., G.. Rita Dudley-Grant, and C. Peter Bankart, eds. *Psychology and Buddhism: From Individual to Global Community*. New York: Kluwer Academic/Plenum Publishers, 2003.

Dockett, Kathleen H. "Buddhist Empowerment: Individual, Organizational, and Societal Transformation." In *Psychology and Buddhism: From Individual to Global Community*, edited by Kathleen H. Dockett, G. Rita Dudley-Grant, and C. Peter Bankart, 173–96. New York: Kluwer Academic/Plenum Publishers, 2003.

Duncan, Simon, and B. Pfau-Effinger, eds. *Gender, Economy and Culture in the European Union*. London and New York: Routledge, 2000.

Dutt, Sukumar. *The Buddha and Five After-Centuries*. Calcutta, India: Sahitya Samsad, 1978.

Ebihara, May. "Interrelation Between Buddhism and Social Systems in Cambodian Peasant Culture." In *Anthropological Studies in Theravada Buddhism*, edited by Manning Nash, 175–96. New Haven, Connecticut: Yale University Press, 1966.

Egge, James R. *Religious Giving and the Invention of Karma in Theravāda Buddhism*. Richmond, UK: Curzon Press, 2002.

Eisenstein, Zillah R., ed. *Capitalist Patriarchy: The Case for Socialist Feminism*. New York and London: Monthly Review Press, 1979.

————. "Developing a Theory of Capitalist Patriarchy and Socialist Feminism." In *Capitalist Patriarchy: The Case for Socialist Feminism*, edited by Zillah R. Eisenstein, 5–40. New York and London: Monthly Review Press, 1979.

————. *Against Empire: Feminisms, Racism, and the West*. London and New York: Zed Books, 2004.

Elam, Diane, and Robyn Wiegman, eds. *Feminism Beside Itself*. London and New York: Routledge, 1995.

Elbedour, Salman, David T. Bastien, and Bruce A. Center. "Identity Formation in the Shadow of Conflict: Projective Drawings by Palestinian and Israeli Arab Children from the West Bank and Gaza." *Journal of Peace Research* 34, no. 2 (May 1997): 217–31.

Enloe, Cynthia. " 'Just Like One of the Family': Domestic Servants in World Politics." In *Bananas Beaches Bases: Making Feminist Sense of International Politics*, 177–94. Berkeley, California: University of California Press, 1989.

Eppsteiner, Fred, ed. *The Path of Compassion: Writings on Socially Engaged Buddhism*, revised 2nd edition. Berkeley, California: Parallax Press, 1988.

Erdosy, George. "City States of North India and Pakistan at the time of the Buddha." In *The Archaeology of Early Historic South Asia*, edited by F. Raymond Allchin, 99–122. Cambridge and New York: Cambridge University Press, 1995.

Falk, Nancy Auer. "An Image of Woman in Old Buddhist Literature: the Daughters of Mara." In *Women and Religion*, edited by Judith Plaskow and Joan Arnold Romero, revised edition. Missoula, Montana: Scholars' Press, 1974.

————. "The Case of the Vanishing Nuns: The Fruits of Ambivalence in Ancient Indian Buddhism." In *Unspoken Worlds: Women's Religious Lives in Non-Western Cultures*, edited by Nancy Auer Falk and Rita M. Gross, 207–24. San Francisco, California: Harper & Row, 1980.

————, and Rita M. Gross, eds. *Unspoken Worlds: Women's Religious Lives in Non-Western Cultures*. San Francisco: Harper & Row, 1980.

Faure, Bernard. *The Power of Denial: Buddhism, Purity, and Gender*. Princeton: Princeton University Press, 2003.

Findly, Ellison Banks, ed. *Women's Buddhism, Buddhism's Women: Tradition, Revision, Renewal*. Boston, Massachusetts: Wisdom Publications, 2000.

————. "Women Teachers of Women: Early Nuns 'Worthy of My Confidence.' " In *Women's Buddhism, Buddhism's Women: Tradition, Revision, Renewal*, edited by Ellison Banks Findly, 133–55. Boston, Massachusetts: Wisdom Publications, 2000.

Fiori, Ernani. "Education and Conscientization." In *Conscientization for Liberation*, edited by Louis M. Colonnese, 123–44. Washington, D.C.: Division for Latin America-USCC, 1971.

Fisher, Ronald J. "Cyprus: The Failure of Mediation and Escalation of an Identity-Based Conflict to an Adversarial Impasse." *Journal of Peace Research* 38, no. 3 (May 2001; Special Issue on Conflict Resolution in Identity-Based Disputes): 307–26.

Fleischman, Paul R. *The Buddha Taught Nonviolence, Not Pacifism*. Onalaska, Washington: Pariyatti Press, 2002.

Forsberg, Gunnel. "The Difference That Space Makes: A Way to Describe the Construction of Local and Regional Gender Contracts." *Norsk Geografisk Tidsskrift-Norwegian Journal of Geography* 55: 161–5.

Foucault, Michél. *Discipline and Punish: The Birth of the Prison*, translated from the French by Alan Sheridan, 2nd edition. New York: Vintage Books, 1995.

Frakes, Chris. "Do the Compassionate Flourish?: Overcoming Anguish and the Impulse towards Violence." *Journal of Buddhist Ethics* 14: 99–128.

Freire, Paulo. *Pedagogy for the Oppressed*. New York: Herder and Herder, 1970.

Fu, Charles Wei-hsün, and Sandra A. Wawrytko, eds. *Buddhist Behavioral Codes and the Modern World: An International Symposium*. Westport, Connecticut and London: Greenwood Press, 1994.

Galtung, Johan. "Cultural Violence." *Journal of Peace Research* 27, no. 3 (August 1990): 291–305.

———. *Buddhism: A Quest for Unity and Peace*. Ratmalana, Sri Lanka: Sarvodaya Book Publishing Services, 1993.

———. *Peace by Peaceful Means: Peace and Conflict, Development and Civilization*. Oslo, Norway: International Peace Research Institute, 1996.

Gier, Nicholas F., and Paul Kjellberg. "Buddhism and the Freedom of the Will: Pali and Mahayanist Responses." In *Freedom and Determinism*, edited by Joseph Keim Campbell, Michael O'Rourke, and David Shier, 277–304. Cambridge, Massachusetts: Massachusetts Institute of Technology Press, 2004.

Goleman, Daniel. *The Meditative Mind: The Varieties of Meditative Experience*. New York: Tarcher, 1996.

Gombrich, Richard F. "Karma and Social Control." *Comparative Studies in Society and History* 17 (1975): 212–20.

Gómez, Luis O. "Some Aspects of Free-Will Question in the Nikāyas." *Philosophy East and West* 25, no. 1 (January 1975): 81–90.

Green, Ronald M. "Buddhist Economic Ethics: A Theoretical Approach." In *Ethics, Wealth, and Salvation: A Study in Buddhist Social Ethics*, edited by Russell F. Sizemore and Donald K. Swearer, 215–34. Columbia, South Carolina: University of South Carolina Press, 1990.

Gregory, Peter N. "Is Critical Buddhism Really Critical?" In *Pruning the Bodhi Tree: The Storm Over Critical Buddhism*, edited by Jamie Hubbard and Paul Swanson, 286–297. Honolulu, Hawai'i: University of Hawai'i Press, 1997.

Gross, Rita M. "Buddhism and Feminism: Toward Their Mutual Transformation." *Eastern Buddhist* 19, nos. 1 and 2 (Spring 1986): 44–58 and 62–74.

———. *Buddhism After Patriarchy: A Feminist History, Analysis, and Reconstruction of Buddhism*. Albany, New York: State University of New York Press, 1993.

———. "Where Are the Women in the Refugee Tree?" In *Religious Feminism and the Future of the Planet: A Buddhist-Christian Conversation*, edited by

Rita M. Gross and Rosemary Radford Ruether, 65–82. New York: The Continuum Publishing Company, 2001.

———. "What Keeps Me in Buddhist Orbit?" In *Religious Feminism and the Future of the Planet: A Buddhist-Christian Conversation*, edited by Rita M. Gross and Rosemary Radford Ruether, 107–120. New York: The Continuum Publishing Company, 2001.

———. "What Buddhists Could Learn from Christians." In *Religious Feminism and the Future of the Planet: A Buddhist-Christian Conversation*, edited by Rita M. Gross and Rosemary Radford Ruether, 163–182. New York: The Continuum Publishing Company, 2001.

———. "The Dharma of Gender." *Contemporary Buddhism* 5, no. 1 (May 2004): 3–13.

———, and Rosemary Radford Ruether. *Religious Feminism and the Future of the Planet: A Christian-Buddhist Conversation*. New York: The Continuum Publishing Company, 2001.

———, and Rosemary Radford Ruether. "Introduction: A Dialogue about Dialogue." In *Religious Feminism and the Future of the Planet: A Buddhist-Christian Conversation*, edited by Rita M. Gross and Rosemary Radford Ruether, 5–21. New York: The Continuum Publishing Company, 2001.

Guenther, Herbert. *Buddhist Philosophy in Theory and Practice*. Baltimore, Maryland: Penguin Books, 1972.

Guijt, Irene, and Meera Kaul Shah, eds. *The Myth of Community: Gender Issues in Participatory Development*, with a foreword by Robert Chambers. London: Intermediate Technology Publications, 1998.

———. "Waking Up to Power, Conflict and Process." In *The Myth of Community: Gender Issues in Participatory Development*, edited by Irene Guijt and Meera Kaul Shah, with a foreword by Robert Chambers, 1–23. London: Intermediate Technology Publications, 1998.

Gutiérrez, Gustavo. *The Power of the Poor in History*, trans. Robert R. Barr. Maryknoll, New York: Orbis Books, 1983.

———. *A Theology of Liberation: History, Politics, and Salvation*, trans. Sister Caridad Inda and John Eagleson, 15th anniversary edition, with a new introduction by the author. Maryknoll, New York: Orbis Books, 1988.

———. *The Density of the Present: Selected Writings*. Maryknoll, New York: Orbis Books, 1999.

Hall, Edward Twitchell. *Beyond Culture*. Garden City, New York: Anchor Press, 1976.

Hallisey, Charles. "Buddhist Ethics: Trajectories." In *The Blackwell Companion to Religious Ethics*, edited by William Schweiker, 312–22. Malden, Massachusetts: Blackwell Publishing, 2005.

Harris, Elizabeth J. "The Female in Buddhism." In *Buddhist Women Across Cultures: Realizations*, edited by Karma Lekshe Tsomo, 49–65. Albany, New York: State University of New York Press, 1999.

Harvey, Peter. *An Introduction to Buddhism: Teachings, History, and Practices*. Cambridge, UK: Cambridge University Press, 1990.

———. "The Mind-Body Relationship in Pali Buddhism: A Philosophical Investigation." *Asian Philosophy* 3, no. 1 (March 1993): 29–41.

———. *An Introduction to Buddhist Ethics: Foundations, Values, and Issues.* Cambridge, UK, and New York: Cambridge University Press, 2000.

———. "Avoiding Unintended Harm to the Environment and the Buddhist Ethic of Intention." *Journal of Buddhist Ethics* 14 (2007): 1–34.

———. "'Freedom of the Will' in the Light of Theravāda Buddhist Teachings." *Journal of Buddhist Ethics* 14 (2007): 35–98.

Heim, Maria. "Toward a 'Wider and Juster Initiative': Recent Comparative Work in Buddhist Ethics." *Religion Compass* 1, no. 1 (2007): 107–19.

Heine, Steven, and Charles S. Prebish, eds. *Buddhism in the Modern World: Adaptations of an Ancient Tradition.* New York: Oxford University Press, 2003.

Hermann, Anne C., and Abigail J. Stewart, eds. *Theorizing Feminism: Parallel Trends in the Humanities and Social Sciences.* Boulder, Colorado: Westview Press, 1994.

Hershock, Peter D. "Family Matters: Dramatic Interdependence and the Intimate Realization of Buddhist Liberation." *Journal of Buddhist Ethics* 7 (2000): 86–104.

Hirakawa, Akira. *Monastic Discipline for the Buddhist Nuns: An English Translation of the Chinese Text of the Mahāsāmghika-Bhiksunī-Vinaya.* Patna, India: Kashi Prasad Jayaswal Research Institute, 1982.

Hofstede, Geert, and Michael Harris Bond. "The Confucius Connection: From Cultural Roots to Economic Growth." *Organizational Dynamics* 16, no. 4 (Spring 1988): 5–21.

Holmes, Prue. "Problematising Intercultural Communication Competence in the Pluricultural Classroom: Chinese Students in a New Zealand University." *Language and Intercultural Communication* 6, no. 1 (2006): 18–34.

Holmes, Robert L., ed. *Nonviolence in Theory and Practice.* Prospect Heights, Illinois: Waveland Press, 1990.

Horner, Isaline Blew. *Women Under Primitive Buddhism: Laywomen and Almswomen*, reprinted. Delhi, India: Motilal Banansidass, 1975.

Hubbard, Jamie, and Paul Swanson, eds. *Pruning the Bodhi Tree: The Storm Over Critical Buddhism.* Honolulu, Hawai'i: University of Hawai'i Press, 1997.

Humble, Morag. "Assessing PRA for Implementing Gender and Development." In *The Myth of Community: Gender Issues in Participatory Development*, edited by Irene Guijt and Meera Kaul Shah, with a foreword by Robert Chambers, 35–45. London: Intermediate Technology Publications, 1998.

Inada, Kenneth K. "The Nature of Emptiness and Buddhist Ethics." *Chung-Hwa Buddhist Journal* 13, no. 2 (May 2000): 255–75.

Ives, Christopher. "Deploying the Dharma: Reflections on the Methodology of Constructive Buddhist Ethics." *Journal of Buddhist Ethics* 15 (2008): 23–44.

Jackson, Roger R., and John J. Makransky, eds. *Buddhist Theology: Critical Reflections by Contemporary Buddhist Scholars*. Richmond, UK: Curzon Press, 2000.

Jackson, Roger R. "Buddhist Theology: Its Historical Context." In *Buddhist Theology: Critical Reflections by Contemporary Buddhist Scholars*, edited by Roger R. Jackson and John J. Makransky, 1–13. Richmond, UK: Curzon Press, 2000.

———. "In Search of a Postmodern Middle." In *Buddhist Theology: Critical Reflections by Contemporary Buddhist Scholars*, edited by Roger R. Jackson and John J. Makransky, 215–46. Richmond, UK: Curzon Press, 2000.

Jakobsen, Janet R. *Working Alliances and the Politics of Difference*. Bloomington, Indiana: Indiana University Press, 1998.

Jayatilleke, Kulatissa Nanda. "The Ethical Theory of Buddhism." *The Mahābodhi* 78 (July 1970): 192–7.

———. *The Message of the Buddha*. London: George Allen and Unwin, 1975; reprinted Kandy: Buddhist Publication Society, 2001.

Jones, Ken. *The New Social Face of Buddhism: A Call to Action*. Boston, Massachusetts: Wisdom Publications, 2003.

Kajiyama Yuichi. "Women in Buddhism." *Eastern Buddhist*, New Series, 15, no. 2 (1982): 53–70.

Kabilsingh, Chatsumarn. *Thai Women in Buddhism*. Berkeley, California: Parallax Press, 1991.

Kalupahana, David J. *Buddhist Philosophy: A Historical Analysis*. Honolulu, Hawai'i: University of Hawai'i Press, 1976.

———. *The Principles of Buddhist Psychology*. Albany, New York: State University of New York Press, 1987.

———. *A History of Buddhist Philosophy: Continuities and Discontinuities*. Honolulu, Hawai'i: University of Hawai'i Press, 1992.

———. *Ethics in Early Buddhism*. Honolulu, Hawai'i: University of Hawai'i Press, 1995.

Kauffman, Linda S., ed. *American Feminist Thought at Century's End: A Reader*. Cambridge, Massachusetts: Blackwell, 1993.

Keown, Damien, comp. *A Dictionary of Buddhism*. Oxford, UK, and New York: Oxford University Press, 2003.

———. *The Nature of Buddhist Ethics*. New York: Palgrave Macmillan, 2001.

Khuankaew, Ouyporn. "Buddhism and Domestic Violence: Using the Four Noble Truths to Deconstruct and Liberate Women's Karma." In *Rethinking Karma: The Dharma of Social Justice*, edited by Jonathan S. Watts, 199–224. Chiang Mai, Thailand: Silkworm Books, 2009.

———. "Buddhism and Violence against Women." In *Violence Against Women in Contemporary World Religion: Roots and Cures*, edited by Daniel C. Maguire and Sa'diyya Shaikh, 174–91. Cleveland, Ohio: Pilgrim Press, 2007.

Kiely, Ray, and Phil Marfleet. *Globalisation and the Third World*. London: Routledge, 1998.

Kindon, Sarah. "Of Mothers and Men: Questioning Gender and Community Myths in Bali." In *The Myth of Community: Gender Issues in Participatory*

Development, edited by Irene Guijt and Meera Kaul Shah, with a foreword by Robert Chambers, 152–64. London: Intermediate Technology Publications, 1998.

King, Sallie B. *Being Benevolence: The Social Ethics of Engaged Buddhism.* Honolulu, Hawai'i: University of Hawai'i Press.

King, Winston L. "A Buddhist Ethic without Karmic Rebirth?" *Journal of Buddhist Ethics* 1 (1994): 33–44.

Kitagawa, Joseph Mitsuo, ed. *The Religious Traditions of Asia: Religion, History, and Culture.* London and New York: Routledge, 2002.

———. "Introduction." In *The Religious Traditions of Asia: Religion, History, and Culture*, edited by Joseph Mitsuo Kitagawa, vii–viii. London and New York: Routledge, 2002.

Kochumuttom, Thomas. "Ethics-Based Society of Buddhism." *Journal of Dharma* 16, no. 4 (October–December 1991): 410–20.

Korten, David C. *When Corporations Rule the World*, 2nd edition. Bloomfield, Connecticut: Kumarian Press, 2001.

Kotler, Arnold, ed. *Engaged Buddhist Reader: Ten Years of Engaged Buddhist Publishing.* Berkeley, California: Parallax Press, 1996.

Kraft, Kenneth, ed. *Inner Peace, World Peace: Essays on Buddhism and Nonviolence.* Albany, New York: State University of New York Press, 1992.

Kumar, Rajesh. "Communicative Conflict in Intercultural Negotiations: The Case of American and Japanese Business Negotiations." *International Negotiation* 4, no. 1 (1999): 63–78.

Kurlansky, Mark. *Nonviolence: Twenty-Five Lessons from the History of a Dangerous Idea*, foreword by His Holiness the Dalai Lama. New York: Random House, 2006.

Lamotte, Étienne. *History of Indian Buddhism: From the Origins to the Śaka Era.* Translated from French by Sara Webb-Boin under the supervision of Jean Dantinne. Paris: Institut Orientaliste de l'Université Catholique de Louvain, 1988.

Lee, Kam-hon, Guang Yang, and John L. Graham. "Tension and Trust in International Business Negotiations: American Executives Negotiating with Chinese Executives." *Journal of International Business Studies* 37 (2006): 623–41.

Levering, Miriam L. "The Dragon Girl and the Abbess of Mo-Shan: Gender and Status in the Ch'an Buddhist Tradition." *Journal of the International Association of Buddhist Studies* 5, no. 1 (1982): 19–35.

Lokamitra, Dharmachari. "Buddhism and Society—the Dynamics of Right Livelihood." Paper presented at the Fourth Chung-Hwa International Conference on Buddhism: The Role of Buddhism in the 21st Century, Taipei, Taiwan, January 18–20, 2002.

Lopez, Donald S., Jr., ed. *Buddhist Hermeneutics.* Honolulu, Hawai'i: University of Hawai'i Press, 1988.

———. "Introduction." In *Buddhist Hermeneutics.* Honolulu, Hawai'i: University of Hawai'i Press, 1988.

————. *Modern Buddhism: Readings for the Unenlightened.* London: Penguin Books, 2002.

Loy, David R. *The Great Awakening: A Buddhist Social Theory.* Boston, Massachusetts: Wisdom Publications, 2003.

————. "The Karma of Women." In *Violence Against Women in Contemporary World Religion: Roots and Cures,* edited by Daniel C. Maguire and Sa'diyya Shaikh, 49–65. Cleveland, Ohio: Pilgrim Press, 2007.

Macy, Joanna. *Mutual Causality in Buddhism and General Systems Theory: The Dharma of Natural Systems.* Albany, New York: State University of New York Press, 1991.

Magliola, Robert. "Afterword." In *Buddhisms and Deconstructions,* edited by Jin Y. Park, 235–70. Lanham, Maryland: Rowman & Littlefield, 2006.

Maguire, Daniel C., and Sa'diyya Shaikh, eds. *Violence Against Women in Contemporary World Religions: Roots and Cures.* Cleveland, Ohio: Pilgrim Press, 2007.

Maguire, Patricia. "Proposing a More Feminist Participatory Research: Knowing and Being Embraced Openly." In *Participatory Research in Health: Issues and Experiences,* edited by Korrie de Koning and Marion Martin, 27–39. London: Zed Books, 1996.

Maha Ghosananda. *Step by Step: Meditations on Wisdom and Compassion.* Berkeley, California: Parallax Press, 1992.

Makransky, John J. "Contemporary Academic Buddhist Theology: Its Emergence and Rationale." In *Buddhist Theology: Critical Reflections by Contemporary Buddhist Scholars,* edited by Roger R. Jackson and John J. Makransky, 14–21. Richmond, UK: Curzon Press, 2000.

————. "Historical Consciousness as an Offering to the Trans-Historical Buddha." In *Buddhist Theology: Critical Reflections by Contemporary Buddhist Scholars,* edited by Roger R. Jackson and John J. Makransky, 111–35. Richmond, UK: Curzon Press, 2000.

————. "Buddhist Perspectives on Truth in Other Religions: Past and Present." *Theological Studies* 64 (2003): 334–61.

Marcoux, Jean-Sébastien. "Body Exchanges: Material Culture, Gender and Stereotypes in the Making." *Home Cultures* 1, issue 1 (2004): 51–60.

Markus, Hazel Rose, and Shinobu Kitayama. "Culture and the Self: Implications for Cognition, Emotion and Motivation." *Psychological Review* 98, no. 2 (1991): 224–53.

McClintock, Anne. "Soft-Soaping Empire: Commodity Racism and Imperial Advertising." In *Traveller's Tales: Narratives of Home and Displacement,* edited by George Robertson, Melinda Mash, Lisa Tickner, Jon Bird, Barry Curtis, and Tim Putnam, 131–54. London and New York: Routledge, 1994.

McClintock, Sara. "Gendered Bodies of Illusion: Finding a Somatic Method in the Ontic Madness of Emptiness." In *Buddhist Theology: Critical Reflections by Contemporary Buddhist Scholars,* edited by Roger R. Jackson and John J. Makransky, 261–74. Richmond, UK: Curzon Press, 2000.

McMahan, David L. *The Making of Buddhist Modernism.* Oxford and New York: Oxford University Press, 2008.

Mead, Margaret. *Sex and Temperament in Three Primitive Societies*. New York: Morrow, 1935.

Misra, G. S. P. *The Age of Vinaya*. New Delhi, India: Munshiram Manoharlal, 1972.

Mrozik, Susanne. "Materialization of Virtue: Buddhist Discourses on Bodies." In *Bodily Citations: Religion and Judith Butler*, edited by Ellen T. Armour and Susan M. St. Ville, 15–47. New York: Columbia University Press, 2006.

Murcott, Susan. *The First Buddhist Women: Translations and Commentary on the Therigatha*. Berkeley, California: Parallax Press, 1991.

Murthy, Ranjani K. "Learning About Participation from Gender Relations of Female Infanticide." In *The Myth of Community: Gender Issues in Participatory Development*, edited by Irene Guijt and Meera Kaul Shah, with a foreword by Robert Chambers, 78–92. London: Intermediate Technology Publications, 1998.

Nash, Manning, ed. *Anthropological Studies in Theravada Buddhism*. New Haven, Connecticut: Yale University Press, 1966.

Nyanaponika Thera, and Bhikkhu Bodhi. "Introduction I." In *Numerical Discourses of the Buddha: An Anthology of Suttas from the Anguttara Nikāya*, selected and translated from the Pāli by Nyanaponika Thera and Bhikkhu Bodhi, 1–10. Walnut Creek, California: AltaMira Press, 1999.

———. "Introduction II." In *Numerical Discourses of the Buddha: An Anthology of Suttas from the Anguttara Nikāya*, selected and translated from the Pāli by Nyanaponika Thera and Bhikkhu Bodhi, 11–30. Walnut Creek, California: AltaMira Press, 1999.

Oakley, Nigel W. "Base Ecclesial Communities and Community Ministry: Some Freirean Points of Comparison and Difference." *Political Theology* 5, no. 4 (2004): 447–65.

Obeyesekere, Gananath. *Imagining Karma: Ethical Transformation in Amerindian, Buddhist, and Greek Rebirth*. Berkeley, California: University of California Press, 2002.

Pacey, Scott. "A Buddhism for the Human World: Interpretations of *Renjian Fojiao* in Contemporary Taiwan." *Asian Studies Review* 29 (March 2005): 61–77.

Park, Jin Y., ed. *Buddhisms and Deconstructions*. Lanham, Maryland: Rowman & Littlefield, 2006.

Peach, Lucinda Joy. "Social Responsibility, Sex Change, and Salvation: Gender Justice in the *Lotus Sūtra*." *Philosophy East and West* 52, no. 1 (January 2002): 50–74.

Perry, Edmund F. "Foreword to the English Edition." In *The Heritage of the Bhikkhu: A Short History of the Bhikkhu in Educational, Cultural, Social, and Political Life*, xi–xv. New York: Grove Press, 1974.

———, and Shanta Ratnayaka. "The Sangha as Refuge: in the Theravāda Buddhist Tradition." In *The Threefold Refuge in the Theravāda Buddhist Tradition*, edited by John Ross Carter, George Doherty Bond, Edmund F. Perry, and Shanta Ratnayaka, 41–55. Chambersburg, Pennsylvania: Anima Books, 1982.

Peters, Rebecca Todd Peters. *In Search of the Good Life: The Ethics of Globalization*. New York and London: Continuum, 2004.

Pew Global Attitudes Project. "Global Opinion Trends 2002–2007." Released on July, 24, 2007. Accessed May 24, 2011. http://pewglobal.org/files/pdf/257.pdf.

Phillips, Anne. *Feminism and Politics*. New York: Oxford University Press, 1998.

Phra Prayudh Payutto (Phra Rājavaramuni). "Foundations of Buddhist Social Ethics." In *Ethics, Wealth, and Salvation: A Study in Buddhist Social Ethics*, edited by Russell F. Sizemore and Donald K. Swearer, 29–53. Columbia, South Carolina: University of South Carolina Press, 1990.

———. *Buddhadhamma: Natural Laws and Values for Life*, translated by Grant A. Olson. Albany, New York: State University of New York Press, 1995.

Plaskow, Judith, and Joan Arnold Romero, eds. *Women and Religion*, revised edition. Missoula, Montana: Scholars' Press, 1974.

Pogge, Thomas. "The First United Nations Millennium Development Goal: A Cause for Celebration?" *Journal of Human Development* 5, no. 3 (November 2004): 377–97.

Pratt, Minnie Bruce. "Identity: Skin Blood Heart." In *Yours in Struggle: Three Feminist Perspectives on Anti-Semitism and Racism*, by Elly Bulkin, Minnie Bruce Pratt, and Barbara Smith, 11–63. New York: Long Haul Press, 1984.

Prebish, Charles S. *Buddhist Monastic Discipline*. University Park, Pennsylvania, and London: Pennsylvania State Press, 1975.

———. "Varying the Vinaya: Creative Responses to Modernity." In *Buddhism in the Modern World: Adaptations of an Ancient Tradition*, edited by Steven Heine and Charles S. Prebish, 45–73. New York: Oxford University Press, 2003.

———. "Cooking the Buddhist Books: The Implications of the New Dating of the Buddha for the History of Early Indian Buddhism" *Journal of Buddhist Ethics* 15 (2008): 1–21.

———, and Damien Keown. *Introducing Buddhism*, 2nd edition. London and New York: Routledge, 2010.

Puntarigvivat, Tavivat. *Bhikkhu Buddhadasa's Dhammic Socialism in Dialogue with Latin American Liberation Theology*. PhD diss., Temple University, 1994.

———. "A Thai Buddhist Perspective." In *What Men Owe to Women: Men's Voices from World Religions*, edited by John C. Raines and Daniel C. Maguire, 211–37. Albany, New York: State University of New York Press, 2001.

Pupatana, Somsuda. "The Development of Peace through the Process of Morality." *Chung-Hwa Buddhist Journal* 13, no. 2 (May 2000): 613–34.

Queen, Christopher S., and Sallie B. King, eds. *Engaged Buddhism: Buddhist Liberation Movements in Asia*. Albany, New York: State University of New York Press, 1996.

Raines, John C., and Daniel C. Maguire, eds. *What Men Owe to Women: Men's Voices from World Religions*. Albany, New York: State University of New York Press, 2001.

Rāhula, Walpola. *What the Buddha Taught*, revised and expanded edition with texts from Suttas and Dhammapada. New York: Grove Press, 1974.

————. *The Heritage of the Bhikkhu: The Buddhist Tradition of Services*, reprint edition. New York: Grove Press, 2003.

Reagon, Bernice Johnson. "Coalition Politics: Turning the Century." In *Feminism and Politics*, edited by Anne Phillips, 242–53. New York: Oxford University Press, 1998.

Rhys Davids, Caroline Augusta Foley. "Introductory Essay." In *A Buddhist Manual of Psychological Ethics*, 3rd edition, xxi-ciii. Oxford, England: The Pāli Text Society, 1974.

Rhys Davids, Thomas William, and William Stede, eds. *The Pāli Text Society's Pāli-English Dictionary*. Oxford, England: The Pāli Text Society, 1995.

Rhys Davids, Thomas William. "*Nibbāna.*" In *The Pāli Text Society's Pāli-English Dictionary*, edited by Thomas William Rhys Davids and William Stede. Oxford, England: The Pāli Text Society, 1995.

Rich, Bruce. *Mortgaging the Earth: The World Bank, Environmental Impoverishment, and the Crisis of Overdevelopment*. Boston, Massachusetts: Beacon Press, 1994.

Robertson, George, Melinda Mash, Lisa Tickner, Jon Bird, Barry Curtis, and Tim Putnam, eds. *Traveller's Tales: Narratives of Home and Displacement*. London and New York: Routledge, 1994.

Robinson, Richard H., Willard L. Johnson, and Thanissaro Bhikkhu. *Buddhist Religions: A Historical Introduction*, 5th edition. Belmont, California: Wadsworth/Thomson Learning, 2005.

Roof, Judith, and Robyn Wiegman, eds. *Who Can Speak? Authority and Critical Identity*. Urbana, Illinois: University of Illinois Press, 1995.

Ruegg, David Seyfort, and Lambert Schmithausen. *Earliest Buddhism and Madhyamaka*. Leiden, Netherlands: E. J. Brill, 1990.

Runzo, Joseph. *Ethics, Religion, and the Good Society: New Directions in a Pluralistic World*. Louisville, Kentucky: Westminster/John Knox Press, 1992.

Saddhatissa, Hammalawa. *Buddhist Ethics*. Boston, Massachusetts: Wisdom Publications, 1997.

Salgado, Nirmala S. "Eight Revered Conditions: Ideological Complicity, Contemporary Reflections, and Practical Realities." *Journal of Buddhist Ethics* 15 (2008): 177–213.

Sangharakshita. *What Is the Sangha: The Nature of Spiritual Community*. Birmingham, UK: Windhorse Publications, 2000.

Schopen, Gregory. "Two Problems in the History of Indian Buddhism, The Layman/Monk Distinction and the Doctrines of the Transference of Merit." In *Bones, Stones, and Buddhist Monks, Collected Papers on the Archaeology, Epigraphy, and Texts of Monastic Buddhism in India*, 23–55. Honolulu, Hawai'i: University of Hawai'i Press, 1997.

————. "The Suppression of Nuns and the Ritual Murder of Their Special Dead in Two Buddhist Monastic Texts." *Journal of Indian Philosophy* 24, no. 6 (December 1996): 563–92.

Schuster, Nancy. "Changing the Female Body: Wise Women and the Bodhisattva Career in Some *Mahāratnakūtasūtras.*" *Journal of the International Association of Buddhist Studies* 4, no. 1 (1981): 24–69.

Schweiker, William, ed. *The Blackwell Companion to Religious Ethics*. Malden, Massachusetts: Blackwell Publishing, 2005.

Seul, Jeffrey R. " 'Ours Is the Way of God': Religion, Identity, and Intergroup Conflict." *Journal of Peace Research* 36, no. 5 (September 1999): 553–69.

Sharp, Gene. "Nonviolent Action: An Active Technique of Struggle." In *Nonviolence in Theory and Practice*, edited by Robert L. Holmes, 147–50. Prospect Heights, Illinois: Waveland Press, 1990.

———. "The Methods of Nonviolent Action." In *Waging Nonviolent Struggle: 20ᵗʰ Century Practice and 21ˢᵗ Century Potential*, 49–65. Boston, Massachusetts: Extending Horizons Books.

Shaw, Sarah, comp. *Buddhist Meditation: An Anthology of Texts from the Pāli Canon*. London and New York: Routledge, 2006.

Shih Chengyen. *Master Chengyen's Still Thoughts*, Vol. 2. Taipei: Tzu-Chi Cultural Publishing, 1994.

Shih Hsing Yun. "Buddhist Perspective on Issues Concerning the Female Gender (Fojiao dui nuxing wenti de kanfa)." *Pu-Men Journal* (Pu-Men xuebao) 18 (November 2003). Accessed May 24, 2011. http://www.fgs.org.tw/master/masterA/books/delectus/discussion/03.htm.

Shih Sheng-yen. "Why Are There More Women Followers of Buddhism Than Men? (Weishenmo xuefo hui nu bi nan duo)" *Dharma Drum Monthly*, June 1, 2004.

Sivaraksa, Sulak. *A Socially Engaged Buddhism*. Bangkok: Thai Inter-Religious Commission for Development, 1988.

———. "Buddhism and Contermporary International Trends." In *Inner Peace, World Peace: Essays on Buddhism and Nonviolence*, edited by Kenneth Kraft, 127–138. Albany, New York: State University of New York Press, 1992.

———. "An Alternative Agenda for a Global Economy." *Seeds of Peace 13*, no. 1 (January–April 1997): 15–6.

———. *Conflict, Culture, Change: Engaged Buddhism in a Globalized World*. Boston, Massachusetts: Wisdom Publications, 2005.

———. "Buddhism in Asia: Challenges & Prospects." *Just Commentary: International Movement for a Just World* 6, no. 9 (September 2006): 9–11.

Sizemore, Russell, and Donald Swearer, eds. *Ethics, Wealth, and Salvation: A Study in Buddhist Social Ethics*. Columbia, South Carolina: University of South Carolina Press, 1990.

Smith, Jonathan Z., and William Scott Green, with the American Academy of Religion, eds. *The HarperCollins Dictionary of Religion*. New York: HarperCollins, 1995.

So, Y. Alvin. *Social Change and Development: Modernization, Dependency, and World-Systems Theories*. Newbury Park, California: Sage Publications, 1990.

Sponberg, Alan. "Attitudes toward Women and the Feminine in Early Buddhism." In *Buddhism, Sexuality, and Gender*, edited by José Ignacio Cabezón, 3–36. Albany, New York: State University of New York Press, 1992.

Stoller, Robert. *Presentations of Gender*. New Haven: Yale University Press, 1985.

Suu Kyi, Aung San. *The Voice of Hope: Conversations with Alan Clements*. With contributions by U Kyi Maung and U Tin U.

Thích Nhât Hanh. *Interbeing: Commentaries on the Tiep Hien Precepts*. Berkeley, California: Parallax Press, 1987.

———. *Being Peace*. Berkeley, California: Parallax Press, 1987.

———. "Community As a Resource." In *Engaged Buddhist Reader: Ten Years of Engaged Buddhist Publishing*, edited by Arnold Kotler, 193–208. Berkeley, California: Parallax Press, 1996.

———. *Interbeing: Fourteen Guidelines for Engaged Buddhism*, 3rd edition. Berkeley, California: Parallax Press, 1998.

———. "The Individual, Society, and Nature." *The Path of Compassion: Writings on Socially Engaged Buddhism*, edited by Fred Eppsteiner, revised 2nd edition, 40–46. Berkeley, California: Parallax Press, 1988.

———. "Ahimsa: The Path of Harmlessness." In *Buddhist Peacework: Creating Cultures of Peace*, edited by David W. Chappell, 155–64. Boston, Massachusetts: Wisdom Publications, 1999.

———, and Daniel Berrigan. *The Raft Is Not the Shore: Conversations Toward A Buddhist-Christian Awareness*, foreword by bell hooks. Maryknoll, New York: Orbis, 2001.

Thomas, Edward J. *The Life of the Buddha as Legend and History*. London: Routledge & Kegan Paul, 1969.

Tsomo, Karma Lekshe, ed. *Buddhist Women Across Cultures: Realizations*. Albany, New York: State University of New York Press, 1999.

———. "Mahāprajāpatī's Legacy: The Buddhist Women's Movement: An Introduction." In *Buddhist Women Across Cultures: Realizations*, edited by Karma Lekshe Tsomo, 1–44. Albany, New York: State University of New York Press, 1999.

———, ed. *Innovative Buddhist Women: Swimming Against the Stream*. Richmond, Surrey: Curzon Press, 2000.

———, ed. *Buddhist Women and Social Justice: Ideals, Challenges, and Achievements*. Albany, New York: State University of New York Press, 2004.

———. "Family, Monastery, and Gender Justice: Reenvisioning Buddhist Institutions." In *Buddhist Women and Social Justice: Ideals, Challenges, and Achievements*, edited by Karma Lekshe Tsomo, 1–19. Albany, New York: State University of New York Press, 2004.

———. "Is the Bhiksunī Vinaya Sexist?" In *Buddhist Women and Social Justice: Ideals, Challenges, and Achievements*, edited by Karma Lekshe Tsomo, 45–72. Albany, New York: State University of New York Press, 2004.

United Nations Development Programme. *Human Development Report 1999: Globalization with a Human Face*. Accessed May 24, 2011. http://hdr.undp.org/en/media/HDR_1999_EN.pdf.

———. *Human Development Report 2003: Millennium Development Goals: A Compact Among Nations to End Human Poverty*. Accessed May 24, 2011. http://hdr.undp.org/en/media/hdr03_complete.pdf.

————. *Human Development Report 2007/2008: Fighting Climate Change: Human Solidarity in a Divided World*. Accessed May 24, 2011. http://hdr.undp. org/en/media/HDR_20072008_EN_Complete.pdf.

Victoria, Brian Daizen. "Engaged Buddhism: A Skeleton in the Closet?" *Journal of Global Buddhism* 2 (2001): 72–91.

Watts, Jonathan, ed. *Rethinking Karma: The Dharma of Social Justice*. Chiang Mai, Thailand: Silkworm Books, 2009.

Weber, Max. *The Sociology of Religion*, translated by Ephraim Fischoff. Boston, Massachusetts: Beacon Press, 1993.

White House. "The Terrorist Threat to the US Homeland." Released on July 17, 2007. Accessed May 24, 2011. http://www.dni.gov/press_ releases/20070717_release.pdf.

Wijayaratna, Mohan. *Buddhist Monastic Life: According to the Texts of the Theravāda Tradition*, translated by Claude Grangier and Steven Collins, with an introduction by Steven Collins. Cambridge and New York: Cambridge University Press, 1990.

Wijayasundara, Senarat. "Restoring the Order of Nuns to the Theravādin Tradition." In *Buddhist Women Across Cultures: Realizations*, edited by Karma Lekshe Tsomo, 79–87. Albany, New York: State University of New York Press, 1999.

Williams, Paul. *Buddhist Thought: A Complete Introduction to the Indian Tradition*, with Anthony Tribe. London and New York: Routledge, 2000.

Wilson, Liz. "Celibacy and the Social World." In *Charming Cadavers: Horrific Figurations of the Feminine in Indian Buddhist Hagiographic Literature*, 15–39. Chicago, Illinois, and London: The University of Chicago Press, 1996.

Yates, Michael D. *Naming the System: Inequality and Work in the Global Economy*. New York: Monthly Review Press, 2003.

Young, Iris Marion. "Throwing Like a Girl: A Phenomenology of Feminine Body Comportment, Motility, and Spatiality." In *The Thinking Muse: Feminism and Modern French Philosophers*, edited by Jeffner Allen and Iris Marion Young, 51–70. Bloomington, Indiana: Indiana University Press, 1989.

Yu, Chai-Shin. *Early Buddhism and Christianity: A Comparative Study of the Founders' Authority, the Community, and the Discipline*. Delhi, India: Motilal Banarsidass, 1981.

Zadek, Simon. "The Practice of Buddhist Economics: Another View." *American Journal of Economics and Sociology* 42, no. 4 (October, 1993): 433–45.

Index

Abhidhamma (Abhidharma), 8, 34,
  67–68, 132
activism/activist, 19, 57, 166–67,
  169, 171, 173, 180n18
(moral) agency/agent, 28, 64, 91,
  100–2, 106, 110, 112, 123, 169
aggression/aversion/ill will/
  hatred/doṣa (dveṣa), 7, 22, 25–26,
  29, 32–34, 39, 45, 68, 84, 95, 106,
  109, 111, 113, 118–25, 128, 132–33,
  136–37, 139, 143, 150, 158, 160,
  162, 168–69, 173–74, 177
altruistic/sympathetic joy, 22, 32,
  68, 118, 136–38, 166
anatta (anātman)/non-Self, 4, 6, 21,
  27–28, 42, 61, 63–66, 72–74, 81, 89,
  91, 97, 100–1, 104, 109–10, 129,
  162–64, 175–76, 184n54, 197n9,
  200n1
androcentrism, 3, 14–16, 27, 55,
  59–61, 73–74, 102, 113, 180n8
arahant (arhat), 33, 46, 50, 58, 60,
  193n96
asceticism, 1, 9, 19–20, 26, 42, 56, 59,
  61, 73, 94–95, 142, 155, 187n100
attachment/clinging, 6, 17–18, 23,
  26, 29, 38, 41, 54, 64, 66, 74, 78,
  111, 119, 121, 123, 128–33, 136–37,
  137, 139, 141, 143, 146, 153, 156,
  159, 161–64, 168, 171, 178, 179n2,
  193n96

(Greg) Bailey and (Ian) Mabbett, 21,
  52, 54, 185n73

benevolence, 124–25, 128, 130,
  135–41, 143, 148, 155–58, 163, 165,
  168, 174
bhikkhu (bhikṣu), 3–4, 9–10, 12–15,
  17–18, 22, 24, 38–39, 47–50,
  52–54, 57–61, 67, 73, 98, 119,
  129–32, 134, 136, 152–56, 177,
  183n36, 185n73, 193n91, 196n142,
  196n143
Bhikkhu Bodhi, 13, 22, 67, 98, 132
bhikkhunī (bhikṣunī), 4, 10, 12, 14–15,
  47, 49–50, 52–54, 57–61, 73, 154,
  156, 183n36, 185n73, 193n91,
  196n143
brāhman/brāhmin, 10–11, 21–23,
  33–34, 36–38, 46, 55–56, 65–66, 81,
  93–94, 131, 185n73, 198n20
Butler, Judith, 6, 21, 64, 75, 83–84,
  87, 91, 98, 100–2, 104, 106

capitalism, 93, 114, 157, 167, 212n29
caste, 2, 31, 36–38, 55–57, 81, 94
causality/causation, 20, 41, 99, 108,
  110, 141, 147, 160, 162, 164, 167,
  170
causes, 1, 20, 92, 111, 113, 127, 137,
  146, 159–60, 162, 171, 179n2
celibacy, 14–15, 42, 54, 56, 58–60,
  196n143
cessation of dukkha (duhkha), see
  nibbāna
Chakravarti, Uma, 53–54, 185n73,
  194n111
clarity, 44, 118, 134–35, 140, 143, 158

233

125, 128–30, 134–35, 141–42,
146–47, 149, 154, 158, 163, 169,
173, 175, 178, 182n29, n30, n31
nobility/nobleness, 27, 31, 36–38,
42, 44, 52–53, 56, 61, 81, 130–32,
140–41, 148, 185n73
non-Self, see *anātta*
nonviolence, 25, 27, 44, 124, 150,
160–61, 165, 171–75, 177–78

opposition/antagonism, ·12, 25–27,
29, 46, 48, 55, 74, 118, 120–24, 158,
160, 162, 167–68, 171–73

participation, 7, 25, 29, 93, 108, 127,
152, 154, 159, 161, 170, 173–74, 177
paṭiccasamuppāda, see co-arising
patience/*khanti* (*kṣānti*), 138–39, 166
patriarchy, 5, 14, 16, 47, 59, 63
Payutto, Phra Prayudh (Phra Rājavaramuni), 9, 34, 142, 146
peace, 3–4, 7, 17, 19, 26, 29, 31, 34,
36, 38, 52, 85, 121–23, 134, 143,
149, 153–54, 156, 159–62, 164–66,
169–78
peace, inner, 3–4, 7, 31, 34, 134, 143,
166, 170, 172, 178
peace, positive/genuine, 160,
164–65, 173, 211n4
performativity, 21, 75–76, 78–80, 88,
100–1, 106, 128, 132–35, 138, 150,
168, 188n108
phenomenon, see *dhamma*
possessive individualism, 53–54,
112, 119, 130, 136
poststructuralism/poststructuralist,
6–7, 21, 24, 27–28, 63–64, 75, 89,
91, 101–2, 177
practical concern/consideration, 4,
8, 10, 23, 31, 34–35, 41, 97, 142–43,
151–52, 159, 170, 176–78
precept/vow, 4, 8–9, 51–52, 55,
141–42, 149–51, 154, 157, 174, 178,
182n29, 182n32, 183n36

repetition, 13, 27, 60, 75, 78, 83–85,
89, 92, 96–97, 100–3, 108–9, 122,

124–25, 136–39, 143, 150, 158,
177
rūpa/material and socio-cultural
forms/material and symbolic
forces, 18, 66–72, 74–75, 78, 81–82,
87, 89, 91, 99, 101, 103–4, 107–8,
110, 118–19, 124, 130–31, 139–40,
149–51, 159–60, 166, 177, 197n20

sammā (*samyak*)/proper/comprehen-
sive, 41, 99, 134–36, 140, 171, 175,
177, 182n29, n30, n31
saṃsāra/cycle of *dukkha*, 19, 72,
124–25, 127, 129–30, 132, 146–48,
158, 160, 166, 170, 178
Sangha, 6, 12, 14–15, 27, 31, 42, 45,
47–54, 56–57, 59–61, 73, 125, 129,
147–50, 152–56, 165, 176, 183n36,
193n91
saṅkhāra (*saṃskāra*)/volitional
construction/mental formation/
disposition, 21–22, 38, 66–72, 74,
78, 81–82, 87, 98–100, 102–4, 107,
109–11, 123–24, 128, 130–31, 134,
139–40, 142–43, 147, 151–53,
158, 162, 164, 168, 172, 174–75,
179n2
Sākya (Śākya) tribe/republic, 2, 15,
53, 56–57, 147, 194n111
seclusion/solitude/isolation, 31,
42, 45–46, 48, 61, 142, 162, 165–
66
sediment/sedimentation, 84, 89,
91–92, 98, 101–3, 106–8, 124–25,
139, 150–51, 166, 170, 174, 176
self-essence/inherent nature, 6,
16, 28, 36–37, 47, 55–56, 60, 65,
72–74, 78–82, 89, 96, 101, 109,
122, 129–32, 161, 163–64, 169, 177,
184n54
self-reconditioning, 28–29, 72, 109,
125, 127–30, 136–37, 139–40,
146–48, 150–52, 157–58, 173, 177
(all) sentient beings, 1, 3–6, 21–22,
64–65, 92, 94, 109–10, 118–20, 128,
130, 135–37, 140, 143–44, 146–48,
152, 161–62, 164–65, 178, 182n32